THE SECRET IS OUT

William Stanek is the artist behind the scenes at World Galleries, and the fiction author Robert Stanek.

BW Fall Arrives at Multnomah Falls in Canvas Print with Floating Frame

Find his art at 360 Studios

360studios.pictorem.com
williamrstanek.com

Note About the Front Matter

The front matter serves as an essential foundation for the series, ensuring that all readers—whether new to the books or returning after some time—can fully grasp the material. It introduces key concepts like the 8 Pillars of Intelligence and the Holistic Intelligence Model, both developed by William Stanek, providing critical context and continuity across the series. This consistent framework enables readers to engage deeply with the content, regardless of where they begin in the series.

For readers already familiar with these concepts, the option to skip directly to the main content is always available, allowing them to dive right into the heart of the book. This structure ensures accessibility for all, while respecting the time of experienced readers.

The Holistic Intelligence Model: The 8 Pillars of Personal and Professional Excellence

The 8 Pillars of Intelligence form the foundation of the Holistic Intelligence Model developed by William Stanek, a transformative framework designed to empower individuals in every dimension of life. This model transcends traditional notions of intelligence by encompassing eight distinct yet interconnected pillars: Emotional Resilience, Creativity Intelligence, Practical Intelligence, Cultural Intelligence, Intrapersonal Intelligence, Interpersonal Intelligence, Ethical Intelligence, and Analytical Intelligence. Each pillar represents a crucial dimension of human capability, addressing intellectual, emotional, ethical, and social competencies essential for thriving in today's dynamic and interconnected world.

At its core, the Holistic Intelligence Model emphasizes the synergy between these eight pillars, recognizing that true excellence arises from the harmonious development of diverse intelligences. By fostering resilience, creativity, practical problem-solving, cultural adaptability, self-awareness, interpersonal skills, ethical grounding, and analytical prowess, individuals are empowered to navigate complex challenges, build meaningful relationships, and achieve sustained success. This comprehensive approach ensures that personal growth is balanced across multiple facets of intelligence, promoting not only professional achievements but also overall well-being and fulfillment.

The model serves as a foundational guide for individuals seeking to enhance their capabilities in a structured and systematic manner. It provides actionable strategies and development pathways for each pillar, enabling continuous improvement and integration of these intelligences into daily life. Whether in leadership roles, creative endeavors, or personal relationships, the Holistic Intelligence Model equips individuals with the tools necessary to excel holistically, fostering a resilient, innovative, and ethically grounded mindset that drives meaningful impact and lasting success.

Pillar 1: Emotional Resilience (ER)

Emotional Resilience (ER) is the foundational pillar of the Holistic Intelligence Model, embodying the capacity to withstand and recover from emotional challenges and setbacks. It equips individuals with the strength to navigate adversity, maintain composure under pressure, and sustain a positive outlook despite difficulties. ER is not merely about bouncing back; it is about growing stronger and more adaptable through life's inevitable trials, thereby fostering long-term psychological well-being and stability.

The significance of Emotional Resilience extends across personal and professional domains. In the workplace, ER enhances performance by enabling individuals to manage stress effectively, stay focused on long-term goals, and lead teams with confidence during crises. Personally, it strengthens relationships by promoting empathy, effective communication, and the ability to support oneself and others through tough times. By cultivating ER, individuals build a robust emotional foundation that supports perseverance, adaptability, and proactive problem-solving, essential traits for sustained success and fulfillment.

Developing Emotional Resilience involves intentional practices such as mindfulness, self-compassion, and building strong social support networks. Strategies include embracing a growth mindset, enhancing coping skills through physical activity and stress management techniques, and fostering self-awareness through reflective practices. Practical applications of ER range from handling workplace stress and leading teams with composure to managing personal challenges and maintaining healthy relationships. By integrating ER with other intelligences, individuals can achieve a balanced and resilient approach to both personal growth and professional excellence.

Pillar 2: Creativity Intelligence (CrQ)

Creativity Intelligence (CrQ) is the pillar that fuels innovation, enabling individuals to generate unique ideas, solve problems innovatively, and adapt to changing environments with a creative mindset. CrQ encompasses a range of cognitive and emotional skills that facilitate the creation and implementation of novel concepts, processes, and products. It is essential for personal fulfillment and organizational success, fostering a culture of continuous improvement and adaptability.

The significance of Creativity Intelligence lies in its ability to drive progress and competitive advantage. In professional settings, CrQ leads to the development of new products, services, and processes that can differentiate an organization in the market. It enhances problem-solving by allowing individuals to approach challenges from unconventional angles, leading to more effective and sustainable solutions. Personally, CrQ contributes to a sense of achievement and satisfaction by enabling individuals to express their creativity and pursue innovative interests.

Enhancing Creativity Intelligence involves cultivating an explorative mindset, fostering adaptive thinking, and strengthening problem-solving proficiency. Strategies include engaging in creative activities, embracing playfulness, practicing divergent thinking, and seeking inspiration from diverse sources. Practical applications of CrQ range from leading innovation projects and strategic planning in the workplace to pursuing creative hobbies and personal goals in everyday life. By integrating CrQ with other intelligences, individuals can harness their creative potential to achieve both personal growth and professional excellence.

Pillar 3: Practical Intelligence (PQ)

Practical Intelligence (PQ), often referred to as "street smarts," is the ability to apply knowledge effectively in real-world situations. It bridges the gap between theoretical understanding and practical application, enabling individuals to navigate everyday complexities with confidence and efficiency. PQ encompasses skills such as effective decision-making, resource management, and adaptability, which are crucial for achieving tangible outcomes in both personal and professional contexts.

The significance of Practical Intelligence is evident in its impact on efficiency and effectiveness. In the workplace, PQ enhances project management, streamlines business processes, and supports strategic planning by ensuring that ideas are implemented successfully. It empowers individuals to solve problems pragmatically, optimize resources, and adapt to changing circumstances, thereby increasing productivity and reducing operational costs. Personally, PQ facilitates effective time management, financial planning, and home organization, contributing to a balanced and organized lifestyle.

Developing Practical Intelligence involves enhancing adaptability and flexibility, strengthening problem-solving and decision-making skills, and improving resource management and optimization. Strategies include engaging in scenario planning, utilizing decision-making frameworks, and practicing continuous improvement techniques. Practical applications of PQ range from managing business operations and executing strategic plans in the workplace to organizing daily tasks and achieving personal financial goals. By integrating PQ with other intelligences, individuals can ensure that their practical skills support their overall growth and success.

Pillar 4: Cultural Intelligence (CQ)

Cultural Intelligence (CQ) is the capability to relate and work effectively across diverse cultural settings. In an increasingly globalized world, CQ is essential for navigating multicultural environments, fostering inclusive workplaces, and building strong, respectful relationships with individuals from different cultural backgrounds. It involves understanding cultural norms, values, and communication styles, and adapting one's behavior to fit various cultural contexts.

The significance of Cultural Intelligence extends to both personal enrichment and professional success. In the workplace, CQ facilitates effective teamwork and collaboration in multicultural teams, enhances cross-cultural communication, and supports market expansion into new regions by understanding local consumer behaviors and business practices. Personally, CQ enriches interactions by promoting mutual respect, reducing misunderstandings, and fostering meaningful relationships with people from diverse backgrounds. It also contributes to personal growth by broadening perspectives and enhancing global awareness.

Enhancing Cultural Intelligence involves increasing cultural awareness, improving adaptability and flexibility, and developing empathy and social competence. Strategies include cultural education, immersion experiences, active listening, and empathy exercises. Practical applications of CQ range from leading multicultural teams and expanding businesses into international markets to building intercultural friendships and participating in diverse community activities. By integrating CQ with other intelligences, individuals can navigate cultural complexities with ease, fostering a harmonious and inclusive environment in all areas of life.

Pillar 5: Intrapersonal Intelligence (IntraQ)

Intrapersonal Intelligence (IntraQ), also known as Reflective Intelligence, is the capacity to understand oneself deeply. It encompasses self-awareness, self-regulation, and the ability to reflect on one's thoughts, emotions, and motivations. IntraQ is fundamental for personal growth, effective decision-making, and aligning actions with personal values and goals, providing a strong foundation for overall well-being and fulfillment.

The significance of Intrapersonal Intelligence lies in its role in fostering self-understanding and personal development. In the workplace, IntraQ enhances leadership by enabling leaders to understand their strengths and weaknesses, manage their emotions, and make decisions that are aligned with their values. It supports career development by helping individuals set clear goals and pursue them with intentionality and self-discipline. Personally, IntraQ contributes to emotional well-being by promoting self-compassion, resilience, and the ability to navigate personal challenges with clarity and purpose.

Developing Intrapersonal Intelligence involves cultivating self-awareness, enhancing emotional regulation, and fostering personal growth and self-reflection. Strategies include journaling, mindfulness meditation, and engaging in reflective practices that promote introspection and self-assessment. Practical applications of IntraQ range from setting and achieving personal goals and managing stress effectively to maintaining authentic relationships and pursuing continuous self-improvement. By integrating IntraQ with other intelligences, individuals can achieve a balanced and insightful approach to personal and professional excellence, ensuring that their actions are purposeful and aligned with their core values.

Pillar 6: Interpersonal Intelligence (InterQ)

Interpersonal Intelligence (InterQ), also known as Social Intelligence, is the ability to understand, communicate, and interact effectively with others. It involves recognizing and interpreting the emotions, motivations, and intentions of others, facilitating meaningful relationships and effective collaboration. InterQ is essential for leadership, teamwork, conflict resolution, and building a supportive social network, making it a critical component of the Holistic Intelligence Model.

The significance of Interpersonal Intelligence is evident in its impact on both personal relationships and professional environments. In the workplace, InterQ enhances team dynamics, fosters collaboration, and supports effective leadership by enabling individuals to inspire and motivate others. It facilitates client relations, conflict management, and networking, contributing to a positive and productive work culture. Personally, InterQ strengthens friendships, family bonds, and community connections by promoting empathy, effective communication, and mutual understanding, leading to more fulfilling and harmonious relationships.

Enhancing Interpersonal Intelligence involves developing empathy and social awareness, improving communication skills, and strengthening conflict management and negotiation abilities. Strategies include active listening, empathy exercises, and engaging in collaborative and team-building activities. Practical applications of InterQ range from leading diverse teams and building strong client relationships in the workplace to maintaining healthy friendships and family relationships in personal life. By integrating InterQ with other intelligences, individuals can foster a supportive and engaging social environment, enhancing both their personal well-being and professional success.

Pillar 7: Ethical Intelligence (EthQ)

Ethical Intelligence (EthQ) serves as the moral compass within the Holistic Intelligence Model, guiding individuals in making principled choices and maintaining integrity in all aspects of life. It involves understanding and adhering to ethical standards, promoting fairness, and demonstrating accountability and responsibility. EthQ is essential for building trust, fostering a positive reputation, and leading with integrity, ensuring that actions are aligned with moral values and societal expectations.

The significance of Ethical Intelligence is profound in both personal and professional contexts. In the workplace, EthQ enhances leadership by promoting ethical decision-making, integrity, and accountability, which are crucial for building trust and credibility within teams and organizations. It supports the development and enforcement of ethical policies, contributing to a culture of responsibility and fairness. Personally, EthQ ensures that individuals uphold their values in their interactions and decisions, fostering honest and trustworthy relationships and contributing positively to their communities.

Developing Ethical Intelligence involves clarifying personal values, enhancing ethical decision-making skills, and fostering integrity and accountability. Strategies include values clarification exercises, utilizing ethical decision-making frameworks, and engaging in continuous ethical education and reflection. Practical applications of EthQ range from leading with integrity and developing ethical policies in the workplace to maintaining honesty and fairness in personal relationships and community engagements. By integrating EthQ with other intelligences, individuals can ensure that their actions are not only effective and innovative but also morally sound and socially responsible, leading to sustained trust and respect.

Pillar 8: Analytical Intelligence (AQ)

Analytical Intelligence (AQ) is the ability to analyze complex problems, think critically, and make informed decisions based on evidence and logical reasoning. It involves breaking down information into manageable parts, identifying patterns, and synthesizing data to derive meaningful conclusions. AQ is essential for effective problem-solving, strategic planning, and informed decision-making in both personal and professional contexts, providing the cognitive tools necessary to navigate and excel in a data-driven world.

The significance of Analytical Intelligence lies in its role in enhancing decision-making and strategic thinking. In the workplace, AQ supports strategic planning by enabling individuals to analyze market trends, assess risks, and develop data-driven strategies that align with organizational goals. It enhances problem-solving capabilities by facilitating the identification of root causes and the development of effective solutions. Personally, AQ contributes to financial management, health tracking, and educational pursuits by enabling individuals to interpret data accurately and make informed decisions that promote well-being and success.

Developing Analytical Intelligence involves enhancing critical thinking, improving problem-solving skills, and strengthening data analysis and interpretation abilities. Strategies include engaging in critical thinking exercises, utilizing data analysis tools and software, and practicing reflective journaling on problem-solving experiences. Practical applications of AQ range from strategic business expansion and process optimization in the workplace to personal financial planning and health management in everyday life. By integrating AQ with other intelligences, individuals can ensure that their analytical capabilities support comprehensive and balanced growth, enabling them to make informed, ethical, and effective decisions across all areas of life.

Conclusion

The Holistic Intelligence Model offers a comprehensive and integrated approach to personal and professional development by encompassing eight pivotal pillars: Emotional Resilience, Creativity Intelligence, Practical Intelligence, Cultural Intelligence, Intrapersonal Intelligence, Interpersonal

Intelligence, Ethical Intelligence, and Analytical Intelligence. Each pillar addresses distinct aspects of human capability, ensuring that individuals develop a balanced and multifaceted intelligence that supports resilience, innovation, ethical integrity, and effective communication. This holistic framework recognizes the interconnectedness of diverse intelligences, emphasizing that true excellence is achieved through the harmonious growth of all these dimensions.

By cultivating each of these eight pillars, individuals are empowered to navigate complex challenges, build meaningful relationships, and achieve sustained success and fulfillment. The model provides actionable strategies and development pathways, enabling continuous improvement and the integration of these intelligences into daily life. Whether in leadership roles, creative endeavors, or personal relationships, the Holistic Intelligence Model equips individuals with the tools necessary to excel holistically, fostering a resilient, innovative, and ethically grounded mindset.

Ultimately, the Holistic Intelligence Model serves as a guiding framework for individuals seeking to enhance their capabilities in a structured and systematic manner. By embracing and developing each pillar, individuals can achieve comprehensive intelligence and excellence, leading to meaningful impact and lasting success in all areas of life. Embrace this model as a transformative journey towards balanced growth, personal fulfillment, and professional achievement.

Letter from the Author

In the realm of leadership and intelligence, there exists a tapestry woven from the threads of experience, wisdom, and an unyielding commitment to excellence. This tapestry has been crafted over the course of three decades, each thread representing a moment of triumph, a lesson learned, or a challenge met head-on. It is a privilege to share these threads with you, dear reader, as we embark on a journey through the corridors of leadership, guided by the principles of the Holistic Intelligence Model.

In these pages, you will discover not only a roadmap to effective leadership but also a comprehensive framework that integrates Emotional Resilience, Creativity Intelligence,

Practical Intelligence, Cultural Intelligence, Intrapersonal Intelligence, Interpersonal Intelligence, Ethical Intelligence, and Analytical Intelligence. These eight pillars form the foundation of a multifaceted intelligence that transcends traditional measures, enabling leaders to navigate complex landscapes with adaptability, innovation, and integrity.

As we delve into the nuances of each pillar, you will gain insights into how these interconnected intelligences work in synergy to foster resilient and dynamic leadership. Whether it's harnessing Emotional Resilience to maintain composure under pressure, leveraging Creativity Intelligence to drive innovation, or applying Ethical Intelligence to uphold integrity, each pillar offers practical strategies and profound wisdom. Together, they unlock doors to innovation, adaptability, and enduring success, providing a holistic approach to leadership that is both practical and inspiring.

This book is not merely a collection of ideas but a distillation of a lifetime's worth of experiences, framed within the Holistic Intelligence Model. It is an offering to leaders, both seasoned and aspiring, who seek to cultivate a balanced and integrated intelligence that supports sustained excellence and fulfillment. It is my sincerest hope that you will find within these pages not only practical guidance but also inspiration to lead with purpose, passion, and resilience, embodying the essence of holistic intelligence in every endeavor.

In the crucible of leadership, one discovers not only the power to guide and influence but also the profound responsibility that comes with it. Over three decades at the intersection of technology, business, and leadership, I have gleaned insights that have shaped my approach to leadership intelligence. From navigating pivotal historical moments to addressing complex technological challenges, these experiences have reinforced the importance of a balanced and integrated intelligence framework.

Throughout my career as a technology consultant and leader, I have learned that the heart of many seemingly insurmountable problems lies not in technological failings but in the nuanced dynamics of leadership and intelligence. This revelation became the cornerstone of my approach, emphasizing that effective leadership is a multifaceted endeavor encompassing Emotional Resilience, Practical Intelligence, Ethical Intelligence, and the other pillars of holistic intelligence. By embracing this integrated framework, leaders can inspire, influence, and adeptly guide teams through even the most formidable challenges.

In this book, and indeed throughout this series, I invite you to embark on a journey of discovery, exploring the intricacies of leading with purpose, adaptability, and a commitment to growth. Together, we will harness the power of holistic intelligence to achieve greater effectiveness, impact, and resilience. May these pages serve as a compass on your own leadership journey, guiding you towards balanced growth and meaningful success.

With warm regards,

William R. Stanek.

Our Foundational Proposition: Navigating the Complex Tapestry of Success

In a world saturated with discussions on various intelligences, our perspective transcends the oversimplified dichotomy of emotional intelligence (EQ) versus intellectual intelligence (IQ). While acknowledging the undeniable importance of emotional intelligence, our exploration delves deeper, recognizing the intricate interplay of the eight pillars of the Holistic Intelligence Model—Emotional Resilience, Creativity Intelligence, Practical Intelligence, Cultural Intelligence, Intrapersonal Intelligence, Interpersonal Intelligence, Ethical Intelligence, and Analytical Intelligence—within the tapestry of effective living and success.

Consider the story of Temple Grandin, a renowned scientist and advocate for individuals with autism. Her unique perspective and creative problem-solving have revolutionized the livestock industry. Grandin's journey reflects the intersection of Practical Intelligence, Emotional Resilience, and Creativity Intelligence, showcasing the versatile dimensions crucial for life, success, and leadership. Similarly, visionaries like Elon Musk demonstrate the indispensable role of Practical Intelligence and Analytical Intelligence in achieving monumental feats. Musk's relentless commitment to innovation highlights how these intelligences synergize to propel progress, rather than overshadow one another.

Meet Frances Arnold, a groundbreaking chemist and engineer awarded the Nobel Prize in Chemistry. Her journey of innovation showcases not only Analytical Intelligence but also Emotional Resilience in a field where women were historically underrepresented. Arnold's creative problem-solving and tenacity redefine the boundaries of intelligence in life, success, and leadership, embodying the harmonious blend of multiple intelligences that drive profound achievements. Steve Jobs, with his unparalleled Analytical Acumen and Creativity Intelligence, demonstrated that visionary success goes beyond emotional intelligence. His ability to distill complex ideas into user-friendly solutions revolutionized industries, emphasizing the symbiotic relationship between Analytical Intelligence and Creativity Intelligence.

Dikembe Mutombo, a former NBA star turned philanthropist, exemplifies the power of Interpersonal Intelligence and Emotional Resilience in life, success, and leadership. Through his humanitarian efforts, Mutombo exhibits an unwavering commitment to uplifting communities, showcasing how Emotional Intelligence and Ethical Intelligence can drive impactful social change. Bill Gates, a luminary in strategic foresight and business acumen, exemplifies the pivotal role of Analytical Intelligence and Practical Intelligence in life, success, and leadership. His capacity to envision the future and strategically navigate challenges underscores the indispensable nature of Holistic Intelligence.

Consider the story of Kip Thorne, a theoretical physicist who played a pivotal role in the discovery of gravitational waves. His ability to navigate ambiguity in the pursuit of groundbreaking discoveries exemplifies the fusion of Analytical Intelligence and Creativity Intelligence, setting an extraordinary example for those working in dynamic environments. Ai Weiwei, a Chinese artist and activist, exemplifies leadership through Creative Intelligence and Ethical Intelligence. His courage in challenging societal norms and fostering change highlights the transformative power of creativity combined with ethical discernment.

Intelligence, we argue, is a multidimensional tapestry that extends beyond the realms of EQ and IQ. The narrative expands to encompass luminaries like Michelle Obama, whose Emotional Resilience has been instrumental in navigating the complexities of public life; Winston Churchill's tenacity reflecting Emotional Resilience and Analytical Intelligence; Indra Nooyi's resourcefulness showcasing Practical Intelligence; Oprah Winfrey's self-belief embodying Intrapersonal Intelligence; Warren Buffett's analytical prowess highlighting Analytical Intelligence; Tim Cook's mindset shifting illustrating Cognitive and Emotional Flexibility; and Malala Yousafzai's challenge reframing, which integrates Ethical Intelligence and Emotional Resilience. These figures collectively weave a narrative that defies simplistic categorizations, embodying the holistic integration of multiple intelligences for impactful existence.

Our proposition revolves around the dynamic interplay of these diverse intelligences, each contributing uniquely to the tapestry of success. It is a paradigm that acknowledges the multifaceted strengths of individuals who excel not by adhering to a rigid framework but by skillfully navigating the intricate dance of the eight pillars of Holistic Intelligence. These exemplars, each embodying specific resilient characteristics, illustrate the power of a multidimensional approach to intelligence. The constellation of essential intelligences for triumphant existence encompasses ethical discernment, cultural acumen, creative ingenuity, relational adeptness, and more, forming a symphony that forges the crucible of true excellence.

This holistic fusion, a testament to the boundless potential of human intellect, breathes life into visionary endeavors, shaping the course of personal and professional journeys, and inspiring generations to come. In our journey to reimagine leadership and success, we must transcend the limiting paradigm of EQ versus IQ. Instead, let us embrace the Holistic Intelligence Model—a comprehensive framework that recognizes and celebrates the manifold facets of intelligence. Through this lens, we equip ourselves to tackle the complexities of modern life with nuance, wisdom, and unwavering determination, fostering a balanced and integrated approach to achieving unparalleled success.

Acknowledgements

Embarking on this journey of exploring the Holistic Intelligence Model and its application to leadership has been a profound experience, one that has been shaped by the guidance and support of numerous individuals. First and foremost, I extend my deepest gratitude to the Chief Officers of Fortune 100, 500, and 1000 companies who entrusted me with their most complex challenges. Your unwavering faith in my ability to devise solutions in seemingly impossible situations has been both humbling and empowering, providing real-world contexts in which the pillars of Emotional Resilience, Practical Intelligence, and Ethical Intelligence have been tested and refined.

I am indebted to the countless leaders I've had the privilege to work alongside throughout my career. Each interaction, each challenge faced together, has contributed to the insights and principles shared in this book. Your dedication to excellence, your unwavering commitment to your teams, and your willingness to embrace innovation have been a constant source of inspiration, highlighting the critical roles of Interpersonal Intelligence and Cultural Intelligence in effective leadership.

To my colleagues and mentors, both past and present, thank you for your invaluable guidance and wisdom. Your collective expertise and diverse perspectives have enriched my understanding of the eight pillars of Holistic Intelligence. It is through our collaborations that many of the concepts explored in these pages have taken shape, particularly in areas such as Analytical Intelligence and Creativity Intelligence, which have been instrumental in developing robust strategies for leadership and personal growth.

I extend a special thanks to those who have provided feedback and insights during the development of this book. Your thoughtful contributions have been instrumental in refining the ideas and ensuring their accessibility to a wide audience. Your willingness to engage in discussions, challenge assumptions, and share your own experiences has been invaluable in shaping the Ethical and Practical aspects of the Holistic Intelligence Model.

This book is a testament to the collective wisdom of leaders, past and present, who have left an indelible mark on the world. It is a tribute to the countless individuals who have demonstrated that leadership is not defined by titles, but by actions, by the impact we have on those we serve. It is a celebration of the potential that lies within each of us to lead with purpose, compassion, and a commitment to positive change, guided by the comprehensive framework of Holistic Intelligence.

Finally, to my family, whose unwavering support has been a constant source of strength, thank you for standing by my side throughout this endeavor. Your belief in me and in the importance of this work has been a driving force. This book is as much a reflection of your encouragement as it is of my own journey through the eight pillars of Holistic Intelligence.

With deepest gratitude,

William R. Stanek

Shifting Mindsets: Transform Thinking, Transform Leadership

The right mindset is a game-changer in leadership.

Elevating Skills, Mindsets, and Strengths for Transformational Leadership in Your Personal and Professional Life

Includes a 2-week Action Plan for Leaders

William Stanek's Leadership Intelligence Mastery Series

William R. Stanek
Author & Series Creator

William Stanek's Leadership Intelligence Mastery Series

Elevating Skills, Mindsets, and Strengths for Transformational Leadership in Your Personal and Professional Life

Shifting Mindsets: Transform Thinking, Transform Leadership

The right mindset is a game-changer in leadership.

Published by Stanek & Associates
in conjunction with
Big Blue Sky Press for Business
www.williamrstanek.com.

Copyright © 2025 William R. Stanek. Seattle, Washington. All rights reserved. Photographs of the author are © HC Stanek. Fine-art photographs and illustrations are © William R. Stanek and were created by the author.

No part of this book may be reproduced, stored in a retrieval system or transmitted in any form or by any means, electronic, mechanical, photocopying, recording, scanning or otherwise, except as permitted by Sections 107 or 108 of the 1976 United States Copyright Act, without the prior written permission of the publisher Requests to the publisher for permission should be sent to the address listed previously.

Stanek & Associates is a trademark of Stanek & Associates and/or its affiliates. All other marks are the property of their respective owners. No association with any real company, organization, person or other named element is intended or should be inferred through use of company names, web site addresses or screens.

This book expresses the views and opinions of the author. The information contained in this book is provided without any express, statutory or implied warranties.

LIMIT OF LIABILITY/DISCLAIMER OF WARRANTY: THE PUBLISHER AND THE AUTHOR MAKE NO REPRESENTATIONS OR WARRANTIES WITH RESPECT TO THE ACCURACY OR COMPLETENESS OF THE CONTENTS OF THIS WORK AND SPECIFICALLY DISCLAIM ALL WARRANTIES, INCLUDING WITHOUT LIMITATION WARRANTIES OF FITNESS FOR A PARTICULAR PURPOSE. NO WARRANTY MAY BE CREATED OR EXTENDD BY SALES OR PROMOTIONAL MATERIALS. THE ADVICE AND DISCUSSION IN THIS BOOK MAY NOT BE SUITABLE FOR EVERY SITUATION. THIS WORK IS SOLD WITH THE UNDERSTANDING THTAT THE PUBLISHER IS NOT ENGAGED IN RENDERING PROFESSIONAL SERVICES AND THAT SHOULD PROFESSIONAL ASSISTANCE BE REQUIRED THE SERVICES OF A COMPETENT PROFESSIONAL SHOULD BE SOUGHT. NEITHER THE PUBLISHERS, AUTHORS, RESELLERS NOR DISTRIBUTORS SHALL BE HELD LIABLE FOR ANY DAMAGES CAUSED OR ALLEGED TO BE CAUSE EITHER

DIRECTLY OR INDIRECTLY HEREFROM. THE REFERENCE OF AN ORGANIZATION OR WEBSITE AS A SOURCE OF FURTHER INFORMATION DOES NOT MEAN THAT THE PUBLISHER OR THE AUTHOR ENDORSES THE INFORMATION THE ORGANIZATION OR WEBSITE MAY PROVIDE OR THE RECOMMENDATIONS IT MAY MAKE. FURTHER, READERS SHOULD BE AWARE THAT WEBSITES LISTED IN THIS BOOK MAY NOT BE AVAILABLE OR MAY HAVE CHANGED SINCE THIS WORK WAS WRITTEN.

Stanek & Associates publishes in a variety of formats, including print, electronic and by print-on-demand. Some materials included with standard print editions may not be included in electronic or print-on-demand editions or vice versa.

Country of First Publication: United States of America.

Cover Design: Creative Designs Ltd.
Editorial Development: Andover Publishing Solutions
Content & Technical Review: L & L Technical Content Services

You can provide feedback related to this book by emailing the author at williamstanek @ aol.com. Please use the <u>name of the book</u> as the subject line.

1st Edition. Version: 1.0.1.0b

> **Note**   I may periodically update this text and the edition and version number shown previously will let you know which version you are working with. If there's a specific feature you'd like me to write about in an update,

message me on Facebook (http://facebook.com/williamstanekauthor). Please keep in mind readership of this book determines how much time I can dedicate to it.

Special Notice for Groups and Teams Are you part of a group or team seeking comprehensive Empowered Leadership© and Inspirational Journeys© training? We offer tailored programs for groups of 12 or more, designed to equip you with the tools and strategies needed to thrive in today's dynamic landscape. Discover the power of collective growth and resilience! For inquiries and customized solutions, please reach out to Jeannie Kim jeannie.kim @ reagentpress.com.

Bulk Orders Available Looking to equip your team or organization with the transformative power of the "Leadership Intelligence Mastery" books? We offer special pricing and customized packages for bulk orders. For more information and to place your order, please contact Jeannie Kim jeannie.kim @ reagentpress.com.

Epigraph

In *The Resilient Leader*, we quoted Nelson Mandela:

> "The greatest glory in living lies not in never falling, but in rising every time we fall." - Nelson Mandela

You might be surprised to learn that Confucius expressed this same idea—more than 2,400 years earlier.

> "Our greatest glory is not in never falling, but in rising every time we fall." – Confucius

This striking parallel highlights the enduring nature of this wisdom. The belief that true strength lies not in avoiding failure but in rising after a fall transcends time, culture, and context. It's a universal truth that has been recognized and articulated by thinkers, philosophers, and leaders throughout history.

This shared understanding speaks to a profound truth about the human experience: resilience and perseverance are timeless virtues. They form the foundation for growth, leadership, and transformation, no matter the era or setting.

This timeless wisdom lies at the core of our exploration of emotional resilience and leadership excellence, serving as a reminder that the principles we study today are deeply rooted in the shared human journey.

Table of Contents

Note About the Front Matter 2
The Holistic Intelligence Model: The 8 Pillars of Personal and Professional Excellence 3
Letter from the Author 15
Our Foundational Proposition: Navigating the Complex Tapestry of Success 18
Acknowledgements 22
Epigraph 30
Table of Contents 31
Part 1. Let's Get Started! 43
   The 8 Pillars of Intelligence As a Framework for Transformative Leadership 44
   Opening Reflection 48
Charting Your Leadership Course 51
Shifting Mindsets: Transform Thinking, Transform Leadership 55
2-Week Action Plan: Empowering Leaders through Mindset and Attitude Shifts 57
Instructions for the Action Plan 70
Shifting Mindsets for Effective Leadership 76
Unpacking Mindset and Attitude in Leadership 85
   Defining Mindset and Attitude in Leadership 87
   The Dynamic Nature of Mindset and Attitude 88
   Dimensions of Attitude in Leadership 89
   The Influence of Mindset and Attitude on Leadership Effectiveness 91

Integrating the Holistic Intelligence Model 92

Practical Strategies for Cultivating a Growth Mindset and Positive Attitude 93

Real-World Example: Satya Nadella's Leadership at Microsoft 95

Defining Mindset and Attitude: Foundations of Effective Leadership... 96

Mindset: The Internal Compass of Leadership 98

Integrating the Holistic Intelligence Model 99

Attitude: The Outward Expression of Inner Beliefs............... 100

The Impact of Attitude on Organizational Culture 102

The Synergy Between Mindset and Attitude.......................... 102

Case Study: Satya Nadella's Transformation of Microsoft 103

Cultivating Mindset and Attitude Through the 8 Pillars 104

Practical Strategies for Leaders 106

The Intricate Dance Between Mindset, Attitude, and Behavior in Leadership 107

Understanding the Triad: Mindset, Attitude, and Behavior 109

The Dynamic Interplay Among Mindset, Attitude, and Behavior.. 111

Practical Strategies for Aligning Mindset, Attitude, and Behavior.. 114

Real-World Examples 115

The Interconnection.. 117

The Psychological Foundations of Mindset and Attitude in Leadership.. 122

Cognitive Processes: The Mental Frameworks of Leadership 124
Attribution Theory: Interpreting Success and Failure 126
Social Cognitive Theory: Learning Through Observation .. 127
Emotional Intelligence: Navigating Emotions in Leadership 127
Self-Regulation and Resilience: Sustaining a Constructive Attitude 128
Social Influence and Norms: Shaping Mindset in Context 129
Self-Concept and Identity: The Leader's Inner Narrative ... 130
Integrating the Holistic Intelligence Model 131
Practical Strategies for Cultivating Psychological Foundations 132
Real-World Example: Dr. Brené Brown's Leadership Insights 133

The Influence of Beliefs and Values on Leadership Mindset **136**

Core Beliefs: The Foundation of Mindset 138
Limiting Beliefs: Overcoming Internal Barriers 139
Values Alignment: Cultivating Authentic Leadership 140
Adaptive Beliefs and Cognitive Flexibility 141
Ethical Framework: Guiding Principles of Leadership 142
Self-Efficacy and Belief in Influence 143
Purpose and Meaning: The Leader's North Star 144
Cultural and Organizational Values 145
Reflective Practice: A Tool for Alignment 146
Integrating the Holistic Intelligence Model 147
Practical Strategies for Leaders 148

Emotional Resilience and Its Impact on Attitude in Leadership **152**
    Understanding Emotional Resilience 156
    The Role of Emotional Resilience in Leadership 157
    Emotional Resilience and the Growth Mindset 160
    Impact on Team and Organizational Culture 161
    Developing Emotional Resilience 162
    Practical Strategies for Leaders 164
    Integrating the Holistic Intelligence Model 165

The Power of Growth Mindset in Leadership **168**
    Embracing Challenges as Opportunities: Turning Obstacles into Stepping Stones 172
    Pioneering Innovation Through Continuous Learning: Cultivating a Culture of Curiosity 173
    Fostering a Learning Culture: Commitment to Development 174
    Encouraging Calculated Risk-Taking: Embracing Uncertainty for Growth 174
    Nurturing Resilience and Adaptability: Building Strength Through Setbacks 175
    Inspiring Purpose and Vision: Leading with Direction 176
    Overcoming Limiting Beliefs: Breaking Barriers to Growth 177
    Promoting Feedback and Development: Cultivating Open Communication 177
    Strengthening Adaptability in a Changing Landscape: Embracing Change 178

Leading by Example: Modeling Growth Mindset Behaviors 179

Empowering and Developing Team Members: Investing in People 180

Promoting Diversity of Thought: Harnessing Collective Intelligence 180

Avoiding the Fixed Mindset Trap: Recognizing and Shifting Limiting Perspectives 181

Creating a Legacy of Growth: Sustaining Impact Beyond Tenure 182

Embracing Change and Continuous Learning: Keys to a Growth Mindset 184

Adapting to Evolving Realities: Proactive Stance Towards Change 188

Fostering a Culture of Adaptability: Creating a Responsive Environment 189

Continuous Learning and Intellectual Curiosity: Learning from Experience 190

Seeking Out New Knowledge: Active Pursuit of Growth ... 190

Encouraging Lifelong Learning in Teams: Building a Learning Organization 191

Embracing Failure as a Learning Opportunity: Cultivating Resilience Through Setbacks 192

Championing Experimentation and Innovation: Creating Safe Spaces for Innovation 193

Remaining Open to Feedback and Critique: Embracing Constructive Criticism 194

Cultivating a Global Perspective: Embracing Diversity and Inclusion 194

Leveraging Technology for Learning: Harnessing Digital Tools 195

Inspiring a Hunger for Knowledge: Leading by Example .. 196

Remaining Humble and Curious: Embracing a Beginner's Mind 197

Embodying Resilience in the Face of Change: Inspiring Confidence Through Stability 197

Overcoming Fixed Mindset Traps: Navigating Challenges to Growth 200

Understanding Fixed Mindset Traps 204

Fostering a Growth Mindset Culture 210

Overcoming Fixed Mindset Traps Individually 213

Fostering a Positive Attitude in Leadership 217

The Importance of a Positive Attitude in Leadership 221

Leading by Example: Embodying Positivity 222

Practicing Gratitude: Cultivating Appreciation 223

Encouraging Open Communication: Building Trust and Transparency 224

Cultivating Optimism: Inspiring Confidence 225

Nurturing a Solutions-Oriented Mindset: Empowering Teams to Overcome Challenges 225

Maintaining Emotional Resilience: Navigating Ups and Downs with Grace 226

Promoting a Culture of Positivity: Embedding Positivity into Organizational DNA 227

Fostering a Sense of Belonging: Creating Inclusive and Supportive Teams 228

Celebrating Successes, Big and Small: Reinforcing Achievements 228

Encouraging Personal Growth and Development: Empowering Team Members 229

Balancing Positivity with Realism: Maintaining Credibility 230

Empowering Autonomy and Ownership: Building Confidence and Motivation 231

Providing Constructive Feedback with Positivity: Focusing on Growth 231

Remaining Adaptable and Flexible: Inspiring Confidence Through Change 232

Demonstrating Empathy and Compassion: Building Strong Relationships 233

Encouraging Work-Life Balance: Prioritizing Well-Being ... 234

The Ripple Effect of Positivity: How Attitude Shapes Organizational Culture 236

Cultivating Trust and Transparency: Building the Foundation of Organizational Culture 240

Fostering a Sense of Belonging and Camaraderie: Building Strong, Cohesive Teams 241

Inspiring Innovation and Creativity: Creating an Environment Where Ideas Flourish 242

Enhancing Resilience and Adaptability: Building Strength Through Positivity 243

Encouraging a Solutions-Oriented Mindset: Focusing on Progress Over Problems 244

Enhancing Employee Well-being and Engagement: Creating a Supportive Work Environment 245

Promoting Accountability and Ownership: Building a Culture of Responsibility 246

Enhancing Customer Focus and Service Excellence: Elevating Organizational Performance 247

Attracting and Retaining Top Talent: Creating a Magnet for Excellence 248

Strengthening Ethical Climate: Embedding Integrity into Organizational DNA 249

Enhancing Organizational Agility: Responding Effectively to Change 250

Driving Organizational Performance and Productivity: Achieving Excellence Through Positivity 251

Strategies for Cultivating a Positive Attitude in Leadership Roles 254

Developing Self-Awareness 259

Transforming Challenges into Opportunities 260

Cultivating Appreciation and Positivity 261

Sustaining Positivity Through Well-Being 262

Fostering Trust and Understanding 262

Enhancing Presence and Composure 263

Instilling Purpose and Motivation 264

Cultivating Resilience and Growth 265

Building Compassionate Connections 265

Fostering Ownership and Confidence 266

Modeling Positivity and Integrity 266

Fostering Growth and Adaptability 267

Motivating Through Appreciation 267

Nurturing Forward-Thinking Mindsets 268

Focusing on Possibilities Over Problems 268
Strengthening Team Dynamics 269
Valuing Every Voice 270
Aligning Individual Roles with Organizational Goals 270
Investing in Growth 271
Building Trust and Collaboration 271

Navigating Challenges and Adversities: Resilience and Attitude in Leadership 274

Resilience: The Bedrock of Leadership 278
Attitude as the Lens for Perception 279
Embracing Challenges for Development 280
Turning Setbacks into Comebacks 281
Cultivating Resilience through Mindset Shifts 282
Embracing Failure as a Stepping Stone 283
The Role of Emotional Intelligence in Resilience 284
Maintaining Positivity in the Face of Adversity 285
Fostering a Resilient Organizational Culture 286
Navigating Challenges with Balanced Perspective 287
Building a Supportive Network 288
Cultivating Physical and Mental Well-being 289
Adopting a Solution-Focused Mindset 290
Learning from Adversity: The Growth Mindset 290
Preparing for Future Challenges 291
Embracing Resilience as a Continuous Journey 292

Building Resilience Through a Positive Attitude: Thriving Amidst Adversity 296

Positivity as the Cornerstone of Resilient Leadership 300

    Channeling Energy into Actionable Solutions 301
    Enhancing Emotional Intelligence through Positivity 302
    Unlocking Creativity in the Face of Adversity 303
    Leveraging Adversity for Growth 304
    Creating a Ripple Effect of Positivity 305
    Embracing Calculated Risks with Confidence 306
    Motivating Teams Through Optimism 307
    Providing Direction Amidst Chaos 308
    Reframing Thoughts to Empower Action 309
    Building a Supportive and Uplifting Environment 309
    Prioritizing Well-being to Sustain Positivity 310
    Using Language to Motivate and Encourage 311
    Positivity as a Continuous Practice 312
    Acknowledging Progress to Maintain Momentum 312
    Visionary Leadership through Positivity 313
    Drawing on Positivity for Resilience 314

Emotional Intelligence and Its Role in Maintaining a Resilient Attitude 317
    Emotional Resilience (ER): The Foundation of Strength 317
    A More Comprehensive Look at Resilience 322
    Synergy between Emotional Resilience and Emotional Intelligence 323
    Integrating Emotional Intelligence and Emotional Resilience with the Holistic Intelligence Model 325
    The Symbiotic Relationship Between Emotional Intelligence and Resilience 331

Case Study: The Transformational Impact of Mindset and Attitude 334

    Analyzing Key Instances Demonstrating the Influence of Mindset and Attitude 336

    Extracting Insights and Strategies from the Case Study 338

    Lessons in Cultivating a Transformational Mindset and Attitude from Akio Yamamoto's Leadership 341

    Practical Takeaways for Leaders Seeking to Shift Their Mindset and Attitude 344

Leadership Case Reviews: Mastering Situations in Shifting Mindsets 347

Tools and Techniques for Shifting Mindset and Attitude towards Effective Leadership 351

    1. Self-Reflection and Journaling 351

    2. Meditation and Mindfulness Practices 352

    3. Positive Affirmations 353

    4. Visualization Techniques 354

    5. Goal-Setting and Action Planning 355

    6. Emotional Resilience Assessments 356

    7. Leadership Coaching and Mentoring 357

    8. Strengths-Based Assessments 358

    9. Feedback Loops 359

    10. Conflict Resolution Training 360

    11. Time Management Tools 361

    12. Cognitive Behavioral Techniques 362

    13. Stress Management Practices 363

    14. Decision-Making Frameworks 364

    15. Networking and Learning Communities 365

16. Continual Learning and Development Plans 366
17. Books and Thought Leaders 367
18. Accountability Partnerships 368
19. Gratitude Practices 369
20. Cognitive Restructuring Techniques 370

Empowering Leaders through Mindset and Attitude Shifts 373

The Transformative Power of Mindset and Attitude 373
Inspiring Change and Driving Organizational Success 374
Unlocking New Levels of Performance and Influence 376
Overcoming Challenges on the Journey to Transformation 377
Empowering Leaders to Inspire, Innovate, and Lead 378
Conclusion: A Call to Action 379

Thoughtful Exploration: Shifting Mindsets for Effective Leadership 381

About the Author: William R. Stanek 385

Biography 386
Connect with William R. Stanek 387

Part 1. Let's Get Started!

Leadership Intelligence Mastery is a groundbreaking series that delves into the evolving landscape of leadership in the 21st century. It challenges the prevailing notion that Emotional Intelligence (EQ) and Intellectual Intelligence (IQ) alone suffice in the complex world of modern leadership. Instead, it introduces the Holistic Intelligence Model, a comprehensive framework that integrates eight essential pillars—Emotional Resilience (ER), Creativity Intelligence (CrQ), Practical Intelligence (PQ), Cultural Intelligence (CQ), Intrapersonal Intelligence (IntraQ), Interpersonal Intelligence (InterQ), Ethical Intelligence (EthQ), and Analytical Intelligence (AQ)—to redefine effective leadership.

In a rapidly changing global economy, leaders are tasked with navigating a myriad of challenges that demand more than traditional intelligence metrics. Leadership Intelligence Mastery recognizes that the divide between EQ and IQ is insufficient. By incorporating the eight pillars of the Holistic Intelligence Model, this series provides a robust framework that goes beyond conventional boundaries of intelligence. At its core, the books spotlight Emotional Resilience (ER) as the linchpin of effective leadership, equipping leaders to bounce back from setbacks, manage stress, and maintain a positive outlook even in the face of adversity.

Moreover, the series carefully dissects the distinctions between Emotional Resilience and EQ, emphasizing that ER transcends and encompasses emotional intelligence. It delves into the cognitive processes associated with understanding and managing emotions in high-pressure scenarios. By introducing the eight pillars of intelligence, including Creativity Intelligence (CrQ) for driving innovation, Cultural Intelligence (CQ) for leading in a globalized world, and Ethical Intelligence (EthQ) for principled leadership, Leadership Intelligence Mastery offers a holistic approach that empowers leaders to thrive in every dimension of their roles.

The 8 Pillars of Intelligence As a Framework for Transformative Leadership

As a Framework for Transformative Leadership, the 8 Pillars of Intelligence represent a revolutionary approach, combining a diverse array of skills and perspectives that empower leaders to excel in today's dynamic environments. These pillars—Emotional Resilience (ER), Creativity Intelligence (CrQ), Practical Intelligence (PQ), Cultural Intelligence (CQ), Intrapersonal Intelligence (IntraQ), Interpersonal Intelligence (InterQ), Ethical Intelligence (EthQ), and Analytical Intelligence (AQ)—transcend traditional notions of intelligence, shaping leaders who are resilient, innovative, and impactful. Together, they form a foundation for a transformative leadership journey that is as practical as it is profound.

1. Emotional Resilience (ER): The Keystone of Leadership

Emotional Resilience is the core pillar that empowers leaders to remain composed under pressure, recover quickly from setbacks, and sustain a positive and focused outlook. It transcends traditional emotional intelligence, embodying a level of emotional fortitude that helps leaders face challenges with grace and inspire confidence in others.

2. Creativity Intelligence (CrQ): Driving Vision and Innovation

Creativity Intelligence equips leaders with the ability to think beyond boundaries, generate novel ideas, and adapt to change. This pillar is vital for problem-solving, fostering innovation, and guiding teams toward visionary solutions. Leaders with high CrQ turn challenges into opportunities for growth and transformation.

3. Practical Intelligence (PQ): Bridging Knowledge and Action

Practical Intelligence—sometimes referred to as "street smarts"—helps leaders effectively apply their knowledge to real-world situations. It emphasizes adaptability, resourcefulness, and sound decision-making in dynamic environments, ensuring that leadership strategies are actionable and results-oriented.

4. Cultural Intelligence (CQ): Leading in a Globalized World

Cultural Intelligence allows leaders to thrive in diverse and interconnected environments. By fostering a deep understanding of cultural norms, values, and practices, this pillar enables leaders to build authentic connections, foster inclusivity, and navigate cross-cultural dynamics with sensitivity and skill.

5. Intrapersonal Intelligence: Leading from Within

Intrapersonal Intelligence focuses on self-awareness and self-regulation, enabling leaders to understand their own emotions, motivations, and values. This pillar empowers leaders to align their actions with their purpose, making decisions rooted in authenticity and inspiring trust among their teams.

6. Interpersonal Intelligence: The Art of Influence and Connection

Interpersonal Intelligence helps leaders build meaningful relationships, foster collaboration, and navigate social dynamics effectively. With strong interpersonal skills, leaders can communicate clearly, resolve conflicts constructively, and create an environment of trust and mutual respect, driving team cohesion and shared purpose.

7. Ethical Intelligence (EthQ): Leadership with Integrity

Ethical Intelligence serves as the moral foundation for principled leadership. By upholding values such as honesty, accountability, and fairness, leaders with strong ethical intelligence make decisions that inspire trust, maintain credibility, and prioritize the greater good. This pillar is essential for building an ethical and sustainable leadership legacy.

8. Analytical Intelligence (AQ): Solving Complexity with Clarity

Analytical Intelligence equips leaders with critical thinking and problem-solving skills needed to make sound, evidence-based decisions. By discerning patterns, evaluating risks, and analyzing data, leaders with strong analytical intelligence navigate complexity with precision and deliver effective, strategic outcomes.

A Symphony of Interconnected Intelligences

Embracing the Holistic Intelligence Model means embarking on a transformative journey where each pillar contributes uniquely to your leadership narrative. Whether you are stepping into a new leadership role, facing unprecedented challenges, or seeking to enhance your personal growth, the eight pillars provide a comprehensive roadmap to guide your path. Integrate Emotional Resilience (ER) to maintain composure and inspire your team during turbulent times, leverage Creativity Intelligence (CrQ) to drive innovation and strategic vision, and apply Practical Intelligence (PQ) to translate ideas into actionable plans. Enhance your leadership effectiveness by cultivating Cultural Intelligence (CQ) to navigate globalized environments, Intrapersonal Intelligence (IntraQ) for self-awareness and authentic decision-making, Interpersonal Intelligence (InterQ) to build strong, collaborative relationships, Ethical Intelligence (EthQ) to uphold integrity and trust, and Analytical Intelligence (AQ) to solve complex problems with clarity and precision.

Together, these pillars form a symphony of intelligences that empower you to lead with resilience, creativity, practicality, cultural sensitivity, self-awareness, interpersonal adeptness, ethical integrity, and analytical prowess. As you integrate these facets into your leadership practice, you will not only excel in your roles but also inspire those around you to achieve their fullest potential, creating a legacy of impactful and sustainable leadership.

Opening Reflection

Before you continue, take a moment to center yourself with the photograph that follows.

As you gaze upon this Hawaiian horizon, where the sun meets the sea, envision your leadership journey stretching out before you. Like the rhythmic crash of waves against the rocky shoreline, your path may be marked by challenges, yet it is also adorned with moments of beauty and triumph. Just as the sun dips below the horizon, signaling the close of one day and the promise of another, your journey in leadership is a series of endings and beginnings. Embrace them all, for they are the threads that weave the tapestry of your growth and resilience.

The interplay of light and shadow in this Hawaiian sky mirrors the dynamic nature of leadership. Each experience, each decision, shapes your narrative, much like the shifting colors of the sky influence the mood of the moment. With each step, you etch your unique story into the sands of time, drawing upon the eight pillars of the Holistic Intelligence Model—from Emotional Resilience (ER) that provides strength during tumultuous times to Creativity Intelligence (CrQ) that sparks innovative solutions. Let the spirit of the islands infuse your path with vitality and inspiration, empowering you to lead with purpose, passion, and resilience.

In this moment, on this shore, you stand at the threshold of a transformative journey. Let the timeless beauty of this photograph serve as a beacon, guiding you back to the essence of your leadership journey. Just as the boardwalk stretches ahead, disappearing into the horizon, your leadership odyssey is filled with boundless opportunities and unforeseen turns. Embrace each step with curiosity and purpose, knowing that every challenge met and every triumph celebrated is a testament to your strength and resilience. Embrace the path, for it is uniquely yours to shape, guided by the comprehensive framework of the Holistic Intelligence Model.

And if ever the winds of uncertainty threaten to steer you off course, return to this photograph. Let the timeless beauty of this moment serve as a beacon, guiding you back to the essence of your leadership journey. Remember, every challenge met, every triumph celebrated, is a testament to your strength and resilience. Embrace the path, for it is uniquely yours to shape.

When faced with crossroads, remember this mountain road. It symbolizes the choices, the uncharted territories, and the possibilities that await. As you stand at the precipice of decisions, know that each step, even the uncertain ones, contributes to your leadership odyssey. Embrace the journey, for every turn leads to growth, to wisdom, to your unique legacy. Keep forging ahead, for the road not taken is the one that defines your extraordinary story.

Charting Your Leadership Course

My journey through the intricacies of leadership has unfolded amidst some of the most pivotal moments in modern history. From the tense era of the Cold War to the turbulent times of the Iraq War, I found myself navigating through significant conflicts that tested our nation's resilience. What distinguishes me is my exceptional ability not only to adapt but to thrive in these high-pressure environments. Time and again, I was thrust into senior leadership positions, defying my relatively junior rank. This speaks volumes about my knack for evaluating critical situations and skillfully guiding those around me—often individuals significantly senior to me—toward resounding success, grounded in the eight pillars of the Holistic Intelligence Model.

My experiences, shaped in the crucible of the military and other arenas, have granted me profound insights: genuine leadership surpasses mere titles or years of service. It revolves around the ability to inspire and influence, to steer a team through even the most daunting challenges. In my role as a technology consultant, I often assumed the mantle of the "fixer" – the one summoned when situations seemed dire and hope was fading. Surprisingly, I discovered that more often than not, the root cause of many seemingly insurmountable problems was not a technological failure but rather a breakdown in leadership and intelligence dynamics. This realization reinforced the importance of Emotional Resilience

(ER), Interpersonal Intelligence (InterQ), and Analytical Intelligence (AQ) in effective leadership.

Recognizing this recurring pattern, my consulting focus naturally evolved toward uncovering people-centric solutions. It became evident that the success of any endeavor, particularly in the fast-paced and constantly evolving landscape of technology, hinges on the human element. This revelation forms the foundation of the principles expounded in our book, emphasizing that effective leadership is a multifaceted endeavor encompassing Emotional Resilience (ER), Practical Intelligence (PQ), Ethical Intelligence (EthQ), and the other pillars of holistic intelligence. By delving into the human dynamics that underpin every facet of professional life, our book provides a comprehensive guide for individuals looking to excel in their roles and lead with authenticity, empathy, and strategic acumen. Through a series of exercises, case studies, reflective practices, and more, readers will gain invaluable insights into honing their own intelligences, fostering a deeper understanding of themselves and those they lead.

Ultimately, this book is a testament to the idea that true leadership is a holistic endeavor, requiring a keen awareness of oneself, an astute understanding of others, and an unwavering commitment to ethical and principled decision-making. It's a call to action for leaders at every level and in every industry to embrace the complexities of human dynamics and harness them as a force for positive change and lasting success. Together, let us embark on this journey of reimagining leadership intelligence, shaping a future where leadership transcends convention and inspires profound transformation.

As you step into this transformative phase, remember that every milestone, every challenge, and every triumph is a thread woven into the tapestry of your leadership journey. Embrace each moment with curiosity and purpose, for it is through this journey that you will discover the true depth of your leadership potential. Let the Holistic Intelligence Model guide you, ensuring that your leadership is resilient, innovative, ethical, and profoundly impactful.

Let your gaze linger on the boardwalk that stretches ahead, disappearing into the horizon. Much like this path, your leadership journey unfurls before you, an odyssey filled with boundless opportunities and unforeseen turns. The distant pagoda-like structure beckons, a symbol of your destination, a testament to your aspirations.

Embrace the ebb and flow, for just as the tides shape the estuary, experiences shape leadership. The interplay of shadows and light in the sky above mirrors the dynamic nature of challenges and triumphs you'll encounter. Each step is a stitch in the fabric of your leadership narrative, weaving together resilience, wisdom, and growth.

With every footfall, you write your own story of leadership. As you traverse this boardwalk, know that you carry with you the potential to create profound impact. The journey itself is your canvas, waiting for the brush strokes of your unique vision. Embrace it with an open heart and a steadfast spirit, for the path you walk is yours to shape and yours to own.

Shifting Mindsets: Transform Thinking, Transform Leadership

2-Week Action Plan: Empowering Leaders through Mindset and Attitude Shifts

Embarking on the journey to enhance your leadership through mindset and attitude shifts requires intentional effort and structured guidance. This 2-week action plan is meticulously designed to help both aspiring leaders and seasoned professionals grasp, apply, and integrate the principles outlined in our book, "Empowering Leaders through Mindset and Attitude Shifts." The plan offers a balanced mix of reading, reflection, practical exercises, and the application of tools and techniques, all while providing the flexibility to tailor it to your specific needs and aspirations. By following this structured framework, you will cultivate a growth-oriented mindset, foster a positive attitude, and develop emotional resilience, ultimately transforming your leadership effectiveness and organizational impact.

Week 1: Building the Foundation of Mindset and Attitude

Day 1: Introduction and Orientation
- **Objective:** Familiarize yourself with the action plan and set intentions for the upcoming two weeks.
- **Time Allocation:** 1-2 hours
- **Action:**
- Review the Table of Contents and understand the structure of the book.
- Read The Holistic Intelligence Model, Letter From the Author and Our Foundational Proposition to understand the unique approach of the book.

- Set personal goals for what you aim to achieve through this action plan.
- Begin a Gratitude Journal to cultivate a positive mindset (15 minutes).

Day 1: Shifting Mindsets for Effective Leadership
- **Objective:** Understand the importance of shifting mindsets in leadership.
- **Time Allocation:** 1-2 hours
- **Actions:**
- Read Shifting Mindsets for Effective Leadership
- Summarize Key Points: Reflect on how shifting your mindset can enhance your leadership effectiveness.
- Set Intentions: Define what mindset shifts you aim to achieve.
- Journaling: Document your current mindset and areas you wish to shift.

Day 2: Unpacking Mindset and Attitude in Leadership
- **Objective:** Deep dive into the definitions and dynamics of mindset and attitude.
- **Time Allocation:** 1-2 hours
- **Actions:**
- Read Unpacking Mindset and Attitude in Leadership
- Reflective Questions:
- How do your current mindset and attitude influence your leadership style?
- What aspects of your mindset and attitude align with effective leadership?
- Practical Exercise: Identify three areas where you can cultivate a growth mindset and positive attitude.

- Journaling: Document your reflections and action steps.

Day 2: The Intricate Dance Between Mindset, Attitude, and Behavior in Leadership

- **Objective:** Explore the relationship between mindset, attitude, and behavior.
- **Time Allocation:** 1-2 hours
- **Actions:**
- Read The Intricate Dance Between Mindset, Attitude, and Behavior in Leadership
- Practical Exercise: Assess how your behavior reflects your current mindset and attitude.
- Journaling: Record instances where your mindset and attitude influenced your behavior positively or negatively.

Day 3: The Psychological Foundations of Mindset and Attitude in Leadership

- **Objective:** Understand the psychological underpinnings of mindset and attitude.
- **Time Allocation:** 3-4 hours
- **Actions:**
- Read The Psychological Foundations of Mindset and Attitude in Leadership
- Reflective Questions:
- How do cognitive processes influence your leadership mindset and attitude?
- In what ways does emotional intelligence play a role in your leadership effectiveness?
- Practical Exercise: Apply attribution theory to a recent success and failure, analyzing your interpretations.

- Journaling: Document insights from applying psychological theories to your leadership experiences.

Day 4: The Influence of Beliefs and Values on Leadership Mindset

- **Objective:** Examine how personal beliefs and values shape leadership mindset.
- **Time Allocation:** 3-4 hours
- **Actions:**
- Read The Influence of Beliefs and Values on Leadership Mindset
- Practical Exercise: Identify your core beliefs and assess how they influence your leadership.
- Values Alignment: Ensure your leadership practices align with your personal and organizational values.
- Journaling: Reflect on any limiting beliefs and strategies to overcome them.

Day 5: Emotional Resilience and Its Impact on Attitude in Leadership

- **Objective:** Understand emotional resilience and its role in shaping leadership attitude.
- **Time Allocation:** 2-3 hours
- **Actions:**
- Read Emotional Resilience and Its Impact on Attitude in Leadership
- Practical Exercise: Assess your current level of emotional resilience.
- Develop Resilience Strategies: Choose and begin implementing at least two strategies to enhance your emotional resilience.

- Journaling: Document your experiences and progress in building emotional resilience.

Day 6: The Power of Growth Mindset in Leadership

- **Objective:** Embrace and implement a growth mindset to drive leadership effectiveness.
- **Time Allocation:** 3-4 hours
- **Actions:**
- Read The Power of Growth Mindset in Leadership
- Reflective Questions:
- How can embracing a growth mindset transform your approach to leadership challenges?
- What steps can you take to foster a culture of continuous learning within your team?
- Practical Exercise: Identify one challenge and reframe it as an opportunity for growth.
- Journaling: Record your mindset shifts and plans to encourage a growth mindset in your leadership practices.

Day 7: Embracing Change and Continuous Learning: Keys to a Growth Mindset

- **Objective:** Cultivate adaptability and continuous learning to maintain a growth mindset.
- **Time Allocation:** 3-4 hours
- **Actions:**
- Read Embracing Change and Continuous Learning: Keys to a Growth Mindset
- Practical Exercise: Identify areas where you can embrace change and continuous learning.
- Implement Learning Strategies: Begin incorporating at least two continuous learning practices into your routine.

- Journaling: Reflect on how embracing change and learning influences your leadership.

Week 2: Applying Tools, Techniques, and Fostering Team Resilience

Day 8: Overcoming Fixed Mindset Traps: Navigating Challenges to Growth

- **Objective:** Identify and overcome fixed mindset traps to foster a growth mindset.
- **Time Allocation:** 1-2 hours
- **Actions:**
- Read Overcoming Fixed Mindset Traps: Navigating Challenges to Growth
- Practical Exercise: Identify common fixed mindset traps you encounter.
- Develop Strategies: Create strategies to overcome these traps and foster a growth mindset.
- Journaling: Document your progress in shifting from fixed to growth mindset.

Day 8: Fostering a Positive Attitude in Leadership

- **Objective:** Develop and maintain a positive attitude to enhance leadership effectiveness and team morale.
- **Time Allocation:** 3-4 hours
- **Actions:**
- Read Fostering a Positive Attitude in Leadership
- Practical Exercise: Implement two strategies to foster a positive attitude within your leadership role.
- Lead by Example: Demonstrate positivity in your daily interactions.

- Journaling: Reflect on the impact of these strategies on your attitude and team morale.

Day 9: The Ripple Effect of Positivity: How Attitude Shapes Organizational Culture

- **Objective:** Understand how a positive attitude influences organizational culture and drives performance.
- **Time Allocation:** 3-4 hours
- **Actions:**
- Read The Ripple Effect of Positivity: How Attitude Shapes Organizational Culture
- Practical Exercise: Assess your current organizational culture and identify areas where a positive attitude can further shape it.
- Develop a Culture Enhancement Plan: Outline specific actions to embed positivity into organizational norms and behaviors.
- Journaling: Document your assessments and planned cultural improvements.

Day 10: Strategies for Cultivating a Positive Attitude in Leadership Roles

- **Objective:** Implement strategies to develop and sustain a positive attitude in leadership.
- **Time Allocation:** 3-4 hours
- **Actions:**
- Read Strategies for Cultivating a Positive Attitude in Leadership Roles
- Practical Exercise: Select three strategies from the chapter to cultivate a positive attitude in your leadership role.
- Implement Strategies: Begin applying these strategies in your daily leadership practices.

- Journaling: Reflect on the effectiveness of these strategies and any adjustments needed.

Day 11: Navigating Challenges and Adversities: Resilience and Attitude in Leadership

- **Objective:** Develop resilience and maintain a positive attitude when facing challenges and adversities.
- **Time Allocation:** 3-4 hours
- **Actions:**
- Read Navigating Challenges and Adversities: Resilience and Attitude in Leadership
- Practical Exercise: Identify a recent challenge and apply resilience strategies to navigate it.
- Develop a Resilience Plan: Create a plan to enhance resilience in future challenges.
- Journaling: Document your experiences and reflections on overcoming adversity.

Day 12: Building Resilience Through a Positive Attitude: Thriving Amidst Adversity

- **Objective:** Leverage a positive attitude to build resilience and thrive in challenging situations.
- **Time Allocation:** 3-4 hours
- **Actions:**
- Read Building Resilience Through a Positive Attitude: Thriving Amidst Adversity
- Reflective Questions:
- How does a positive attitude contribute to your resilience as a leader?
- In what ways can you channel positive energy into actionable solutions during adversity?

- Practical Exercise: Identify and implement strategies from Chapter 14 to build resilience through positivity.
- Journaling: Reflect on how these strategies impact your ability to thrive amidst adversity and your overall leadership effectiveness.

Day 13: Emotional Intelligence and Its Role in Maintaining a Resilient Attitude

- **Objective:** Deepen your understanding of emotional intelligence (EI) and its synergy with emotional resilience in leadership.
- **Time Allocation:** 1-2 hours
- **Actions:**
- Read Emotional Intelligence and Its Role in Maintaining a Resilient Attitude
- Reflective Questions:
- How does emotional intelligence contribute to your emotional resilience?
- In what ways can you leverage EI to enhance your leadership effectiveness?
- Practical Exercise: Analyze the case study provided and identify key strategies that can be applied to your leadership approach.
- Develop an EI Enhancement Plan: Create actionable steps to improve your emotional intelligence based on the insights gained.
- Journaling: Document your reflections, strategies, and progress in enhancing EI and resilience.

Day 13: Exploring Case Study: The Transformational Impact of Mindset and Attitude

- **Objective:** Learn from real-life examples of transformational impact of mindset and attitude on leadership.
- **Time Allocation:** 1.5 – 2.5 hours
- **Action:**
- Read and analyze Case Study: The Transformational Impact of Mindset and Attitude.
- Extract key strategies and lessons learned.
- Reflect on how these strategies can be integrated into your leadership approach.
- Journal your reflections and action points.

Day 14: Tools and Techniques for Shifting Mindset and Attitude towards Effective Leadership

- **Objective:** Master various tools and techniques to shift mindset and attitude, enhancing leadership effectiveness.
- **Time Allocation:** 3-4 hours
- **Actions:**
- Read Tools and Techniques for Shifting Mindset and Attitude towards Effective Leadership
- Practical Exercise: Select three tools or techniques that resonate most with your leadership needs and develop a plan to implement them.
- Implement Tools: Begin applying the selected tools in your daily routine.
- Reflect and Adjust: Monitor the effectiveness of these tools and make necessary adjustments.
- Journaling: Document your experiences, challenges, and successes in using these tools and techniques.

Review: Empowering Leaders through Mindset and Attitude Shifts

- **Objective:** Integrate all learned concepts to empower yourself to lead with a transformed mindset and attitude.
- Time Allocation: 4-5 hours
- **Actions:**
- Read Empowering Leaders through Mindset and Attitude Shifts
- **Comprehensive Integration:**
- Review All Chapters: Briefly revisit key points from all the chapters to reinforce understanding.
- Create an Integrated Action Plan: Combine insights and strategies from all chapters to develop a comprehensive leadership development plan.
- Implement Key Strategies: Select and begin using at least two strategies from Tools and Techniques that align with your goals.
- Engage with a Mentor or Coach: Seek feedback on your progress and refine your action plan based on their insights.

Final Reflection:

- How have your mindset and attitude shifts impacted your leadership?
- What continuous practices will you adopt to sustain and further develop your leadership effectiveness?
- How can you support your team in their own mindset and attitude shifts?
- Journaling: Reflect on your overall growth, key takeaways, and ongoing strategies for maintaining mindset and attitude shifts.
- development.

Tools and Resources

To support your journey through this action plan, consider leveraging the following tools and resources:

- **Journaling Apps:** Tools like Day One, Evernote, or Microsoft OneNote to document your reflections, insights, and progress.
- **Mindfulness Apps:** Applications such as Headspace, Calm, or Insight Timer for guided meditation and mindfulness exercises.
- **Goal-Setting Worksheets:** Templates to define and track your personal development goals, available on platforms like Canva or Google Docs.
- **Books by William Stanek:** Dive deeper into leadership and personal development by exploring the Leadership Intelligence Mastery Library by William Stanek. These books provide invaluable insights and practical strategies to enhance your growth and understanding.
- **Resilience Workshops:** Participate in or organize workshops focused on building emotional resilience and adaptive thinking.

Building a resilient and effective leadership mindset is an ongoing journey that extends beyond these two weeks. Use this action plan as a foundation to develop and strengthen your mindset and attitude continuously. By committing to these practices, you not only enhance your own leadership capabilities but also inspire and empower your team to develop their own resilience. This collective strength contributes to a more adaptable, innovative, and high-performing organization capable of thriving in the face of adversity.

Next Steps:
- Review and Adjust the Action Plan: Tailor the activities to better fit your personal and professional schedule.
- Engage Your Team: Share this action plan with your team members to foster a collective commitment to resilience and growth.
- Track Your Progress: Use your gratitude journal and personal development plan to monitor your growth and make necessary adjustments.
- Seek Continuous Improvement: Regularly revisit the strategies and tools discussed in the book to further enhance your emotional resilience and leadership effectiveness.
- By following this 2-week action plan, you lay a strong foundation for integrating mindset and attitude shifts into your leadership role, setting the stage for enduring success and a thriving organizational culture.

Instructions for the Action Plan

The action plan offers a structured approach to integrate the strategies discussed in this book into your leadership style, whether you're starting your leadership journey or looking to enhance your existing leadership skills.

While the action plan is initially structured as a two-week schedule, it's important to note that both the schedule and all other aspects of the plan can be fully customized to align with your individual needs and preferences:

- **Personalization**   Tailor the suggested activities to align with your current level of leadership experience, preferences, and specific leadership context.

- **Allocate Flexible Time**   Recognize that the suggested schedule and time allocations are flexible. Adjust them to accommodate your availability and preferences. Focus on quality engagement rather than rigid adherence to schedules and time frames.

- **Reflect and Internalize**   After completing each session or activity, take time to reflect on the insights gained. Internalize how they can be applied to your unique leadership challenges and opportunities.

As an added component, contemplate including the following optional activities as part of the action plan:

- **Discussion Forums**   Engage with fellow leaders in discussions related to the content. Share experiences, insights, and challenges for mutual learning. This platform caters to leaders at various stages of their careers.

- **Weekly Q&A Sessions**   Attend live Q&A sessions to seek clarifications, share progress, and gain additional guidance from peers and experts. These sessions are beneficial for both aspiring leaders and experienced professionals looking to exchange insights.

- **Resource Library**   Explore the supplementary materials provided to deepen your understanding and application of resilience concepts. This resource is valuable regardless of your level of leadership experience.

Here are some overarching tips to assist you on your journey:

- **Consistency is Key**   Engage consistently with the material and activities to embed resilience practices into your leadership style, regardless of your current leadership level.

- **Balance Learning and Application**   Strike a balance between learning from the book and actively applying the concepts in your leadership role. This approach is beneficial for leaders at all stages.

- **Document Progress**   Keep a journal to record your reflections, insights, and challenges. Track your growth in resilience over time. This practice is valuable for leaders at any point in their journey.

- **Seek Feedback**   Encourage open communication with your team or peers. Seek feedback on your leadership style and adjust your approach based on their input. This applies to leaders at any stage of their careers.

- **Stay Open-Minded**   Embrace new ideas and perspectives. Be open to adapting your leadership style based on the insights gained. This attitude is crucial for leaders at all levels.

- **Celebrate Milestones**   Acknowledge and celebrate your achievements, no matter how small. Recognize your growth in resilience. This practice is relevant for leaders at any stage of their careers.

By following the structured action plan, you will not only gain a deeper understanding but also develop practical skills. The journey towards transformative leadership is ongoing, and each step you take contributes to your continued growth and development, regardless of your level of experience.

For aspiring leaders when the action plans suggest applying concepts to your leadership role, keep the following in mind:

- **Understand the Concept**   Begin by thoroughly understanding the concept or principle outlined in the action plan. Take time to grasp its significance and how it contributes to effective leadership.

- **Reflect on Relevance**   Consider how this concept applies to your current leadership aspirations and goals. Reflect on specific situations or scenarios where you can implement this principle.

- **Identify Opportunities**   Even if you haven't held formal leadership positions yet, there are likely opportunities within your academic, professional, or personal life where you can exhibit leadership qualities. Look for chances to take initiative, influence others positively, or demonstrate resilience.

- **Experiment and Practice** Apply the concept in these identified opportunities. Experiment with different approaches and observe the outcomes. Pay attention to what works well and what may require adjustments.

- **Seek Feedback** Don't hesitate to ask for feedback from mentors, supervisors, or peers who have experience in leadership roles. Their insights can provide valuable guidance on how you can further develop and apply these leadership skills.

- **Reflect on Learnings** After applying the concept, take time to reflect on the experience. Consider what went well, what challenges you faced, and what you learned from the process.

- **Document Achievements** Keep a record of instances where you successfully applied the concept. This documentation serves as tangible evidence of your developing leadership abilities and can be valuable when discussing your leadership potential in future endeavors.

- **Continuously Learn and Adapt** Aspire to be a lifelong learner. Stay open to new ideas and seek opportunities for growth. Adapt your approach based on the insights gained from applying leadership concepts.

Leadership is not solely defined by titles or formal positions. As an aspiring leader, you have the capacity to demonstrate leadership qualities in various capacities. Embrace these opportunities to cultivate and showcase your leadership potential. Each step you take now lays the foundation for your future leadership journey.

Lastly, whether you're an aspiring leader or an experienced one, keep the following points in mind:

- **Consistency and Patience**   Developing leadership skills is a journey that requires consistency and patience. It's important to acknowledge that growth takes time, and each step forward, no matter how small, is a valuable progression.

- **Adaptability**   Leadership is a dynamic field, and the ability to adapt to changing circumstances and environments is crucial. Remain open to new ideas, feedback, and emerging trends in leadership.

- **Leverage Networks**   Building a network of mentors, peers, and industry contacts can provide valuable insights and opportunities for growth. Don't hesitate to seek advice or engage in discussions with others who have experience in leadership.

- **Embrace Failure**   Failure is a natural part of the learning process. It's important to view setbacks as opportunities for growth and learning. Embrace challenges, learn from mistakes, and use them as stepping stones toward future success.

- **Self-Care and Well-Being**   Effective leadership starts with taking care of oneself. Prioritize physical, emotional, and mental well-being to ensure you have the energy and resilience needed to lead effectively.

- **Setting Personal Goals** Consider setting specific, measurable goals related to your leadership development. These goals can provide a clear direction for your journey and serve as milestones to track your progress.

- **Seek Additional Resources** Beyond the book, there are numerous resources available to support leadership development. This may include workshops, courses, seminars, and industry-specific publications. Stay curious and explore these opportunities.

- **Reflection and Continuous Improvement** Regularly take time to reflect on your leadership journey. Consider what has been effective, areas for improvement, and the direction you want to take in your leadership development.

- **Celebrate Achievements** Acknowledge and celebrate your achievements, no matter how small. Recognizing your progress can boost confidence and motivation, reinforcing your commitment to leadership growth.

- **Stay Inspired** Find sources of inspiration that resonate with you. Whether it's books, TED talks, podcasts, or biographies of influential leaders, seek out content that fuels your passion for leadership.

Leadership is a multifaceted skill that evolves over time. Embrace the process, stay committed to your growth, and remain open to new experiences and knowledge. The journey toward becoming an effective leader is not only professionally fulfilling but also personally enriching.

Shifting Mindsets for Effective Leadership

In the dynamic landscape of leadership, success isn't solely determined by skills and strategies; it's equally reliant on the often underestimated factors of mindset and attitude. These intangible elements form the bedrock upon which effective leadership is built. A leader's mindset shapes their perspective, influences decision-making, and ultimately defines their impact on the organization and its members.

A leader's mindset is akin to a compass that guides their actions. It encompasses beliefs, values, and outlook toward challenges and opportunities. A growth mindset empowers leaders to adapt, learn, and innovate in the face of adversity, while a fixed mindset can limit potential and hinder progress.

Attitude is the outward manifestation of one's mindset. It's reflected in a leader's demeanor, energy, and resilience. A positive attitude can galvanize teams, foster collaboration, and inspire collective achievement. Conversely, a negative attitude can stifle growth and erode morale.

The Holistic Intelligence Model and its 8 Pillars of Intelligence provide a comprehensive framework for understanding how shifting mindsets enhances leadership effectiveness. Each pillar offers insights into how leaders can transform their thinking and, consequently, their leadership impact.

1. Emotional Resilience (ER): Building Inner Strength

Emotional Resilience is the keystone that enables leaders to handle stress, recover from setbacks, and maintain a balanced outlook.

- **Mindset Integration:** Cultivating a resilient mindset allows leaders to view challenges as temporary obstacles rather than insurmountable barriers.
- **Application:** Leaders can develop coping strategies and stress management techniques to enhance their emotional resilience.

Example: Nelson Mandela demonstrated extraordinary emotional resilience by maintaining hope and purpose during his 27 years of imprisonment, emerging as a unifying leader for South Africa.

2. Creativity Intelligence (CrQ): Embracing Innovation

Creativity Intelligence fuels the ability to generate new ideas and think outside the box.

- **Mindset Integration:** Adopting an innovative mindset encourages leaders to challenge conventional thinking and embrace novel solutions.
- **Application:** Leaders can foster a culture of creativity by encouraging experimentation and valuing diverse perspectives.

Example: Steve Jobs' innovative mindset led to groundbreaking products that revolutionized multiple industries.

3. Practical Intelligence (PQ): Bridging Thought and Action

Practical Intelligence helps leaders apply knowledge effectively in real-world situations.

- **Mindset Integration:** A pragmatic mindset ensures that ideas are not just theoretical but are translated into actionable strategies.
- **Application:** Leaders can focus on developing problem-solving skills and making informed decisions that drive results.

Example: Indra Nooyi's practical intelligence was evident in her strategic decisions that led PepsiCo to diversify its product portfolio successfully.

4. Cultural Intelligence (CQ): Leading with Inclusivity

Cultural Intelligence enables leaders to navigate and embrace diversity.

- **Mindset Integration:** An inclusive mindset values different cultures, perspectives, and experiences, fostering a collaborative environment.
- **Application:** Leaders can enhance their cultural intelligence by learning about different cultures and adapting their communication styles accordingly.

Example: Satya Nadella prioritized cultural transformation at Microsoft by promoting inclusivity and empathy.

5. Intrapersonal Intelligence: Self-Awareness and Personal Growth

Intrapersonal Intelligence focuses on understanding oneself.

- **Mindset Integration:** A reflective mindset encourages continuous personal development and self-regulation.
- **Application:** Leaders can engage in self-assessment and mindfulness practices to increase self-awareness.

Example: Oprah Winfrey's intrapersonal intelligence has been a cornerstone of her authentic leadership style.

6. Interpersonal Intelligence: Connecting with Others

Interpersonal Intelligence enhances communication and relationship-building.

- **Mindset Integration:** An empathetic mindset prioritizes understanding and connecting with others.
- **Application:** Leaders can develop active listening skills and foster open dialogue within their teams.

Example: Jacinda Ardern's empathetic approach strengthened her connection with New Zealanders during times of crisis.

7. Ethical Intelligence (EthQ): Upholding Integrity

Ethical Intelligence provides a moral compass for leaders.

- **Mindset Integration:** An integrity-driven mindset ensures that decisions are aligned with ethical principles.

- **Application:** Leaders can establish clear values and lead by example to build trust.

Example: Warren Buffett is renowned for his ethical approach to business and investing.

8. Analytical Intelligence (AQ): Making Informed Decisions

Analytical Intelligence involves critical thinking and problem-solving.

- **Mindset Integration:** A strategic mindset leverages data and logic to make sound decisions.
- **Application:** Leaders can enhance their analytical skills through continuous learning and embracing evidence-based approaches.

Example: Bill Gates utilized analytical intelligence to drive Microsoft's success and later address global health issues through his foundation.

By integrating the 8 Pillars into their mindset, leaders can:

- **Enhance Decision-Making:** Combining analytical and practical intelligence leads to effective strategies.
- **Foster Innovation:** Creativity intelligence, coupled with a growth mindset, drives innovation.
- **Build Resilience:** Emotional resilience supports leaders in navigating adversity.
- **Promote Inclusivity:** Cultural and interpersonal intelligence foster diverse and collaborative teams.
- **Maintain Integrity:** Ethical intelligence ensures trustworthiness and credibility.

- **Encourage Self-Development:** Intrapersonal intelligence leads to continual personal and professional growth.

Practical Strategies for Shifting Mindsets Using the 8 Pillars

1. Develop Emotional Resilience

- **Mindfulness Practices:** Incorporate techniques such as meditation to enhance emotional regulation.
- **Stress Management:** Identify stressors and develop coping mechanisms.

2. Cultivate Creativity Intelligence

- **Encourage Curiosity:** Ask open-ended questions and explore new ideas.
- **Innovation Workshops:** Facilitate sessions that stimulate creative thinking.

3. Enhance Practical Intelligence

- **Problem-Solving Exercises:** Engage in real-world scenarios to apply knowledge.
- **Mentorship Programs:** Learn from experienced leaders who exemplify practical wisdom.

4. Boost Cultural Intelligence

- **Cultural Training:** Participate in workshops that increase cultural awareness.
- **Diverse Teams:** Build teams with varied backgrounds to enrich perspectives.

5. Strengthen Intrapersonal Intelligence

- **Self-Reflection Journals:** Regularly write about personal experiences and insights.

- **Goal Setting:** Define personal and professional objectives aligned with core values.

6. Improve Interpersonal Intelligence
- **Active Listening:** Practice listening without interrupting and provide thoughtful feedback.
- **Team-Building Activities:** Foster strong relationships through collaborative experiences.

7. Uphold Ethical Standards
- **Ethics Training:** Engage in discussions and training on ethical dilemmas.
- **Transparent Policies:** Implement and communicate clear ethical guidelines.

8. Sharpen Analytical Skills
- **Data Analysis Training:** Learn to interpret and utilize data effectively.
- **Critical Thinking Exercises:** Challenge assumptions and explore alternative solutions.

Real-World Application: A Case Study

Transforming Leadership

Background: A technology company faced stagnant growth due to a fixed mindset culture resistant to change.

Action Steps:
- **Leadership Training:** Implemented programs focusing on the 8 Pillars to shift mindsets.
- **Cultural Transformation:** Emphasized inclusivity and innovation through diverse teams.

- **Ethical Commitment:** Reinforced ethical practices to rebuild trust with stakeholders.

Outcomes:

- **Increased Innovation:** Launch of new products resulting from creative collaboration.
- **Enhanced Employee Engagement:** Higher morale and reduced turnover.
- **Sustainable Growth:** Achieved through strategic decision-making and ethical leadership.

Reflection Questions

- **Emotional Resilience:** How do you manage stress and setbacks? What strategies can you implement to enhance your resilience?
- **Creativity Intelligence:** In what ways can you foster innovation within your team or organization?
- **Practical Intelligence:** How effectively do you translate ideas into action? Where can you improve?
- **Cultural Intelligence:** How do you adapt your leadership style to accommodate diverse perspectives?
- **Intrapersonal Intelligence:** What are your core values, and how do they influence your leadership?
- **Interpersonal Intelligence:** How can you improve your communication to strengthen relationships?
- **Ethical Intelligence:** Are your decisions aligned with ethical principles? How do you ensure integrity?
- **Analytical Intelligence:** How do you utilize data and critical thinking in your decision-making process?

Action Plan

- **Assess Your Mindset:** Use the reflection questions to identify areas for growth.
- **Set Specific Goals:** Develop a plan to enhance each pillar relevant to your leadership context.
- **Engage in Continuous Learning:** Commit to personal and professional development aligned with the Holistic Intelligence Model.
- **Lead by Example:** Demonstrate the mindset and behaviors you wish to see in your organization.

Shifting to a growth-oriented, adaptive mindset is transformative for leadership effectiveness. By integrating the Holistic Intelligence Model's 8 Pillars, leaders can unlock new levels of potential, inspire their teams, and drive lasting success.

References

Carol Dweck's "Mindset: The New Psychology of Success"

Daniel Goleman's work on Emotional Intelligence

Howard Gardner's Theory of Multiple Intelligences

William Stanek's Holistic Intelligence Model

Unpacking Mindset and Attitude in Leadership

Core Reading

Leadership, at its core, is a mental endeavor. It requires a specific frame of mind and a set of attitudes that go beyond the technical skills and competencies. Mindset, in this context, refers to the overarching belief system and perspective a leader holds. It dictates how they perceive challenges, opportunities, and their own capabilities.

Attitude, on the other hand, is the emotional and behavioral manifestation of one's mindset. It's the way a leader presents themselves, responds to situations, and influences the morale and motivation of their team. A positive attitude can be contagious, creating an environment of enthusiasm and productivity, while a negative one can have a detrimental ripple effect.

To truly understand the impact of mindset and attitude on leadership, it's crucial to recognize that they are not fixed attributes. They can be cultivated, honed, and refined over time. Leaders have the agency to consciously shape their mindset and attitude, thereby influencing their effectiveness and the organizational culture they foster.

One of the foundational elements of mindset in leadership is the distinction between a fixed mindset and a growth mindset. A leader with a fixed mindset believes that their abilities and intelligence are static traits. They may shy away from challenges, fearing failure as a reflection of their inherent limitations. On the other hand, a leader with a growth mindset sees challenges as opportunities for learning and growth. They believe that with effort and dedication, they can develop new skills and overcome obstacles.

Attitude, in leadership, is a multifaceted facet that encompasses various dimensions. It includes emotional intelligence, which involves the ability to recognize, understand, and manage one's own emotions, as well as effectively influence the emotions of others. Leaders with high emotional intelligence are adept at navigating complex interpersonal dynamics and creating a positive work environment.

Another critical aspect of attitude is resilience. In the fast-paced and often unpredictable world of leadership, setbacks and failures are inevitable. A leader's ability to bounce back, learn from adversity, and maintain a forward-looking perspective is a testament to their resilience. It not only sets an example for their team but also instills confidence in their ability to navigate challenges.

Attitude extends to the leader's approach to decision-making. A leader with a proactive attitude takes initiative, seizes opportunities, and is unafraid to make difficult decisions. They possess a sense of agency and a willingness to take responsibility for the outcomes of their choices. This contrasts with a reactive attitude, where a leader may be more passive and hesitant in their decision-making, potentially missing out on valuable opportunities.

Unpacking mindset and attitude in leadership reveals their profound influence on a leader's effectiveness. They form the lens through which a leader perceives and responds to the world around them. Recognizing the malleability of these attributes empowers leaders to intentionally cultivate a mindset and attitude that align with their goals and aspirations.

Defining Mindset and Attitude in Leadership

Mindset refers to the overarching belief system and perspective a leader holds. It dictates how they interpret experiences, perceive challenges, and assess their own capabilities. A leader's mindset influences their approach to problem-solving, innovation, and growth. It acts as an internal compass guiding decisions and behaviors.

Fixed Mindset vs. Growth Mindset: Psychologist Carol Dweck introduces the concepts of a fixed mindset and a growth mindset.

- **Fixed Mindset:** Belief that abilities and intelligence are static. Leaders may avoid challenges, fear failure, and feel threatened by the success of others.
- **Growth Mindset:** Belief that abilities can be developed through dedication and hard work. Leaders embrace challenges, persist despite setbacks, and see effort as a path to mastery.

Embracing a growth mindset aligns with the Emotional Resilience (ER) pillar of the Holistic Intelligence Model, enabling leaders to navigate adversity with optimism and determination.

Attitude is the emotional and behavioral manifestation of one's mindset. It's how a leader presents themselves, responds to situations, and influences the morale and motivation of their team. Attitude reflects a leader's emotional state and can significantly impact the organizational climate.

- **Positive Attitude:** Encourages enthusiasm, fosters a supportive environment, and inspires team members to perform at their best.
- **Negative Attitude:** Can lead to low morale, decreased productivity, and a toxic work environment.

Developing a positive attitude connects with Interpersonal Intelligence, enhancing a leader's ability to build strong relationships and communicate effectively.

The Dynamic Nature of Mindset and Attitude

Mindset and attitude are not fixed traits; they are dynamic and can be cultivated over time. Leaders have the agency to consciously shape their mindset and attitude through self-awareness and intentional practice. This growth is central to the Intrapersonal Intelligence pillar, which focuses on self-understanding and self-regulation.

- **Self-Awareness:** Recognizing one's own beliefs, emotions, and biases.

- **Self-Regulation:** Managing one's emotional responses and behaviors in alignment with desired outcomes.

By developing intrapersonal intelligence, leaders can adapt their mindset and attitude to better align with their goals and the needs of their organization.

Dimensions of Attitude in Leadership

Attitude in leadership encompasses several critical dimensions:

1. Emotional Intelligence

Emotional Intelligence (EQ) involves the ability to recognize, understand, and manage one's own emotions, as well as to influence the emotions of others positively.

- **Self-Management:** Controlling impulsive feelings and behaviors.
- **Social Awareness:** Understanding the emotions, needs, and concerns of others.
- **Relationship Management:** Developing and maintaining good relationships, inspiring others, and managing conflict.

High EQ is essential for navigating complex interpersonal dynamics and creating a positive work environment, resonating with the Interpersonal Intelligence pillar.

2. Resilience and Adaptability

In the fast-paced world of leadership, setbacks are inevitable. Resilience is the capacity to recover quickly from difficulties.

Resilient Leaders:

- Maintain a positive outlook.
- Learn from failures.
- Adapt to changing circumstances.

Adaptability complements resilience, reflecting a leader's willingness to adjust their strategies and behaviors in response to new information or environments. This flexibility is critical for innovation and aligns with the Creativity Intelligence (CrQ) pillar.

3. Proactive vs. Reactive Approach

Proactive Leaders:

- Anticipate challenges and opportunities.
- Take initiative and are decisive.
- Embrace responsibility for outcomes.

Reactive Leaders:

- Respond only when necessary.
- May be hesitant or avoid decision-making.
- Risk missing opportunities due to inaction.

A proactive attitude is essential for effective leadership and is supported by the Analytical Intelligence (AQ) pillar, enabling leaders to make informed, strategic decisions.

The Influence of Mindset and Attitude on Leadership Effectiveness

Mindset and attitude significantly impact various aspects of leadership:

1. Decision-Making

Leaders with a growth mindset and positive attitude:

- Approach problems with creativity and open-mindedness.
- Are more likely to take calculated risks.
- Make decisions that encourage innovation and long-term success.

This approach is enhanced by Practical Intelligence (PQ), ensuring that decisions are grounded and actionable.

2. Organizational Culture

Leaders set the tone for the organization's culture:

- **Positive Culture:** Encourages collaboration, trust, and continuous learning.
- **Negative Culture:** May foster fear, resistance to change, and stagnation.

By embodying a growth mindset and positive attitude, leaders cultivate a culture that aligns with the Ethical Intelligence (EthQ) pillar, promoting integrity and shared values.

3. Team Performance

Leaders influence team dynamics through their attitude:

- **Motivation:** Positive leaders inspire and motivate their teams.
- **Engagement:** Teams are more engaged when leaders demonstrate enthusiasm and support.
- **Productivity:** A constructive environment leads to higher productivity and better outcomes.

Integrating the Holistic Intelligence Model

The 8 Pillars of the Holistic Intelligence Model offer a comprehensive framework for enhancing mindset and attitude in leadership:

- **Emotional Resilience (ER):** Cultivating the ability to cope with stress and recover from adversity strengthens a leader's mindset.
- **Creativity Intelligence (CrQ):** Encouraging innovative thinking and embracing new ideas fosters a forward-thinking attitude.
- **Practical Intelligence (PQ):** Applying knowledge effectively bridges the gap between ideas and action, reinforcing a proactive approach.
- **Cultural Intelligence (CQ):** Understanding and appreciating diverse perspectives enriches a leader's mindset and promotes inclusivity.
- **Intrapersonal Intelligence:** Enhancing self-awareness and self-regulation empowers leaders to consciously shape their mindset and attitude.
- **Interpersonal Intelligence:** Building strong relationships and effective communication skills positively influence team dynamics.

- **Ethical Intelligence (EthQ):** Upholding integrity guides leaders to make principled decisions, shaping an ethical organizational culture.
- Analytical Intelligence (AQ): Utilizing critical thinking and data analysis supports strategic decision-making and problem-solving.

By integrating these pillars, leaders develop a holistic approach to mindset and attitude, enhancing their overall effectiveness.

Practical Strategies for Cultivating a Growth Mindset and Positive Attitude

1. Self-Reflection and Assessment

- **Journaling:** Reflect on experiences, emotions, and reactions to identify patterns.
- **Feedback:** Seek constructive feedback from peers and mentors to gain insight into areas for improvement.

2. Embrace Continuous Learning

- **Professional Development:** Engage in workshops, courses, and reading to expand knowledge and skills.
- **Curiosity:** Adopt a learner's mindset by asking questions and exploring new ideas.

3. Develop Emotional Intelligence

- **Mindfulness Practices:** Incorporate meditation or deep-breathing exercises to enhance self-awareness.
- **Empathy Exercises:** Practice putting yourself in others' shoes to better understand their perspectives.

4. Foster Resilience and Adaptability

- **Set Realistic Goals:** Break larger objectives into manageable steps to build confidence.
- **Learn from Setbacks:** Analyze failures to extract lessons and inform future actions.

5. Cultivate a Proactive Attitude

- **Goal Setting:** Define clear, actionable objectives for yourself and your team.
- **Take Initiative:** Identify areas where you can make a positive impact and act on them.

6. Enhance Cultural Intelligence

- **Cultural Exposure:** Engage with diverse groups and learn about different cultures.
- **Inclusive Practices:** Encourage diverse viewpoints and create an environment where all voices are heard.

7. Uphold Ethical Standards

- **Define Core Values:** Clarify your personal and organizational values to guide decisions.
- **Lead by Example:** Demonstrate integrity in all actions to build trust and credibility.

8. Strengthen Analytical Skills

- **Critical Thinking Exercises:** Challenge assumptions and consider alternative perspectives.
- **Data Literacy:** Improve your ability to interpret and use data effectively in decision-making.

Real-World Example: Satya Nadella's Leadership at Microsoft

When Satya Nadella became CEO of Microsoft, he recognized the need for a cultural and mindset shift within the company.

- **Growth Mindset:** Promoted a culture where learning from failures was encouraged.
- **Positive Attitude:** Emphasized empathy and collaboration, transforming internal dynamics.
- **Holistic Approach:** Integrated innovation (Creativity Intelligence), inclusivity (Cultural Intelligence), and ethical practices (Ethical Intelligence) into the company's core values.

As a result, Microsoft experienced renewed innovation, employee engagement, and market success.

—

Unpacking mindset and attitude in leadership reveals their profound influence on effectiveness and organizational outcomes. Recognizing that these attributes are malleable empowers leaders to intentionally cultivate a mindset and attitude that align with their goals and aspirations.

By integrating the principles of the Holistic Intelligence Model, leaders can enhance their capabilities across multiple dimensions, leading to transformative personal growth and positive impact on their teams and organizations. Embracing a growth mindset and positive attitude is not just beneficial—it's essential for navigating the complexities of modern leadership.

Defining Mindset and Attitude: Foundations of Effective Leadership

Core Reading

At the heart of leadership lies the intricate interplay of mindset and attitude, two foundational pillars that shape the trajectory of a leader's journey. These twin elements constitute the bedrock upon which effective leadership is built. To comprehend their profound impact, it is imperative to dissect and understand each component individually.

Mindset, the first cornerstone, is the lens through which a leader interprets and navigates the world. It encapsulates a set of beliefs, values, and assumptions that underlie a leader's perceptions, decisions, and actions. This mental framework determines how challenges are approached, risks are assessed, and opportunities are seized. It is the compass that guides a leader's journey, influencing the routes they choose and the destinations they aim for.

In leadership, there are primarily two archetypes of mindsets: fixed and growth. A fixed mindset is characterized by a belief in static abilities. Leaders with this mindset tend to view talents and intelligence as innate, unchangeable traits. Challenges are perceived as threats, and failures are often internalized as personal inadequacies. In contrast, a growth mindset embraces the idea that abilities can be developed through dedication, effort, and learning. Leaders with a growth mindset relish challenges, seeing them as stepping stones to mastery.

Attitude, the second pillar, is the outward manifestation of a leader's internal landscape. It encompasses the emotional tone, disposition, and behavioral responses that a leader exhibits. Attitude is the brushstroke that colors interactions, influences team dynamics, and sets the tone for organizational culture. It is the energy source that fuels motivation, resilience, and collaboration within a team.

Within the realm of attitude, emotional intelligence plays a pivotal role. This capacity to recognize, understand, and manage one's own emotions, as well as empathize with the emotions of others, is the cornerstone of effective leadership. Leaders who possess high emotional intelligence are adept at fostering an inclusive and supportive environment. They can navigate complex interpersonal dynamics with grace and tact.

Attitude encompasses resilience, a quality that enables leaders to bounce back from setbacks, learn from failures, and persevere in the face of adversity. A resilient leader not only sets a powerful example but also instills confidence and fortitude in their team members. This contagious spirit of tenacity becomes a driving force within the organization.

In addition to emotional intelligence and resilience, attitude extends to the leader's decision-making approach. Proactivity, a key facet of attitude, is the willingness to take initiative and assume responsibility for outcomes. Leaders with a proactive attitude seize opportunities, tackle challenges head-on, and make informed, timely decisions. This proactive stance not only catalyzes progress but also fosters a culture of empowerment within the team.

Defining mindset and attitude unveils their pivotal role in shaping effective leadership. They serve as the foundation upon which leadership acumen is constructed. Acknowledging their profound impact empowers leaders to intentionally cultivate a growth-oriented mindset and a positive, proactive attitude.

Mindset: The Internal Compass of Leadership

Mindset is the lens through which a leader interprets and navigates the world. It encapsulates a set of beliefs, values, and assumptions that underlie a leader's perceptions, decisions, and actions. This mental framework determines how challenges are approached, risks are assessed, and opportunities are seized. It is the compass that guides a leader's journey, influencing the routes they choose and the destinations they aim for.

In leadership, there are primarily two archetypes of mindsets, as identified by psychologist Carol Dweck:

Fixed Mindset: Characterized by the belief that abilities and intelligence are static traits. Leaders with this mindset tend to:

- **Avoid Challenges:** Viewing them as threats to their perceived competence.
- **Give Up Easily:** Facing obstacles, they may retreat rather than persist.

- **Ignore Useful Feedback:** Dismissing constructive criticism as irrelevant.
- **Feel Threatened by Others' Success:** Viewing others' achievements as a reflection of their own inadequacies.

Growth Mindset: Embraces the idea that abilities can be developed through dedication, effort, and learning. Leaders with a growth mindset:

- **Embrace Challenges:** Seeing them as opportunities to grow.
- **Persist in the Face of Setbacks:** Demonstrating resilience and tenacity.
- **Learn from Criticism:** Valuing feedback as a tool for improvement.
- **Find Inspiration in Others' Success:** Using it as motivation to enhance their own abilities.

Integrating the Holistic Intelligence Model

The concept of mindset aligns closely with several pillars of the Holistic Intelligence Model:

- **Intrapersonal Intelligence:** Enhances self-awareness and self-regulation, allowing leaders to recognize their mindset and make conscious efforts to cultivate a growth-oriented perspective.
- **Analytical Intelligence (AQ):** Supports critical thinking and reflection, enabling leaders to challenge their own assumptions and embrace new ways of thinking.
- **Emotional Resilience (ER):** A growth mindset fosters emotional resilience by framing challenges as learning

opportunities, thus reducing stress and enhancing adaptability.

Attitude: The Outward Expression of Inner Beliefs

Attitude is the outward manifestation of a leader's internal landscape. It encompasses the emotional tone, disposition, and behavioral responses that a leader exhibits. Attitude is the brushstroke that colors interactions, influences team dynamics, and sets the tone for organizational culture. It is the energy source that fuels motivation, resilience, and collaboration within a team.

Key Components of Attitude in Leadership

1. Emotional Intelligence (EQ)

Within the realm of attitude, emotional intelligence plays a pivotal role. This capacity to recognize, understand, and manage one's own emotions, as well as empathize with the emotions of others, is the cornerstone of effective leadership.

- **Self-Awareness:** Understanding one's emotions and their impact on others.
- **Self-Regulation:** Managing emotions to respond appropriately.
- **Motivation:** Harnessing emotions to stay focused on goals.
- **Empathy:** Recognizing and appreciating others' feelings.
- **Social Skills:** Building relationships and navigating social complexities.

Integration with the Holistic Intelligence Model: Emotional intelligence aligns with both Intrapersonal Intelligence (self-awareness) and Interpersonal Intelligence (empathy and social skills), enhancing a leader's ability to connect with and inspire others.

2. Resilience

Resilience is the quality that enables leaders to bounce back from setbacks, learn from failures, and persevere in the face of adversity.

- **Adaptability:** Adjusting to new conditions with a positive outlook.
- **Persistence:** Continuing efforts despite difficulties.
- **Optimism:** Maintaining a hopeful and constructive perspective.

Integration with the Holistic Intelligence Model: Resilience is a key aspect of Emotional Resilience (ER), supporting leaders in maintaining stability and composure under pressure.

3. Proactivity

Proactivity is the willingness to take initiative and assume responsibility for outcomes.

- **Initiative:** Acting without being prompted by others.
- **Responsibility:** Owning decisions and their consequences.
- **Forward-Thinking:** Anticipating future challenges and opportunities.

Integration with the Holistic Intelligence Model: Proactivity is connected to Practical Intelligence (PQ), which involves applying knowledge effectively to achieve goals.

4. Ethical Orientation

Attitude also reflects a leader's commitment to ethical principles.

- **Integrity:** Upholding moral and ethical standards.
- **Accountability:** Being answerable for actions and decisions.
- **Fairness:** Treating others justly and equitably.

Integration with the Holistic Intelligence Model: This aligns with Ethical Intelligence, guiding leaders to make principled decisions.

The Impact of Attitude on Organizational Culture

A leader's attitude significantly influences:

- **Team Morale:** A positive attitude boosts confidence and enthusiasm among team members.
- **Communication:** An open and respectful attitude fosters transparent and effective dialogue.
- **Innovation:** An encouraging attitude promotes creativity and experimentation.

The Synergy Between Mindset and Attitude

Mindset and attitude are deeply interconnected:

- **Mindset Shapes Attitude:** A leader's beliefs influence their emotional responses and behaviors.
- **Attitude Reinforces Mindset:** Consistent behaviors and emotional expressions can strengthen underlying beliefs.

This synergy affects:

- **Decision-Making:** A growth mindset combined with a proactive attitude leads to innovative and effective solutions.
- **Team Dynamics:** Leaders who model positive attitudes inspire similar behaviors in their teams.
- **Organizational Success:** The combined effect enhances adaptability, resilience, and overall performance.

Case Study: Satya Nadella's Transformation of Microsoft

When Satya Nadella became CEO of Microsoft, he recognized the need to shift the company's culture:

- **Mindset Shift:** Encouraged a move from a fixed to a growth mindset across the organization.
- **Attitude Transformation:** Emphasized empathy, collaboration, and inclusivity.
- Outcomes:

Innovation: Revival of creativity leading to new products and services.

Employee Engagement: Increased morale and collaboration.

Market Performance: Significant growth in market value and competitiveness.

Nadella's leadership exemplifies how aligning mindset and attitude can drive organizational transformation.

Cultivating Mindset and Attitude Through the 8 Pillars

1. Enhancing Intrapersonal Intelligence

- **Self-Reflection:** Regularly assess personal beliefs and assumptions.
- **Mindfulness Practices:** Increase self-awareness and emotional regulation.
- **Goal Setting:** Align personal values with professional objectives.

2. Developing Emotional Resilience (ER)

- **Stress Management:** Utilize techniques like deep breathing and meditation.
- **Positive Reframing:** View challenges as opportunities for growth.
- **Support Systems:** Build networks for encouragement and advice.

3. Strengthening Interpersonal Intelligence

- **Active Listening:** Fully engage in conversations, acknowledging others' perspectives.
- **Empathy Exercises:** Practice understanding others' emotions and motivations.
- **Conflict Resolution Skills:** Learn to navigate disagreements constructively.

4. Applying Practical Intelligence (PQ)

- **Decision-Making Skills:** Use practical reasoning to make effective choices.
- **Problem-Solving:** Approach obstacles methodically and creatively.

- **Action Orientation:** Translate ideas into tangible results.

5. Fostering Ethical Intelligence

- **Ethical Training:** Participate in workshops on ethics and compliance.
- **Transparency:** Communicate openly about decisions and their rationale.
- **Lead by Example:** Demonstrate ethical behavior consistently.

6. Cultivating Cultural Intelligence (CQ)

- **Cultural Awareness:** Educate yourself on different cultural practices and norms.
- **Adaptability:** Adjust communication styles to suit diverse audiences.
- **Inclusivity:** Promote diversity and inclusion within the team.

7. Enhancing Analytical Intelligence (AQ)

- **Critical Thinking:** Challenge assumptions and evaluate evidence objectively.
- **Data Literacy:** Develop skills in analyzing and interpreting data.
- **Strategic Planning:** Use analytical insights to inform long-term strategies.

8. Encouraging Creativity Intelligence (CrQ)

- **Innovation Mindset:** Encourage experimentation and tolerate failures as learning experiences.
- **Brainstorming Sessions:** Facilitate collaborative idea generation.

- **Continuous Learning:** Stay curious and open to new information.

Practical Strategies for Leaders

- **Adopt a Learning Orientation:** Embrace continuous improvement for yourself and your team.
- **Model Desired Behaviors:** Demonstrate the mindset and attitude you wish to see.
- **Provide Feedback and Recognition:** Reinforce positive behaviors and acknowledge efforts.
- **Create a Supportive Environment:** Foster psychological safety where team members feel valued and heard.

Defining mindset and attitude unveils their pivotal role in shaping effective leadership. They are the foundational elements that influence how leaders think, behave, and impact others. By intentionally cultivating a growth-oriented mindset and a positive, proactive attitude—integrated with the Holistic Intelligence Model's 8 Pillars—leaders can enhance their effectiveness and drive meaningful change within their organizations.

The Intricate Dance Between Mindset, Attitude, and Behavior in Leadership

Core Reading

In the tapestry of effective leadership, mindset, attitude, and behavior form an inseparable triad, each thread influencing and being influenced by the others. Understanding this dynamic interplay is essential for leaders striving to maximize their impact and inspire meaningful change.

Mindset, as the foundational element, lays the groundwork for both attitude and behavior. It is the fertile soil from which attitudes and actions sprout. A leader's mindset shapes their beliefs about what is possible and sets the parameters for their vision. For instance, a leader with a growth mindset approaches challenges as opportunities for learning and growth. This outlook informs their attitude, leading to a positive and constructive approach to difficulties.

Attitude is the bridge that connects mindset to behavior. It is the lens through which a leader interprets their environment and responds to stimuli. A leader's attitude manifests in their demeanor, communication style, and interactions with team members. An optimistic attitude, for example, can inspire and motivate others, creating an atmosphere of positivity and enthusiasm. Conversely, a negative or complacent attitude can stifle creativity and hinder progress.

Behavior, in turn, is the tangible expression of mindset and attitude. It is the culmination of thought and feeling translated into action. A leader's behavior encompasses their decision-making, communication, problem-solving, and conflict resolution. For instance, a leader with a growth mindset and a proactive attitude is more likely to take calculated risks, pursue innovation, and encourage a culture of continuous improvement.

The alignment of these three components is crucial for leadership effectiveness. A leader may possess a growth-oriented mindset and a positive attitude, but if their behavior does not reflect these attributes, their impact will be limited. Conversely, a leader who demonstrates congruence between their mindset, attitude, and behavior exudes authenticity, fostering trust and credibility within their team.

The interplay between mindset, attitude, and behavior is not static. It is subject to evolution and adaptation. A leader's mindset can evolve over time through learning, exposure to new experiences, and deliberate efforts to challenge and expand existing beliefs. Attitude, too, can be refined through self-awareness and intentional cultivation of emotional intelligence.

Behavior can serve as a feedback loop, influencing and reinforcing mindset and attitude. When leaders witness the positive outcomes of their behaviors aligned with a growth mindset and a proactive attitude, it reinforces their belief in the efficacy of this approach. This, in turn, perpetuates a cycle of positive reinforcement, strengthening their commitment to these foundational principles.

The intricate dance between mindset, attitude, and behavior forms the essence of effective leadership. Leaders who grasp the synergistic relationship between these elements can leverage them as powerful tools for driving meaningful change.

Understanding the Triad: Mindset, Attitude, and Behavior

Mindset is the fertile soil from which attitudes and actions sprout. It encompasses the set of beliefs, values, and assumptions that shape a leader's perception of what is possible, setting the parameters for their vision and goals.

Growth Mindset vs. Fixed Mindset: As introduced by psychologist Carol Dweck, leaders with a growth mindset view challenges as opportunities for learning and development, whereas those with a fixed mindset may see obstacles as insurmountable barriers.

Integration with the Holistic Intelligence Model:

- **Intrapersonal Intelligence:** Enhances self-awareness, allowing leaders to recognize and develop their mindset.
- **Emotional Resilience (ER):** Supports leaders in maintaining a positive mindset even in the face of adversity.
- **Analytical Intelligence (AQ):** Enables leaders to critically assess their beliefs and adapt their mindset accordingly.

Attitude serves as the bridge between mindset and behavior. It is the lens through which a leader interprets their environment and responds to stimuli, manifesting in their demeanor, communication style, and interactions with others.

- **Optimistic Attitude:** Inspires and motivates, fostering an atmosphere of positivity and enthusiasm.
- **Negative Attitude:** Can stifle creativity, hinder progress, and create a toxic work environment.

Integration with the Holistic Intelligence Model:

- **Interpersonal Intelligence:** Enhances a leader's ability to communicate effectively and build positive relationships.
- **Emotional Intelligence:** Allows leaders to manage their emotions and influence the emotions of others constructively.
- **Cultural Intelligence (CQ):** Enables leaders to adopt attitudes that are sensitive and adaptable to diverse cultural contexts.

Behavior is the tangible expression of mindset and attitude, encompassing decision-making, problem-solving, communication, and conflict resolution.

- **Aligned Behavior:** When behavior reflects a growth mindset and positive attitude, it leads to actions that promote innovation, collaboration, and progress.
- **Misaligned Behavior:** Discrepancies between mindset, attitude, and behavior can lead to mistrust and reduced effectiveness.

Integration with the Holistic Intelligence Model:

- **Practical Intelligence (PQ):** Helps leaders apply their mindset and attitude effectively in real-world situations.
- **Ethical Intelligence:** Guides leaders to behave in ways consistent with ethical principles and values.
- **Creativity Intelligence (CrQ):** Encourages innovative behaviors that drive organizational growth.

The Dynamic Interplay Among Mindset, Attitude, and Behavior

The alignment of mindset, attitude, and behavior is crucial for leadership effectiveness. Congruence among these elements fosters authenticity, which is essential for building trust and credibility within a team.

- **Authentic Leadership:** Leaders who consistently align their beliefs, attitudes, and actions are perceived as genuine and trustworthy.
- **Impact on Team Dynamics:** Such alignment enhances team cohesion, motivation, and performance.

The interplay between mindset, attitude, and behavior is not static; it evolves over time through learning and experience.

- **Mindset Evolution:** Exposure to new ideas and challenges can expand a leader's mindset.
- **Attitude Refinement:** Self-awareness and emotional intelligence enable leaders to adjust their attitudes to better serve their goals.
- **Behavioral Adaptation:** Reflecting on the outcomes of actions allows leaders to modify behaviors for improved effectiveness.

Feedback Loops:

- **Positive Reinforcement:** Successful behaviors reinforce a growth mindset and positive attitude.
- **Learning from Failure:** Setbacks provide opportunities to reassess and realign mindset, attitude, and behavior.

By integrating the 8 Pillars of Intelligence, leaders can enhance the synergy between mindset, attitude, and behavior:

1. Emotional Resilience (ER):
- **Mindset:** Cultivate resilience by embracing challenges as growth opportunities.
- **Attitude:** Maintain optimism and composure under pressure.
- **Behavior:** Demonstrate perseverance and encourage the same in others.

2. Creativity Intelligence (CrQ):
- **Mindset:** Foster openness to new ideas and innovative thinking.
- **Attitude:** Encourage curiosity and a willingness to explore uncharted territories.
- **Behavior:** Implement creative solutions and inspire innovation in the team.

3. Practical Intelligence (PQ):
- **Mindset:** Focus on practical problem-solving and application of knowledge.
- **Attitude:** Exhibit pragmatism and adaptability.
- **Behavior:** Translate ideas into actionable plans and results.

4. Cultural Intelligence (CQ):

- **Mindset:** Value diversity and seek to understand different perspectives.
- **Attitude:** Show respect and openness towards cultural differences.
- **Behavior:** Adapt leadership styles to be effective across cultures.

5. Intrapersonal Intelligence:

- **Mindset:** Engage in self-reflection to understand personal beliefs and motivations.
- **Attitude:** Maintain self-confidence balanced with humility.
- **Behavior:** Make decisions aligned with personal values and vision.

6. Interpersonal Intelligence:

- **Mindset:** Believe in the importance of strong relationships and teamwork.
- **Attitude:** Display empathy and active listening.
- **Behavior:** Foster collaboration and resolve conflicts constructively.

7. Ethical Intelligence:

- **Mindset:** Commit to integrity and ethical principles.
- **Attitude:** Uphold fairness and accountability.
- **Behavior:** Act transparently and encourage ethical practices.

8. Analytical Intelligence (AQ):

- **Mindset:** Value critical thinking and evidence-based decision-making.

- **Attitude:** Maintain objectivity and openness to new information.
- **Behavior:** Analyze situations thoroughly before acting.

Practical Strategies for Aligning Mindset, Attitude, and Behavior

1. Self-Assessment and Reflection

- **Mindset Evaluation:** Use assessments to identify whether you lean towards a fixed or growth mindset.
- **Attitude Check:** Reflect on your emotional responses and how they affect your leadership.
- **Behavioral Analysis:** Observe whether your actions consistently reflect your beliefs and attitudes.
- **Holistic Intelligence Pillars Involved:** Intrapersonal Intelligence, Analytical Intelligence

2. Cultivating Emotional Intelligence

- **Enhance Self-Awareness:** Practice mindfulness to become more attuned to your emotions.
- **Develop Empathy:** Engage with team members to understand their perspectives.
- **Holistic Intelligence Pillars Involved:** Emotional Resilience, Interpersonal Intelligence

3. Setting Intentional Goals

- **Align Goals with Values:** Ensure your objectives reflect your core beliefs.
- **Behavioral Objectives:** Define specific actions that embody your desired mindset and attitude.
- **Holistic Intelligence Pillars Involved:** Practical Intelligence, Ethical Intelligence

4. Seeking Continuous Learning and Growth

- **Embrace Challenges:** Take on tasks that push you out of your comfort zone.
- **Learn from Experiences:** Reflect on outcomes to inform future decisions.
- **Holistic Intelligence Pillars Involved:** Creativity Intelligence, Analytical Intelligence

5. Building Supportive Environments

- **Foster Open Communication:** Encourage honest dialogue within your team.
- **Promote a Growth Culture:** Lead by example in valuing learning and development.
- **Holistic Intelligence Pillars Involved:** Cultural Intelligence, Interpersonal Intelligence

Real-World Examples

1. Satya Nadella, CEO of Microsoft

Mindset:

- Adopted a growth mindset, emphasizing learning over knowing.
- Encouraged a shift from a "know-it-all" to a "learn-it-all" culture.

Attitude:

- Demonstrated empathy and inclusivity.
- Fostered a collaborative environment.

Behavior:

- Implemented organizational changes promoting innovation and agility.
- Invested in employee development and cross-functional teams.

Integration with Holistic Intelligence:

- **Intrapersonal Intelligence:** Self-reflected on leadership style to drive cultural change.
- **Cultural Intelligence:** Navigated diverse global markets effectively.
- **Ethical Intelligence:** Committed to ethical AI development and corporate responsibility.

2. Indra Nooyi, Former CEO of PepsiCo

Mindset:

- Embraced a long-term, sustainable growth mindset.
- Advocated for "Performance with Purpose."

Attitude:

- Showed optimism about integrating social responsibility with profitability.
- Maintained resilience in the face of skepticism.

Behavior:

- Led initiatives to make products healthier.
- Invested in environmental sustainability.

Integration with Holistic Intelligence:

- **Ethical Intelligence:** Prioritized ethical considerations in business strategies.
- **Practical Intelligence:** Balanced immediate business needs with future societal trends.
- **Cultural Intelligence:** Recognized and adapted to global consumer preferences.

The Interconnection

Mindset influences attitude, which in turn shapes behavior. A leader's belief system (mindset) affects how they feel about situations (attitude), leading to corresponding actions (behavior). This interplay is critical in leadership effectiveness.

Integration with the Holistic Intelligence Model:

1. Intrapersonal Intelligence:

Self-Awareness: Recognizing how one's mindset affects attitude and behavior allows leaders to make conscious adjustments. Self-reflection helps in identifying areas for growth and aligning actions with intentions.

2. Interpersonal Intelligence:

Empathy and Communication: Understanding how one's attitude impacts others is essential. Leaders who are aware of their influence can adjust their behavior to motivate and engage their teams effectively.

3. Emotional Resilience (ER):

Managing Emotional Responses: Leaders who regulate their emotions can maintain a positive attitude, even in challenging situations. This stability influences their behavior, promoting consistent and constructive interactions.

4. Analytical Intelligence (AQ):

Critical Evaluation: Analyzing the outcomes of behaviors helps leaders understand the effectiveness of their mindset and attitude. Data-driven insights enable leaders to make informed adjustments to their approach.

5. Ethical Intelligence (EthQ):

Integrity in Action: Ethical considerations ensure that a leader's behavior aligns with moral principles. An ethical mindset fosters an attitude of responsibility, guiding behaviors that build trust and respect.

6. Cultural Intelligence (CQ):

Adaptability: Leaders with high cultural intelligence adjust their mindset and attitude to respect cultural differences. This adaptability enhances their behavior in diverse environments, promoting inclusivity.

7. Creativity Intelligence (CrQ):

Innovative Approaches: A mindset open to new ideas fosters a creative attitude. Leaders who embrace creativity in their thinking are more likely to engage in innovative behaviors, driving organizational growth.

8. Practical Intelligence (PQ):

Effective Implementation: A pragmatic mindset leads to an action-oriented attitude. Leaders apply practical intelligence to translate ideas into effective behaviors that achieve results.

Case Example: The Holistic Leader

Consider a leader facing a significant organizational change:

Mindset: Believes that challenges are opportunities for growth (Growth Mindset).

Attitude: Approaches the change with optimism and confidence.

Behavior: Communicates a clear vision, involves the team in planning, and takes decisive action.

Holistic Intelligence Integration:

Emotional Resilience (ER): Manages stress associated with change, providing stability for the team.

Creativity Intelligence (CrQ): Generates innovative solutions to navigate the change effectively.

Practical Intelligence (PQ): Applies strategies that are feasible and effective in the real world.

Cultural Intelligence (CQ): Considers the diverse perspectives within the team, fostering inclusive decision-making.

Intrapersonal Intelligence: Reflects on personal responses to change, ensuring authentic leadership.

Interpersonal Intelligence: Communicates effectively, building trust and collaboration.

Ethical Intelligence (EthQ): Maintains integrity, making decisions that are ethically sound.

Analytical Intelligence (AQ): Uses data and evidence to inform strategies, assessing risks and opportunities.

—

The intricate dance between mindset, attitude, and behavior forms the essence of effective leadership. Leaders who understand and harness the synergistic relationship among these elements can leverage them as powerful tools for driving meaningful change. By intentionally aligning mindset, attitude, and behavior—and integrating the principles of the Holistic Intelligence Model—leaders can unleash their full potential and inspire transformative impact within their organizations.

Reflection Questions

1. Mindset:

Do you perceive challenges as threats or opportunities?

How can you shift your mindset to embrace growth more fully?

2. Attitude:

How does your attitude influence your team's morale and productivity?

What steps can you take to foster a more positive attitude?

3. Behavior:

Are your actions consistent with your stated values and beliefs?

How can you adjust your behavior to better align with your desired leadership impact?

Action Plan

1. Assess Alignment: Regularly evaluate the congruence between your mindset, attitude, and behavior.

2. Set Development Goals: Identify areas for growth within the 8 Pillars of the Holistic Intelligence Model.

3. Implement Changes: Take actionable steps to adjust your mindset, attitude, and behavior.

4. Seek Feedback: Encourage input from peers and team members to gain different perspectives.

The Psychological Foundations of Mindset and Attitude in Leadership

Core Reading

Understanding the psychological underpinnings of mindset and attitude is fundamental to unlocking their full potential in leadership. These foundational elements are shaped by a complex interplay of cognitive processes, emotional intelligence, and social dynamics. By delving into these psychological foundations, leaders can gain insights into how to cultivate a growth-oriented mindset and a positive, proactive attitude, enhancing their effectiveness and impact.

At the core of mindset and attitude lie cognitive processes that govern how leaders perceive and interpret the world around them. This includes processes such as perception, attention, memory, and reasoning. For instance, a leader's selective attention can influence their attitude by focusing on either opportunities or challenges. Similarly, memory biases can shape their mindset by reinforcing certain beliefs or experiences.

A critical aspect of mindset is how leaders attribute success and failure. Attribution theory posits that individuals tend to attribute outcomes to either internal or external factors. A leader with a growth mindset is more likely to attribute success to effort and persistence, fostering a belief in their ability to improve. Conversely, a fixed mindset may lead to attributing success or failure to innate traits, potentially stifling growth.

Leaders do not develop their mindset and attitude in isolation. Social cognitive theory highlights the role of observation and modeling in shaping behavior and beliefs. Leaders often draw inspiration and learning from observing the behaviors and attitudes of others, whether they be mentors, colleagues, or historical figures. This social learning process contributes significantly to the formation of their leadership mindset.

Emotional intelligence, encompassing the ability to recognize, understand, and manage one's own emotions as well as the ability to influence the emotions of others, plays a pivotal role in attitude formation. Leaders with high emotional intelligence are better equipped to navigate complex interpersonal dynamics, fostering positive attitudes within their teams.

The capacity for self-regulation, or the ability to manage one's thoughts, emotions, and behaviors, is intimately tied to mindset and attitude. Leaders who can regulate their responses to challenges and setbacks are more likely to maintain a constructive attitude. Additionally, resilience—the ability to bounce back from adversity—nurtures a growth-oriented mindset, as leaders view setbacks as temporary and surmountable.

The social environment in which leaders operate exerts a profound influence on their mindset and attitude. Social norms, or the accepted behaviors and attitudes within a group, can either reinforce existing mindsets or challenge them. Effective leaders recognize the potential impact of social influence and actively shape their environments to foster positive attitudes and growth-oriented mindsets.

How leaders perceive themselves, their strengths, and their identity as a leader significantly shapes their mindset and attitude. Leaders with a strong, positive self-concept are more likely to approach challenges with confidence and maintain a growth-oriented mindset. This self-assuredness radiates through their attitude, influencing how they interact with their teams.

The psychological foundations of mindset and attitude in leadership are intricate and multifaceted. Leaders navigate a complex interplay of cognitive processes, emotional intelligence, social dynamics, and self-perception. Understanding these foundational elements equips leaders with the awareness and tools to intentionally shape their mindset and attitude, ultimately enhancing their effectiveness in leadership roles.

Cognitive Processes: The Mental Frameworks of Leadership

At the core of mindset and attitude lie cognitive processes that govern how leaders perceive and interpret the world around them. These processes include perception, attention, memory, and reasoning. They form the mental frameworks that influence a leader's beliefs, decisions, and actions.

Perception and Attention
- **Selective Attention:** Leaders often focus on specific aspects of their environment, which can shape their

attitudes. For example, a leader who focuses on opportunities rather than obstacles is more likely to develop a positive and proactive attitude.

- **Framing Effect:** The way information is presented can influence perception and decision-making. Leaders aware of cognitive biases can adjust their mindset to consider multiple perspectives.

Integration with the Holistic Intelligence Model:

- **Analytical Intelligence (AQ):** Enhances critical thinking and helps leaders recognize and overcome cognitive biases.
- **Emotional Resilience (ER):** Supports leaders in maintaining a balanced perspective under stress.

Memory and Reasoning

- **Confirmation Bias:** Leaders may favor information that confirms their existing beliefs. Recognizing this bias allows leaders to adopt a more open-minded mindset, essential for growth and innovation.
- **Reflective Thinking:** Engaging in reflective practices enhances decision-making and problem-solving abilities.

Integration with the Holistic Intelligence Model:

- **Intrapersonal Intelligence:** Encourages self-reflection to understand personal thought patterns.
- **Practical Intelligence (PQ):** Facilitates effective application of knowledge in real-world situations.

Attribution Theory: Interpreting Success and Failure

Attribution Theory explores how individuals explain the causes of events and behaviors. In leadership, this theory is crucial in understanding how leaders interpret success and failure.

Internal vs. External Attribution

- **Internal Attribution:** Leaders attribute outcomes to personal factors like effort and ability. This fosters a sense of control and responsibility.
- **External Attribution:** Outcomes are attributed to external factors such as luck or circumstances, which may reduce a leader's perceived control.

Growth Mindset and Attribution

- **Effort and Persistence:** Leaders with a growth mindset attribute success to hard work and learning, aligning with Practical Intelligence (PQ) by applying knowledge effectively.
- **Fixed Mindset Pitfalls:** Attributing failure to innate ability can hinder development and stifle Creativity Intelligence (CrQ).

Integration with the Holistic Intelligence Model:

- **Emotional Resilience (ER):** Helps leaders bounce back from setbacks by focusing on factors they can control.
- **Intrapersonal Intelligence:** Enhances self-awareness regarding attribution styles.

Social Cognitive Theory: Learning Through Observation

Social Cognitive Theory, developed by Albert Bandura, highlights the role of observation, imitation, and modeling in learning behaviors and attitudes.

Role Modeling in Leadership
- **Vicarious Learning:** Leaders develop mindset and attitudes by observing mentors, peers, and industry leaders.
- **Behavioral Modeling:** By embodying the qualities they wish to instill, leaders can influence their teams' mindset and attitude, enhancing Interpersonal Intelligence.

Self-Efficacy
- **Belief in Capabilities:** Confidence in one's ability to execute tasks influences mindset and behavior.
- **Enhancing Self-Efficacy:** Setting achievable goals and celebrating successes bolster self-concept, connecting to Intrapersonal Intelligence.

Integration with the Holistic Intelligence Model:

- **Cultural Intelligence (CQ):** Understanding and adapting to diverse role models from different cultures.
- **Ethical Intelligence:** Modeling ethical behavior reinforces organizational values.

Emotional Intelligence: Navigating Emotions in Leadership

Emotional Intelligence (EQ) encompasses the ability to recognize, understand, and manage one's own emotions and influence the emotions of others. It's pivotal in forming attitudes and building relationships.

Components of Emotional Intelligence
- **Self-Awareness:** Understanding one's emotions, strengths, and limitations.
- **Self-Regulation:** Managing emotions and impulses effectively.
- **Motivation:** Harnessing emotions to pursue goals.
- **Empathy:** Recognizing and responding to others' emotions.
- **Social Skills:** Building relationships and managing conflict.

Impact on Leadership:
- Leaders with high EQ can foster positive attitudes within their teams, leading to better collaboration and morale.

Integration with the Holistic Intelligence Model:

- **Interpersonal Intelligence:** Enhances communication and relationship-building.
- **Intrapersonal Intelligence:** Deepens self-understanding and emotional management.

Self-Regulation and Resilience: Sustaining a Constructive Attitude

Self-Regulation refers to the ability to control one's thoughts, emotions, and behaviors in pursuit of long-term goals. Resilience is the capacity to recover from setbacks.

Self-Regulation Strategies
- **Mindfulness Practices:** Increase awareness of emotional states, aiding in regulation.

- **Goal Setting:** Clear objectives guide behavior and focus attention.

Building Resilience

- **Cognitive Reframing:** Viewing challenges as opportunities aligns with Emotional Resilience (ER).
- **Support Networks:** Engaging with mentors and peers provides resources for coping.

Integration with the Holistic Intelligence Model:

- **Emotional Resilience (ER):** Strengthens the ability to handle stress and adversity.
- **Practical Intelligence (PQ):** Applies adaptive strategies effectively.

Social Influence and Norms: Shaping Mindset in Context

The social environment exerts a profound influence on leaders' mindset and attitude through social norms and group dynamics.

Social Norms

- **Descriptive Norms:** Behaviors typical within a group.
- **Injunctive Norms:** Behaviors perceived as approved by the group.

Impact on Leadership

- Leaders can be influenced by organizational culture but also have the power to shape it.
- Cultivating a positive environment enhances Cultural Intelligence (CQ), promoting inclusivity and adaptability.

Groupthink and Conformity
- **Awareness of Groupthink:** Helps leaders encourage diverse perspectives and critical thinking.
- **Balancing Conformity with Innovation:** Key to fostering Creativity Intelligence (CrQ).

Integration with the Holistic Intelligence Model:

- **Ethical Intelligence:** Guides leaders to challenge unethical norms.
- **Creativity Intelligence (CrQ):** Encourages innovation within social structures.

Self-Concept and Identity: The Leader's Inner Narrative

Self-Concept is how leaders perceive themselves, encompassing self-esteem, identity, and the perceived role within an organization.

Developing a Leadership Identity
- **Personal Values and Beliefs:** Clarifying these helps align mindset and behavior.
- **Authenticity:** Being true to oneself enhances trust and credibility.

Impact on Mindset and Attitude
- A strong, positive self-concept leads to confidence in facing challenges.

Integration with the Holistic Intelligence Model:

- **Intrapersonal Intelligence:** Promotes self-awareness and personal growth.
- **Ethical Intelligence:** Ensures alignment between personal values and ethical leadership.

Integrating the Holistic Intelligence Model

The psychological foundations discussed correspond with the 8 Pillars of the Holistic Intelligence Model, providing a comprehensive framework for leaders to develop mindset and attitude.

- **1. Emotional Resilience (ER):** Building resilience through self-regulation and reframing challenges.
- **2. Creativity Intelligence (CrQ):** Encouraging innovation by overcoming cognitive biases and fostering an open mindset.
- **3. Practical Intelligence (PQ):** Applying knowledge and learning from experiences to enhance decision-making.
- **4. Cultural Intelligence (CQ):** Understanding social norms and influences to navigate diverse environments.
- **5. Intrapersonal Intelligence:** Deepening self-awareness and self-concept to align actions with values.
- **6. Interpersonal Intelligence:** Utilizing emotional intelligence to build strong relationships.
- **7. Ethical Intelligence:** Grounding mindset and attitude in ethical principles to guide behavior.
- **8. Analytical Intelligence (AQ):** Employing critical thinking to overcome cognitive biases and make informed decisions.

Practical Strategies for Cultivating Psychological Foundations

1. Enhance Cognitive Processes

- **Challenge Assumptions:** Engage in critical thinking exercises.
- **Lifelong Learning:** Stay curious and open to new information.
- **Holistic Intelligence Pillars:** Analytical Intelligence, Practical Intelligence

2. Foster a Growth Mindset

- **Attribution Training:** Recognize the role of effort over innate ability.
- **Set Incremental Goals:** Build confidence through small successes.
- **Holistic Intelligence Pillars:** Intrapersonal Intelligence, Emotional Resilience

3. Develop Emotional Intelligence

- **Self-Reflection:** Regularly assess emotional responses.
- **Empathy Practice:** Actively listen and respond to others' feelings.
- **Holistic Intelligence Pillars:** Interpersonal Intelligence, Intrapersonal Intelligence

4. Build Resilience and Self-Regulation

- **Stress Management Techniques:** Incorporate relaxation methods.
- **Resilience Training:** Participate in programs that build coping skills.

- **Holistic Intelligence Pillars:** Emotional Resilience, Practical Intelligence

5. Leverage Social Learning
- **Mentorship:** Seek guidance from experienced leaders.
- **Networking:** Engage with diverse groups to broaden perspectives.
- **Holistic Intelligence Pillars:** Cultural Intelligence, Interpersonal Intelligence

6. Strengthen Self-Concept
- **Personal Branding:** Define your leadership identity and values.
- **Feedback Solicitation:** Use input from others to refine self-perception.
- **Holistic Intelligence Pillars:** Intrapersonal Intelligence, Ethical Intelligence

Real-World Example: Dr. Brené Brown's Leadership Insights

Dr. Brené Brown, a research professor and leadership consultant, emphasizes the importance of vulnerability and authenticity in leadership.

- **Emotional Intelligence:** Advocates for leaders to be self-aware and empathetic.
- **Resilience:** Encourages embracing failure as a learning opportunity.
- **Self-Concept:** Highlights the power of aligning actions with personal values.

Integration with the Holistic Intelligence Model:

- **Intrapersonal Intelligence:** Fosters self-awareness and authenticity.
- **Emotional Resilience (ER):** Builds strength through vulnerability.
- **Ethical Intelligence:** Promotes integrity and ethical leadership.

The psychological foundations of mindset and attitude in leadership are intricate and multifaceted. By understanding cognitive processes, emotional intelligence, social dynamics, and self-perception, leaders are better equipped to intentionally shape their mindset and attitude. Integrating the Holistic Intelligence Model's 8 Pillars provides a structured approach to developing these foundational elements, ultimately enhancing leadership effectiveness.

As we continue, we will explore practical strategies for cultivating and leveraging these psychological foundations for transformative leadership, delving deeper into how leaders can apply these insights in real-world contexts.

Reflection Questions

1. Cognitive Processes: How do your perception and attention influence your leadership decisions?

2. Attribution Style: Do you tend to attribute successes and failures to internal or external factors?

3. Emotional Intelligence: In what areas can you improve your emotional awareness and regulation?

4. Social Influence: How does your organizational culture shape your mindset and attitude?

5. Self-Concept: How does your self-perception align with your leadership goals?

Action Plan

1. Self-Assessment: Utilize assessments to evaluate your emotional intelligence and cognitive biases.

2. Set Development Goals: Identify specific psychological foundations to strengthen.

3. Engage in Training: Participate in workshops or courses on emotional intelligence, resilience, or cognitive development.

4. Seek Feedback: Encourage input from peers and mentors to gain different perspectives.

References

"Mindset: The New Psychology of Success" by Carol S. Dweck

"Emotional Intelligence" by Daniel Goleman

Albert Bandura's Social Cognitive Theory

"Rising Strong" by Brené Brown

The Influence of Beliefs and Values on Leadership Mindset

Core Reading

Beliefs and values are the bedrock upon which a leader's mindset is constructed. They form the lenses through which leaders perceive the world, make decisions, and interact with others. Understanding how beliefs and values shape leadership mindset is crucial for developing self-awareness and cultivating a purpose-driven approach to leadership.

At the heart of a leader's mindset are their core beliefs, which are deeply ingrained convictions about themselves, others, and the world. These beliefs act as filters, influencing how leaders interpret information and make meaning of their experiences. For instance, a leader with a belief in the potential for growth and development is more likely to approach challenges with a constructive mindset.

On the flip side, leaders may also hold limiting beliefs that constrain their potential. These are often self-imposed barriers that stem from past experiences, societal conditioning, or fear of failure. Identifying and challenging these limiting beliefs is a critical step in shifting towards a more empowered and growth-oriented mindset.

Values, representing what a leader holds dear and considers important, play a pivotal role in shaping mindset. When a leader's actions and decisions align with their core values, it reinforces a sense of authenticity and purpose. This alignment fosters a positive mindset, as leaders feel a sense of congruence between their beliefs, values, and actions.

Effective leaders possess adaptive beliefs, which allow them to adjust their perspectives and approaches in response to changing circumstances. This cognitive flexibility is an essential component of a growth-oriented mindset. Leaders who are open to revising their beliefs based on new information are better equipped to navigate complex and dynamic environments.

A leader's ethical framework, encompassing their moral principles and sense of integrity, profoundly influences their mindset. Leaders who prioritize ethical considerations in their decision-making process tend to cultivate a mindset rooted in fairness, accountability, and transparency. This ethical orientation shapes their attitude towards challenges and interactions with stakeholders.

Believing in one's ability to exert influence and make a positive impact is a cornerstone of an effective leadership mindset. Leaders with high self-efficacy exhibit confidence in their capacity to lead and inspire change. This belief empowers them to approach challenges with a proactive and solution-oriented mindset.

Leaders who infuse their roles with a sense of purpose and meaning are more likely to cultivate a resilient and growth-oriented mindset. Having a clear understanding of why they lead and the impact they aspire to make provides a North Star that guides their attitude and decision-making.

The culture and values of the organization in which a leader operates also influence their mindset. Leaders who align with the prevailing organizational values are more likely to exhibit a positive attitude and approach challenges in a manner consistent with the organizational ethos.

Engaging in regular self-reflection allows leaders to assess the alignment between their beliefs, values, and actions. This introspective process enables them to identify areas where their mindset may benefit from refinement or adjustment.

Beliefs and values serve as the foundation upon which a leader's mindset is constructed. They shape perception, decision-making, and behavior, ultimately influencing a leader's effectiveness. Recognizing the profound impact of beliefs and values empowers leaders to intentionally cultivate a mindset that aligns with their aspirations and the needs of their teams and organizations.

Core Beliefs: The Foundation of Mindset

At the heart of a leader's mindset are their core beliefs, which are deeply ingrained convictions about themselves, others, and the world. These beliefs act as filters, influencing how leaders interpret information and make meaning of their experiences.

- **Positive Core Beliefs:** A leader who believes in the potential for growth and development is more likely to approach challenges with optimism and a constructive mindset. This aligns with the concept of a growth mindset, as introduced by psychologist Carol Dweck.
- **Impact on Leadership:** Core beliefs shape a leader's approach to innovation, risk-taking, and problem-solving. Leaders with empowering beliefs foster environments that encourage learning and adaptability.

Integration with the Holistic Intelligence Model:

- **Intrapersonal Intelligence:** Enhances self-awareness, allowing leaders to recognize and understand their core beliefs.
- **Emotional Resilience (ER):** Positive core beliefs support resilience, enabling leaders to navigate adversity effectively.

Limiting Beliefs: Overcoming Internal Barriers

On the flip side, leaders may hold limiting beliefs that constrain their potential. These are often self-imposed barriers stemming from past experiences, societal conditioning, or fear of failure.

Examples of Limiting Beliefs:

- "I must have all the answers to be an effective leader."
- "Failure is a sign of incompetence."

Consequences: Limiting beliefs can lead to avoidance of challenges, stifling innovation and growth.

Challenging Limiting Beliefs:

- **Self-Reflection:** Identifying and questioning the validity of these beliefs.
- **Reframing:** Transforming limiting beliefs into empowering ones.

Integration with the Holistic Intelligence Model:

- **Intrapersonal Intelligence:** Self-reflection helps identify and address limiting beliefs.
- **Analytical Intelligence (AQ):** Critical thinking aids in evaluating and altering unhelpful beliefs.
- **Emotional Resilience (ER):** Overcoming limiting beliefs enhances resilience.

Values Alignment: Cultivating Authentic Leadership

Values represent what a leader holds dear and considers important. They play a pivotal role in shaping mindset.

Authenticity and Purpose: When a leader's actions and decisions align with their core values, it reinforces a sense of authenticity and purpose.

Positive Outcomes:

- Increased trust and credibility.
- Enhanced motivation and engagement.

Values in Decision-Making: Leaders who prioritize values-driven decisions are more likely to maintain ethical standards and inspire their teams.

Integration with the Holistic Intelligence Model:

- **Ethical Intelligence:** Values alignment strengthens ethical decision-making.
- **Intrapersonal Intelligence:** Understanding one's values is key to aligning actions accordingly.
- **Interpersonal Intelligence:** Authentic leadership fosters strong relationships.

Case Example:

Howard Schultz, former CEO of Starbucks, emphasized company values such as community and social responsibility, guiding business decisions and cultivating a strong organizational culture.

Adaptive Beliefs and Cognitive Flexibility

Effective leaders possess adaptive beliefs, allowing them to adjust perspectives and approaches in response to changing circumstances.

Cognitive Flexibility:

- **Definition:** The mental ability to switch between thinking about two different concepts or to think about multiple concepts simultaneously.
- **Importance:** Essential for innovation and problem-solving in dynamic environments.

Embracing Change:

- Leaders open to revising their beliefs based on new information are better equipped to navigate complexity.

Benefits:
- Enhanced creativity.
- Improved adaptability.

Integration with the Holistic Intelligence Model:

- **Creativity Intelligence (CrQ):** Cognitive flexibility fuels creativity and innovation.
- **Analytical Intelligence (AQ):** Supports critical evaluation of existing beliefs.
- **Practical Intelligence (PQ):** Applying adaptive beliefs to real-world situations.

Real-World Example:

Satya Nadella, CEO of Microsoft, fostered a culture of learning and adaptability, shifting the company towards cloud computing and AI.

Ethical Framework: Guiding Principles of Leadership

A leader's ethical framework, encompassing their moral principles and sense of integrity, profoundly influences their mindset.

Ethical Orientation:

- Prioritizing fairness, accountability, and transparency.
- Making decisions that consider the broader impact on stakeholders.

Impact on Mindset:
- Cultivates trust and respect.
- Shapes attitudes toward challenges and interactions.

Integration with the Holistic Intelligence Model:

- **Ethical Intelligence:** Central to developing an ethical framework.
- **Intrapersonal Intelligence:** Self-awareness of one's ethical principles.
- **Cultural Intelligence (CQ):** Understanding ethical considerations in diverse contexts.

Case Study:

Paul Polman, former CEO of Unilever, integrated sustainability and ethical practices into the company's strategy, promoting long-term value over short-term gains.

Self-Efficacy and Belief in Influence

Believing in one's ability to exert influence and make a positive impact is a cornerstone of an effective leadership mindset.

Self-Efficacy:

- **Definition:** Confidence in one's ability to execute behaviors necessary to produce specific performance attainments.

Effects on Leadership:

- Enhances motivation and persistence.

- Encourages a proactive and solution-oriented mindset.

Developing Self-Efficacy:

- Setting and achieving small goals.
- Reflecting on past successes.

Integration with the Holistic Intelligence Model:

- **Intrapersonal Intelligence:** Recognizing and enhancing self-efficacy.
- **Emotional Resilience (ER):** Confidence supports resilience in the face of challenges.
- **Interpersonal Intelligence:** Belief in influence enhances leadership presence.

Example:

Sheryl Sandberg, COO of Facebook, emphasizes the importance of self-belief and leaning into opportunities, inspiring others to do the same.

Purpose and Meaning: The Leader's North Star

Leaders who infuse their roles with a sense of purpose and meaning are more likely to cultivate a resilient and growth-oriented mindset.

Clarity of Purpose:

- Understanding the "why" behind leadership actions.
- Aligning personal purpose with organizational goals.

Benefits:
- Sustains motivation.
- Guides decision-making and prioritization.

Integration with the Holistic Intelligence Model:

- **Intrapersonal Intelligence:** Deepens self-understanding of purpose.
- **Emotional Resilience (ER):** Purpose provides strength during adversity.
- **Ethical Intelligence:** Ensures purpose aligns with ethical standards.

Case Example:

Simon Sinek's "Start With Why" emphasizes that leaders who articulate a clear purpose inspire others and drive successful organizations.

Cultural and Organizational Values

The culture and values of the organization in which a leader operates also influence their mindset.

Alignment with Organizational Values:

- Leaders who resonate with the organization's ethos are more engaged.
- Promotes consistency in actions and decisions.

Cultural Intelligence (CQ):

- Understanding and navigating organizational culture effectively.

- Adapting leadership style to fit cultural contexts.

Integration with the Holistic Intelligence Model:

- **Cultural Intelligence (CQ):** Key to aligning with organizational values.
- **Interpersonal Intelligence:** Builds relationships within the cultural context.
- **Ethical Intelligence:** Maintains integrity within organizational norms.

Example:

Tony Hsieh, former CEO of Zappos, prioritized company culture and core values, leading to exceptional customer service and employee satisfaction.

Reflective Practice: A Tool for Alignment

Engaging in regular self-reflection allows leaders to assess the alignment between their beliefs, values, and actions.

Introspective Processes:

- Journaling.
- Meditation and mindfulness.
- Seeking feedback.

Benefits:
- Identifies areas for growth.
- Enhances self-awareness and authenticity.

Integration with the Holistic Intelligence Model:

- Intrapersonal Intelligence: Core to reflective practice.
- Analytical Intelligence (AQ): Critical evaluation of one's beliefs and actions.
- Emotional Resilience (ER): Reflection aids in processing experiences.

Practical Strategies:

- **Feedback:** Gathers perspectives from peers, subordinates, and superiors.

Personal Development Plans: Sets goals based on reflection outcomes.

Integrating the Holistic Intelligence Model

By understanding the influence of beliefs and values on leadership mindset, leaders can leverage the 8 Pillars of the Holistic Intelligence Model to enhance their effectiveness:

1. Emotional Resilience (ER): Beliefs in growth and purpose strengthen resilience.

2. Creativity Intelligence (CrQ): Adaptive beliefs promote innovative thinking.

3. Practical Intelligence (PQ): Values alignment ensures practical decisions align with core principles.

4. Cultural Intelligence (CQ): Aligning with organizational values enhances cultural fit.

5. Intrapersonal Intelligence: Self-awareness of beliefs and values is foundational.

6. Interpersonal Intelligence: Authenticity in beliefs fosters strong relationships.

7. Ethical Intelligence: Ethical frameworks guide principled leadership.

8. Analytical Intelligence (AQ): Critical evaluation of beliefs ensures they serve the leader's goals.

Practical Strategies for Leaders

1. Identify and Clarify Core Beliefs and Values
- Self-Assessment Tools: Utilize instruments like the Values in Action (VIA) Survey.
- Journaling: Reflect on experiences that shaped your beliefs.

2. Challenge Limiting Beliefs
- Cognitive Restructuring: Replace negative beliefs with positive affirmations.
- Coaching and Mentorship: Seek support to identify and overcome barriers.

3. Align Actions with Values
- Decision-Making Frameworks: Incorporate values into strategic planning.
- Lead by Example: Demonstrate values through consistent behavior.

4. Cultivate Adaptive Beliefs

- Embrace Lifelong Learning: Stay open to new ideas and perspectives.
- Flexibility Training: Engage in activities that require adaptability.

5. Strengthen Ethical Foundations

- Ethics Training: Participate in workshops on ethical leadership.
- Establish Ethical Guidelines: Create clear policies reflecting core values.

6. Enhance Self-Efficacy

- Set Achievable Goals: Build confidence through small wins.
- Celebrate Successes: Acknowledge accomplishments to reinforce belief in abilities.

7. Define Purpose and Meaning

- Vision Statements: Articulate your leadership purpose.
- Align with Organizational Mission: Connect personal and organizational goals.

8. Engage in Reflective Practice

- Regular Reflection Sessions: Schedule time for introspection.
- Feedback Loops: Continuously seek and act on feedback.

—

Beliefs and values serve as the foundation upon which a leader's mindset is constructed. They shape perception, decision-making, and behavior, ultimately influencing a leader's effectiveness. Recognizing the profound impact of beliefs and values empowers leaders to intentionally cultivate a mindset that aligns with their aspirations and the needs of their teams and organizations.

By integrating the principles of the Holistic Intelligence Model, leaders can develop a well-rounded approach to nurturing their beliefs and values, leading to transformative leadership and organizational success.

Reflection Questions

1. Core Beliefs: What are your most deeply held beliefs, and how do they influence your leadership?

2. Limiting Beliefs: Are there any beliefs that may be hindering your growth? How can you challenge them?

3. Values Alignment: Do your actions consistently reflect your core values?

4. Purpose: What is your personal leadership purpose, and how does it guide your decisions?

Action Plan

1. Self-Assessment: Identify your core beliefs and values.

2. Set Development Goals: Focus on areas where beliefs and values can enhance your leadership.

3. Implement Strategies: Apply practical steps to align beliefs, values, and actions.

4. Monitor Progress: Regularly review and adjust your approach.

Emotional Resilience and Its Impact on Attitude in Leadership

Core Reading

Emotional resilience is a cornerstone of effective leadership and serves as the first pillar in the Holistic Intelligence Model. It refers to a leader's ability to adapt and bounce back from adversity, maintaining composure and a constructive attitude in the face of challenges. Understanding how emotional resilience shapes a leader's attitude is essential for fostering a positive and impactful leadership style.

Leaders often encounter difficult situations, whether it's managing conflicts within teams, facing organizational crises, or addressing individual setbacks. Emotional resilience equips leaders with the capacity to navigate these challenges with grace and a constructive attitude. Instead of being overwhelmed by adversity, resilient leaders maintain a composed demeanor and approach difficulties as opportunities for growth.

Emotional resilience is closely linked to maintaining a positive outlook and optimistic attitude. Resilient leaders possess a belief in their ability to overcome challenges and view setbacks as temporary rather than insurmountable. This positive mindset is infectious and can inspire team members to approach difficulties with a similar attitude.

Leaders with high emotional resilience are adept at managing stress and preventing it from negatively impacting their attitude. They possess coping mechanisms that allow them to stay focused and composed even in high-pressure situations. This ability to regulate their emotions contributes to a more even-keeled and positive attitude.

Emotional resilience fosters empathy, which is a critical component of a leader's attitude towards their team members. Resilient leaders are attuned to the emotions and experiences of others, allowing them to respond with compassion and understanding. This empathetic attitude creates a supportive and inclusive team environment.

Resilient leaders demonstrate high levels of emotional intelligence, which includes self-awareness and an understanding of their own emotional responses. This self-awareness enables them to regulate their emotions effectively and avoid allowing negative emotions to dictate their attitude or decision-making.

Maintaining a resilient attitude allows leaders to approach conflicts and difficult conversations with a constructive mindset. They don't shy away from providing honest feedback or addressing conflicts, but do so in a manner that fosters growth and collaboration rather than resentment.

Resilient leaders serve as role models for their team members. By demonstrating emotional resilience, they set an example of how to approach challenges with a positive and solution-oriented attitude. This modeling behavior can have a cascading effect, inspiring team members to develop their own resilience and constructive attitudes.

A resilient attitude is closely tied to a leader's ability to adapt to change. Leaders who are emotionally resilient are more likely to embrace change as an opportunity for growth rather than a disruption. They approach change with a flexible and open-minded attitude, which can be contagious within the organization.

Emotional resilience is intertwined with a growth mindset, the belief that abilities and intelligence can be developed with effort and dedication. Leaders with a growth mindset approach challenges with a positive attitude, viewing them as opportunities to learn and improve.

One of the hallmarks of emotional resilience is the ability to maintain composure even in high-stakes situations. Leaders who remain calm and collected inspire confidence in their team members and project an attitude of competence and control.

A leader's emotional resilience contributes to their trustworthiness and credibility. When team members see their leader maintaining a positive attitude and effectively handling challenges, it builds trust in their leadership capabilities.

Resilient leaders approach problems with a solution-oriented attitude. They are more likely to think creatively and seek innovative solutions to challenges, rather than becoming bogged down by obstacles.

Leaders with high emotional resilience have the capacity to foster a culture of resilience within their teams and organizations. They actively encourage team members to develop their own resilience and approach challenges with a constructive attitude.

Emotional resilience also encompasses a leader's ability to prioritize their own well-being. Leaders who practice self-care and prioritize their physical and mental health are better equipped to maintain a positive attitude and navigate challenges effectively.

Resilient leaders take proactive steps to build resilience in their teams. They provide support, resources, and mentorship to help team members develop their own emotional resilience and constructive attitudes.

While maintaining a positive attitude, emotionally resilient leaders also balance optimism with a realistic assessment of challenges. They acknowledge difficulties and setbacks, but approach them with a belief in their ability to find solutions.

A resilient attitude allows leaders to view setbacks as opportunities for learning and growth. They analyze what went wrong, extract lessons, and apply them to future situations, reinforcing a constructive approach to challenges.

Emotional resilience doesn't mean suppressing emotions, but rather acknowledging and processing them in a healthy way. Leaders who are emotionally resilient have the capacity to express and manage their emotions in a manner that doesn't detract from their effectiveness.

Resilient leaders have a long-term perspective that extends beyond immediate challenges. They understand that setbacks are part of the journey towards success and maintain a forward-looking attitude.

In times of crisis, a leader's emotional resilience is particularly critical. It enables them to provide steady and reassuring guidance to their teams, even in the face of uncertainty and adversity.

Emotional resilience profoundly influences a leader's attitude and approach to challenges. Leaders who cultivate emotional resilience are better equipped to maintain a positive, constructive, and solution-oriented mindset, even in the most demanding circumstances. This attitude not only benefits the leader personally but also has a positive impact on their team and organization as a whole.

Understanding Emotional Resilience

Definition and Importance

Emotional Resilience (ER): The capacity to withstand stressors and remain stable in the face of challenges. It involves bouncing back from setbacks and using experiences as opportunities for growth.

Impact on Leadership: Leaders with high emotional resilience can navigate complex situations without being overwhelmed, thereby influencing their team's morale and productivity positively.

Connection to Attitude

Positive Outlook: Emotional resilience fosters an optimistic attitude, enabling leaders to view setbacks as temporary and surmountable.

Stress Management: Resilient leaders effectively manage stress, preventing it from negatively impacting their decisions and interactions.

Integration with the Holistic Intelligence Model:

- Emotional Resilience is the keystone that supports and enhances all other intelligences in the model.

The Role of Emotional Resilience in Leadership

1. Navigating Adversity with Composure

Grace Under Pressure: Resilient leaders maintain a composed demeanor during crises, setting a calming example for their teams.

Opportunity Mindset: They approach difficulties as opportunities for learning and improvement.

Example:

Nelson Mandela: Demonstrated remarkable resilience during his imprisonment, emerging as a leader who united a nation.

2. Fostering a Positive Outlook and Optimism

Infectious Positivity: A leader's optimistic attitude can inspire team members to adopt a similar mindset.

Motivation and Morale: Positive leaders boost team morale, enhancing engagement and productivity.

Integration with the Holistic Intelligence Model:

- **Interpersonal Intelligence:** Enhances the ability to communicate optimism effectively.
- **Intrapersonal Intelligence:** Self-awareness of one's attitude and its impact on others.

3. Effective Stress Management

Coping Mechanisms: Resilient leaders employ strategies such as mindfulness, exercise, or time management to handle stress.

Maintaining Performance: Effective stress management ensures consistent decision-making and leadership presence.

Practical Strategies:

- **Mindfulness Meditation:** Incorporate daily practices to enhance focus and reduce stress.
- **Time Management Techniques:** Prioritize tasks to prevent overwhelm.

4. Enhancing Empathy and Understanding

Emotional Intelligence (EQ): Resilience is linked to higher EQ, allowing leaders to connect with team members on an emotional level.

Supportive Environment: Empathetic leaders foster a culture of trust and openness.

Integration with the Holistic Intelligence Model:

- **Interpersonal Intelligence:** Empathy strengthens relationships and team cohesion.
- **Cultural Intelligence (CQ):** Understanding diverse perspectives enhances empathy.

5. Conflict Resolution and Constructive Feedback

Approach to Conflict: Resilient leaders address conflicts directly yet tactfully, aiming for collaborative solutions.

Feedback Culture: They provide and receive feedback constructively, promoting growth.

Example:

Satya Nadella: Encouraged a feedback-rich culture at Microsoft, enhancing innovation and collaboration.

6. Role Modeling Resilience

Leading by Example: Demonstrating resilience encourages team members to develop their own.

Cascading Effect: A resilient leader fosters a resilient organization.

Integration with the Holistic Intelligence Model:

- **Ethical Intelligence:** Leading with integrity strengthens the leader's influence.
- **Practical Intelligence (PQ):** Applying resilience in practical ways guides the team effectively.

Emotional Resilience and the Growth Mindset

Cultivating a Growth Mindset

Belief in Development: Resilient leaders embrace the idea that abilities can improve through effort.

Embracing Challenges: View obstacles as opportunities to expand skills.

Integration with the Holistic Intelligence Model:

- **Creativity Intelligence (CrQ):** A growth mindset fuels innovation.
- **Analytical Intelligence (AQ):** Critical thinking aids in learning from experiences.

Adaptability and Change Management

Flexible Attitude: Resilient leaders adapt to change positively.

Driving Transformation: They lead change initiatives effectively, minimizing resistance.

Example:

Mary Barra, CEO of General Motors, navigated the company through significant technological shifts with adaptability and resilience.

Impact on Team and Organizational Culture

1. Maintaining Composure Under Pressure

Confidence Building: Teams gain confidence when leaders remain calm during crises.

Decision-Making: Composure leads to better strategic decisions.

2. Fostering Trust and Credibility

Consistency: Resilient leaders are reliable, enhancing trust.

Transparency: Open communication during challenges builds credibility.

3. Promoting Innovative Thinking and Problem-Solving

Solution-Oriented: Focus on finding solutions rather than dwelling on problems.

Encouraging Creativity: Create an environment where new ideas are welcomed.

Integration with the Holistic Intelligence Model:

- **Creativity Intelligence (CrQ):** Encourages exploration of novel solutions.
- **Practical Intelligence (PQ):** Implements innovative ideas effectively.

4. Building Resilience in Teams

Support and Resources: Provide tools for team members to develop resilience.

Mentorship: Guide team members through challenges.

Practical Strategies:

- **Resilience Training Programs:** Implement workshops to build team resilience.
- **Peer Support Networks:** Encourage collaboration and mutual support.

Developing Emotional Resilience

1. Self-Care and Well-Being

Physical Health: Regular exercise, adequate sleep, and a balanced diet.

Mental Health: Mindfulness, meditation, and hobbies.

Integration with the Holistic Intelligence Model:

- **Intrapersonal Intelligence:** Recognizing personal needs and taking action.
- **Emotional Resilience (ER):** Strengthening the ability to handle stress.

2. Acknowledging and Processing Emotions

Emotional Awareness: Recognize and understand one's emotions.

Healthy Expression: Communicate feelings constructively.

Practical Strategies:

- **Journaling:** Reflect on experiences and emotions.
- **Counseling or Coaching:** Seek professional support when needed.

3. Maintaining a Long-Term Perspective

Goal Setting: Focus on long-term objectives to navigate short-term setbacks.

Vision Alignment: Ensure personal and organizational goals are in harmony.

Integration with the Holistic Intelligence Model:

- **Analytical Intelligence (AQ):** Strategic planning for future success.
- **Ethical Intelligence:** Aligning actions with core values.

Real-World Examples

1. Angela Merkel, Former Chancellor of Germany

Emotional Resilience: Demonstrated calm leadership during the European financial crisis and refugee influx.

Impact: Maintained stability and confidence in her leadership domestically and internationally.

2. Barack Obama, Former President of the United States

Composure: Known for his calm demeanor during economic challenges and national crises.

Empathy: Showed deep understanding and connection with diverse groups.

Practical Strategies for Leaders

1. Develop Stress Management Techniques

Mindfulness and Meditation: Practice regularly to enhance focus and reduce anxiety.

Physical Activity: Incorporate exercise into routine for mental and physical benefits.

2. Enhance Emotional Intelligence

Self-Assessment: Use tools like William Stanek's Resilient Growth Self-Assessment and the 8 Pillars of Leadership: Self-Assessment.

Training Programs: Participate in workshops to improve EQ skills.

3. Foster a Supportive Network

Mentorship: Seek guidance from experienced leaders.

Peer Groups: Engage with leadership communities for shared learning.

4. Encourage Open Communication

Feedback Culture: Create an environment where feedback is welcomed and valued.

Active Listening: Practice attentive listening to understand team needs.

5. Promote Work-Life Balance

Set Boundaries: Encourage reasonable working hours and time off.

Flexible Policies: Offer options like remote work or flexible schedules.

Integrating the Holistic Intelligence Model

By enhancing emotional resilience, leaders can strengthen other intelligences within the Holistic Intelligence Model:

- **Emotional Resilience (ER):** Foundation for stability and adaptability.
- **Creativity Intelligence (CrQ):** Resilience encourages risk-taking and innovation.
- **Practical Intelligence (PQ):** Maintains focus on actionable solutions.
- **Cultural Intelligence (CQ):** Resilient leaders navigate cultural differences effectively.

- **Intrapersonal Intelligence:** Deepens self-awareness and self-regulation.
- **Interpersonal Intelligence:** Builds stronger relationships through empathy and support.
- **Ethical Intelligence:** Upholds integrity during challenging times.
- **Analytical Intelligence (AQ):** Enhances critical thinking under pressure.

—

Emotional resilience profoundly influences a leader's attitude and approach to challenges. Leaders who cultivate emotional resilience are better equipped to maintain a positive, constructive, and solution-oriented mindset, even in the most demanding circumstances. This attitude not only benefits the leader personally but also has a positive impact on their team and organization as a whole.

By intentionally developing emotional resilience and integrating it with the Holistic Intelligence Model, leaders can enhance their overall effectiveness, inspire their teams, and drive organizational success.

Reflection Questions

1. Self-Assessment: How do you currently respond to stress and setbacks? What emotions arise, and how do they influence your attitude?

2. Development Areas: Which aspects of emotional resilience do you wish to strengthen?

3. Impact on Others: How does your level of emotional resilience affect your team's morale and performance?

Action Plan

1. Set Personal Goals: Identify specific resilience skills to develop.

2. Create a Support System: Engage mentors, coaches, or peers for guidance.

3. Implement Daily Practices: Incorporate stress management and self-care into your routine.

4. Monitor Progress: Regularly reflect on improvements and adjust strategies as needed.

The Power of Growth Mindset in Leadership

Core Reading

Growth mindset is a foundational concept that holds immense significance in the realm of leadership. It refers to the belief that abilities and intelligence can be developed through dedication, hard work, and a commitment to learning. Understanding the profound influence of a growth mindset on leadership is crucial for fostering an environment of continuous improvement and innovation.

Leaders with a growth mindset view challenges as opportunities for growth and development rather than as insurmountable obstacles. They approach difficulties with a sense of curiosity and a belief in their ability to learn from them. This mindset empowers them to tackle complex issues with confidence and determination.

A growth mindset is closely associated with an inclination towards innovation. Leaders who believe in the potential for growth are more likely to encourage creativity and experimentation within their teams. They recognize that new ideas and approaches can lead to breakthroughs and improvements in the organization's processes and outcomes.

Leaders with a growth mindset actively promote a culture of continuous learning within their teams. They understand that ongoing education and skill development are essential for personal and organizational growth. This commitment to learning permeates the team's work ethic and contributes to a culture of excellence.

Leaders with a growth mindset are more inclined to support calculated risk-taking. They recognize that taking risks can lead to valuable learning experiences and breakthrough achievements. This attitude encourages team members to step out of their comfort zones and explore new avenues for innovation and progress.

A growth mindset is closely intertwined with emotional resilience. Leaders who believe in the potential for growth are better equipped to bounce back from setbacks and maintain a positive attitude in the face of challenges. They see setbacks as opportunities for learning and use them as stepping stones towards future success.

Leaders with a growth mindset have a compelling vision for the future and inspire their teams to pursue that vision. They communicate the importance of continuous improvement and growth, instilling a sense of purpose and direction within their teams.

A growth mindset enables leaders to challenge and overcome limiting beliefs, both in themselves and in their teams. They recognize that preconceived notions about capabilities can stifle progress, and they actively work to dismantle these barriers to growth.

Leaders with a growth mindset place a high value on feedback and developmental opportunities. They actively seek out input from their teams and provide constructive feedback in return. This open communication fosters an environment of trust and collaboration, where everyone is invested in each other's growth and success.

A growth mindset contributes to the development of stronger and more cohesive teams. Leaders who believe in the potential for growth are more likely to invest in the development of their team members, recognizing that a skilled and empowered team is a cornerstone of organizational success.

Leaders with a growth mindset approach problems with a solution-oriented attitude. They view challenges as puzzles to be solved rather than insurmountable barriers. This mindset encourages creative problem-solving and drives the team towards innovative solutions.

In an ever-changing business landscape, adaptability is a crucial trait for leaders. A growth mindset equips leaders with the ability to adapt to new circumstances and embrace change as an opportunity for growth and improvement.

Leaders with a growth mindset take ownership of their actions and decisions. They recognize that mistakes are part of the learning process and are willing to take responsibility for them. This accountability sets a powerful example for their teams and establishes a culture of integrity.

A growth mindset fuels intellectual curiosity and a hunger for knowledge. Leaders who believe in the potential for growth are more likely to seek out new information, explore diverse perspectives, and stay updated on industry trends. This intellectual curiosity drives innovation and keeps the organization on the cutting edge.

A growth mindset instills a sense of confidence in leaders. They have faith in their ability to learn and adapt, which translates into a demeanor of competence and assurance. This confidence inspires trust and respect from their teams.

Leaders with a growth mindset are vigilant about avoiding the limitations of a fixed mindset. They recognize that a fixed mindset, which believes that abilities are static and unchangeable, can hinder progress and innovation. They actively work to cultivate and reinforce a growth mindset within themselves and their teams.

Leaders with a growth mindset empower their team members to take ownership of their own development. They provide resources, mentorship, and opportunities for growth, encouraging each team member to cultivate their own growth mindset and pursue continuous improvement.

Perhaps most importantly, leaders with a growth mindset lead by example. They embody the principles of continuous learning, resilience, and a passion for improvement. Their actions speak louder than words, inspiring their teams to adopt a growth-oriented mindset.

A growth mindset is open to diverse perspectives and approaches. Leaders with this mindset actively seek out input from team members with different backgrounds, experiences, and expertise. This diversity of thought leads to more well-rounded and innovative solutions.

Leaders with a growth mindset leave a lasting legacy of progress and improvement. Their influence extends beyond their time in leadership, as they inspire a culture of growth that continues to thrive even in their absence.

In essence, a growth mindset is a cornerstone of effective leadership. It shapes a leader's attitude, behaviors, and approach to challenges, ultimately driving continuous improvement and innovation within the organization.

Embracing Challenges as Opportunities: Turning Obstacles into Stepping Stones

Leaders with a growth mindset view challenges not as insurmountable obstacles but as opportunities for growth and development. They approach difficulties with curiosity and a belief in their ability to learn and adapt. This perspective empowers them to tackle complex issues with confidence and determination, fostering a culture where challenges are welcomed and seen as catalysts for advancement.

Integration with the Holistic Intelligence Model:

- **Emotional Resilience (ER):** Embracing challenges enhances resilience, enabling leaders to bounce back from setbacks.
- **Creativity Intelligence (CrQ):** Viewing challenges creatively leads to innovative solutions.
- **Analytical Intelligence (AQ):** Applying critical thinking to navigate complexities.

Case Example:

Elon Musk, CEO of Tesla and SpaceX, consistently embraces monumental challenges, such as revolutionizing space travel and sustainable energy, demonstrating a relentless growth mindset.

Pioneering Innovation Through Continuous Learning: Cultivating a Culture of Curiosity

A growth mindset is closely associated with an inclination towards innovation. Leaders who believe in the potential for growth encourage creativity and experimentation within their teams. They recognize that new ideas and approaches can lead to breakthroughs, improving organizational processes and outcomes.

Integration with the Holistic Intelligence Model:

- **Creativity Intelligence (CrQ):** Fosters an environment where creativity thrives.
- **Cultural Intelligence (CQ):** Embraces diverse perspectives, enhancing innovation.
- **Practical Intelligence (PQ):** Translates innovative ideas into actionable strategies.

Practical Strategies:

- **Innovation Workshops:** Implement sessions to brainstorm and develop new ideas.
- **Learning Opportunities:** Encourage continuous education through training and development programs.

Fostering a Learning Culture: Commitment to Development

Leaders with a growth mindset actively promote a culture of continuous learning. They understand that ongoing education and skill development are essential for personal and organizational growth. This commitment permeates the team's work ethic, contributing to a culture of excellence and adaptability.

Integration with the Holistic Intelligence Model:

- **Intrapersonal Intelligence:** Encourages self-awareness and personal growth.
- **Interpersonal Intelligence:** Facilitates collaborative learning.
- **Ethical Intelligence:** Upholds integrity in the pursuit of knowledge.

Case Example:

Satya Nadella, CEO of Microsoft, transformed the company culture by promoting a "learn-it-all" mindset over a "know-it-all" attitude, leading to renewed innovation and success.

Encouraging Calculated Risk-Taking: Embracing Uncertainty for Growth

Leaders with a growth mindset support calculated risk-taking, recognizing that it can lead to valuable learning experiences and breakthrough achievements. This attitude encourages team members to step out of their comfort zones and explore new avenues for innovation and progress.

Integration with the Holistic Intelligence Model:

- **Emotional Resilience (ER):** Manages the emotional impact of risk.
- **Analytical Intelligence (AQ):** Assesses risks effectively.
- **Practical Intelligence (PQ):** Implements risk strategies wisely.

Practical Strategies:

- **Safe-to-Fail Experiments:** Allow team members to test ideas without fear of negative repercussions.
- **Celebrate Failures:** Acknowledge and learn from unsuccessful attempts as part of the growth process.

Nurturing Resilience and Adaptability: Building Strength Through Setbacks

A growth mindset is intertwined with emotional resilience. Leaders who believe in the potential for growth are better equipped to bounce back from setbacks and maintain a positive attitude in the face of challenges. They see setbacks as opportunities for learning and use them as stepping stones toward future success.

Integration with the Holistic Intelligence Model:

- **Emotional Resilience (ER):** Core to bouncing back from adversity.
- **Intrapersonal Intelligence:** Reflects on experiences for personal development.
- **Cultural Intelligence (CQ):** Adapts to diverse situations and perspectives.

Case Example:

J.K. Rowling, author of the Harry Potter series, overcame numerous rejections before achieving success, exemplifying resilience and a growth mindset.

Inspiring Purpose and Vision: Leading with Direction

Leaders with a growth mindset have a compelling vision for the future and inspire their teams to pursue that vision. They communicate the importance of continuous improvement, instilling a sense of purpose and direction within their teams.

Integration with the Holistic Intelligence Model:

- **Ethical Intelligence:** Aligns vision with core values.
- **Interpersonal Intelligence:** Communicates vision effectively.
- **Analytical Intelligence (AQ):** Strategizes to achieve long-term goals.

Practical Strategies:

- **Vision Workshops:** Collaborate with teams to define and align on a shared vision.
- **Storytelling:** Use narratives to convey purpose and motivate others.

Overcoming Limiting Beliefs: Breaking Barriers to Growth

A growth mindset enables leaders to challenge and overcome limiting beliefs, both in themselves and their teams. They recognize that preconceived notions about capabilities can stifle progress and actively work to dismantle these barriers.

Integration with the Holistic Intelligence Model:

- **Intrapersonal Intelligence:** Self-awareness to identify personal limiting beliefs.
- **Interpersonal Intelligence:** Supports team members in overcoming their barriers.
- **Ethical Intelligence:** Encourages honesty and transparency.

Practical Strategies:

- **Coaching and Mentoring:** Provide guidance to help others recognize and overcome limitations.
- **Mindset Training:** Implement programs focused on developing a growth mindset.

Promoting Feedback and Development: Cultivating Open Communication

Leaders with a growth mindset place a high value on feedback and developmental opportunities. They actively seek input from their teams and provide constructive feedback in return, fostering an environment of trust and collaboration.

Integration with the Holistic Intelligence Model:

- **Interpersonal Intelligence:** Enhances communication and relationship-building.
- **Ethical Intelligence:** Maintains integrity in feedback processes.
- **Cultural Intelligence (CQ):** Respects diverse perspectives in feedback.

Practical Strategies:

- **Feedback:** Implement systems for comprehensive feedback.
- **Regular Check-Ins:** Schedule consistent one-on-one meetings for development discussions.

Popular feedback models include 360-Degree Feedback, the Feedforward Approach and the Holistic Feedback System (HFS) developed by William Stanek.

Strengthening Adaptability in a Changing Landscape: Embracing Change

In an ever-changing business environment, adaptability is crucial. A growth mindset equips leaders with the ability to embrace change as an opportunity for growth and improvement, rather than resisting it.

Integration with the Holistic Intelligence Model:

- **Emotional Resilience (ER):** Manages emotions during transitions.
- **Practical Intelligence (PQ):** Adjusts strategies effectively.
- **Cultural Intelligence (CQ):** Navigates changes in diverse contexts.

Case Example:

Reed Hastings, CEO of Netflix, pivoted the company's business model from DVD rentals to streaming services, demonstrating adaptability and a growth mindset.

Leading by Example: Modeling Growth Mindset Behaviors

Leaders with a growth mindset lead by example, embodying principles of continuous learning, resilience, and a passion for improvement. Their actions inspire their teams to adopt a similar mindset.

Integration with the Holistic Intelligence Model:

- **Ethical Intelligence:** Sets standards through ethical behavior.
- **Interpersonal Intelligence:** Influences others positively.
- **Intrapersonal Intelligence:** Reflects personal commitment to growth.

Practical Strategies:

- **Continuous Learning:** Engage in ongoing education and share learnings with the team.
- **Transparency:** Share personal growth experiences and lessons learned.

Empowering and Developing Team Members: Investing in People

Leaders with a growth mindset empower their team members to take ownership of their development. They provide resources, mentorship, and opportunities for growth, recognizing that a skilled and empowered team is essential for organizational success.

Integration with the Holistic Intelligence Model:

- **Interpersonal Intelligence:** Builds strong relationships.
- **Practical Intelligence (PQ):** Develops team competencies.
- **Emotional Resilience (ER):** Supports team members in building resilience.

Practical Strategies:

- **Personal Development Plans:** Collaborate with team members to set and achieve growth goals.
- **Training Opportunities:** Offer access to workshops, courses, and learning materials.

Promoting Diversity of Thought: Harnessing Collective Intelligence

A growth mindset is open to diverse perspectives and approaches. Leaders actively seek input from team members with different backgrounds and expertise, leading to more well-rounded and innovative solutions.

Integration with the Holistic Intelligence Model:

- **Cultural Intelligence (CQ):** Values diversity and inclusion.
- **Creativity Intelligence (CrQ):** Leverages diverse ideas for innovation.
- **Ethical Intelligence:** Ensures fairness and respect in collaboration.

Practical Strategies:

- **Inclusive Meetings:** Encourage participation from all team members.
- **Diversity Initiatives:** Implement policies that promote diversity and inclusion.

Avoiding the Fixed Mindset Trap: Recognizing and Shifting Limiting Perspectives

Leaders with a growth mindset are vigilant about avoiding the limitations of a fixed mindset, which believes that abilities are static and unchangeable. They actively work to cultivate and reinforce a growth mindset within themselves and their teams.

Integration with the Holistic Intelligence Model:

- **Intrapersonal Intelligence:** Monitors personal mindset tendencies.
- **Interpersonal Intelligence:** Guides others away from fixed mindset thinking.
- **Analytical Intelligence (AQ):** Critically evaluates beliefs and assumptions.

Practical Strategies:

- **Mindset Workshops:** Educate teams on growth vs. fixed mindsets.
- **Language Awareness:** Use language that promotes growth, such as "not yet" instead of "can't."

Creating a Legacy of Growth: Sustaining Impact Beyond Tenure

Leaders with a growth mindset leave a lasting legacy of progress and improvement. Their influence extends beyond their time in leadership, as they inspire a culture of growth that continues to thrive.

Integration with the Holistic Intelligence Model:

- **Ethical Intelligence:** Builds a legacy rooted in integrity.
- **Cultural Intelligence (CQ):** Embeds growth mindset into organizational culture.
- **Practical Intelligence (PQ):** Ensures sustainable practices are in place.

Case Example:

Jack Ma, founder of Alibaba Group, fostered a culture of innovation and entrepreneurship, leaving a lasting impact on the company's ethos.

A growth mindset is a cornerstone of effective leadership. It shapes a leader's attitude, behaviors, and approach to challenges, ultimately driving continuous improvement and innovation within the organization. By integrating the principles of the Holistic Intelligence Model, leaders can cultivate and reinforce a growth mindset, enhancing their effectiveness and inspiring their teams.

Reflection Questions

1. Self-Assessment: Do you currently embrace challenges as opportunities for growth?

2. Team Dynamics: How can you foster a growth mindset within your team?

3. Limiting Beliefs: Are there any fixed mindset tendencies you need to address?

Action Plan

1. Identify Areas for Growth: Reflect on personal and team areas that could benefit from a growth mindset.

2. Implement Strategies: Apply practical steps such as training, feedback systems, and mentorship programs.

3. Monitor Progress: Regularly review the impact of these initiatives and adjust as needed.

Embracing Change and Continuous Learning: Keys to a Growth Mindset

Core Reading

In the dynamic landscape of leadership, the ability to embrace change and engage in continuous learning is pivotal to the development and sustenance of a growth mindset. Leaders who understand the transformative potential of these principles position themselves and their teams for sustained success and innovation.

Change is a constant in the world of leadership. Whether it be shifts in industry trends, technological advancements, or global events, leaders must be agile and adaptable. Embracing change is not merely a reaction, but a proactive stance towards evolving realities. Leaders with a growth mindset see change as an opportunity for progress and a chance to explore new horizons.

Leaders set the tone for organizational culture. When they exhibit a willingness to adapt, it encourages a similar outlook among team members. This culture of adaptability permeates the organization, creating a dynamic and responsive environment that is better equipped to navigate challenges and seize opportunities.

Continuous learning is a cornerstone of a growth mindset. Leaders recognize that every experience, whether a triumph or a setback, holds valuable lessons. They approach each situation with a curiosity and a hunger for knowledge, extracting insights that contribute to personal and organizational growth.

Leaders with a growth mindset actively seek out opportunities for learning. They are avid readers, attend workshops, engage in industry conferences, and seek mentorship. This thirst for knowledge not only expands their own skill set but also positions them as a well-informed and forward-thinking leader within their organization.

Leaders play a crucial role in fostering a culture of continuous learning among their teams. They provide resources, support, and encouragement for professional development. By recognizing and rewarding a commitment to learning, leaders cultivate a team of individuals who are motivated to grow and contribute to the organization's success.

A growth mindset encourages a 'beginner's mind' approach, where leaders approach situations with an open, curious, and non-judgmental perspective. This approach allows for fresh insights and innovative solutions, unencumbered by preconceived notions or past experiences.

In a growth mindset, failure is not viewed as a setback, but as a stepping stone towards improvement. Leaders understand that failure provides invaluable feedback and an opportunity to iterate and evolve. They encourage their teams to view failures in the same light, creating an environment where innovation flourishes.

Leaders with a growth mindset champion experimentation and innovation. They create safe spaces for team members to take calculated risks and explore new approaches. This willingness to innovate leads to the development of breakthrough solutions and keeps the organization at the forefront of its industry.

Leaders with a growth mindset are receptive to feedback, regardless of its source. They recognize that constructive criticism is a catalyst for growth and improvement. This openness to feedback not only fosters personal development but also sets an example for their teams to embrace a culture of continuous improvement.

In an increasingly interconnected world, leaders with a growth mindset recognize the importance of understanding global perspectives and trends. They seek opportunities for cross-cultural learning and embrace diversity of thought. This global outlook positions them to lead effectively in an ever-changing international landscape.

Leaders with a growth mindset are committed to staying informed about industry trends and emerging technologies. They understand that being at the forefront of advancements is essential for maintaining a competitive edge. This proactive approach ensures that their organizations are well-positioned to adapt to changing market dynamics.

In today's digital age, technology provides unprecedented access to learning resources. Leaders with a growth mindset leverage these tools to facilitate continuous learning. They encourage their teams to explore online courses, webinars, and virtual conferences, harnessing the power of technology for professional development.

Leaders with a growth mindset inspire a hunger for knowledge within their teams. They communicate the value of continuous learning and provide opportunities for skill development. By setting an example and creating a learning-centric environment, they ignite a passion for growth among their team members.

Leaders can create communities or forums where team members can share insights, articles, and resources related to personal and professional growth. This community-building approach fosters a culture of continuous learning and provides a platform for individuals to support each other in their development journeys.

A growth mindset is characterized by humility and curiosity. Leaders acknowledge that there is always more to learn and understand. They approach situations with a sense of wonder and a willingness to explore new perspectives, even as experienced leaders.

Embracing change requires resilience, and leaders with a growth mindset embody this trait. They navigate uncertainties and challenges with a sense of purpose and determination. Their ability to remain steadfast in the face of change inspires confidence.

Adapting to Evolving Realities: Proactive Stance Towards Change

Change is a constant in the world of leadership. Whether it's shifts in industry trends, technological advancements, or global events, leaders must be agile and adaptable. Embracing change is not merely a reaction but a proactive stance towards evolving realities.

- **Viewing Change as Opportunity:** Leaders with a growth mindset see change as an avenue for progress and exploration.
- **Agility and Flexibility:** They adjust strategies and approaches to align with new developments.

Integration with the Holistic Intelligence Model:

- **Emotional Resilience (ER):** Helps leaders remain composed during transitions.
- **Practical Intelligence (PQ):** Enables the practical application of new strategies.
- **Cultural Intelligence (CQ):** Facilitates understanding and adapting to diverse cultural shifts.

Case Example:

Amazon consistently embraced change by expanding from an online bookstore to a global e-commerce and technology leader, demonstrating adaptability and a commitment to innovation.

Fostering a Culture of Adaptability: Creating a Responsive Environment

Leaders set the tone for organizational culture. When they exhibit a willingness to adapt, it encourages a similar outlook among team members.

- **Encouraging Flexibility:** Promote policies that allow for adaptive work practices.
- **Empowering Teams:** Give team members autonomy to make decisions in response to change.

Integration with the Holistic Intelligence Model:

- **Interpersonal Intelligence:** Builds strong relationships that support adaptability.
- **Ethical Intelligence:** Ensures that changes align with core values and ethics.
- **Intrapersonal Intelligence:** Self-awareness helps leaders model adaptability authentically.

Practical Strategies:

- **Adaptive Leadership Training:** Provide programs that develop adaptability skills.
- **Open Communication Channels:** Maintain transparency about changes to reduce uncertainty.

Continuous Learning and Intellectual Curiosity: Learning from Experience

Continuous learning is a cornerstone of a growth mindset. Leaders recognize that every experience, whether a triumph or a setback, holds valuable lessons.

- **Reflective Practices:** Regularly analyze successes and failures to extract insights.
- **Knowledge Sharing:** Encourage the dissemination of learnings within the team.

Integration with the Holistic Intelligence Model:

- **Analytical Intelligence (AQ):** Enhances the ability to learn from data and experiences.
- **Intrapersonal Intelligence:** Promotes self-reflection and personal growth.
- **Interpersonal Intelligence:** Facilitates sharing and collaborative learning.

Case Example:

Indra Nooyi, former CEO of PepsiCo, emphasized learning from global markets to drive innovation and growth, showcasing intellectual curiosity and continuous learning.

Seeking Out New Knowledge: Active Pursuit of Growth

Leaders with a growth mindset actively seek out opportunities for learning.

- **Professional Development:** Attend workshops, conferences, and pursue further education.
- **Mentorship and Networking:** Engage with other leaders to gain new perspectives.

Integration with the Holistic Intelligence Model:

- **Cultural Intelligence (CQ):** Broadens understanding through exposure to diverse ideas.
- **Emotional Resilience (ER):** Embraces learning even when it challenges existing beliefs.
- **Creativity Intelligence (CrQ):** Sparks innovative thinking through new knowledge.

Practical Strategies:

- **Learning Goals:** Set specific objectives for personal development.
- **Resource Allocation:** Invest time and resources in learning activities.

Encouraging Lifelong Learning in Teams: Building a Learning Organization

Leaders play a crucial role in fostering a culture of continuous learning among their teams.

- **Providing Resources:** Offer access to training, workshops, and educational materials.
- **Recognizing Development:** Acknowledge and reward efforts towards learning and growth.

Integration with the Holistic Intelligence Model:

- **Interpersonal Intelligence:** Builds trust and encourages open communication.
- **Ethical Intelligence:** Supports fair opportunities for development.
- **Practical Intelligence (PQ):** Enhances team capabilities and performance.

Practical Strategies:

- **Learning Management Systems:** Implement platforms for ongoing education.
- **Knowledge Sharing Sessions:** Schedule regular meetings for team members to share insights.

Embracing Failure as a Learning Opportunity: Cultivating Resilience Through Setbacks

In a growth mindset, failure is not viewed as a setback but as a stepping stone towards improvement.

- **Normalizing Failure:** Create an environment where mistakes are seen as part of the learning process.
- **Analyzing Failures:** Encourage teams to dissect what went wrong to prevent future issues.

Integration with the Holistic Intelligence Model:

- **Emotional Resilience (ER):** Strengthens the ability to recover from failures.
- **Analytical Intelligence (AQ):** Uses critical thinking to learn from mistakes.
- **Ethical Intelligence:** Maintains integrity when addressing failures.

Case Example:

Thomas Edison famously viewed each unsuccessful attempt as a step closer to success, embodying the philosophy, "I have not failed. I've just found 10,000 ways that won't work."

Championing Experimentation and Innovation: Creating Safe Spaces for Innovation

Leaders with a growth mindset champion experimentation and innovation.

- **Encouraging Risk-Taking:** Support team members in exploring new ideas without fear of reprimand.
- **Innovation Labs:** Establish dedicated spaces or times for creative thinking.

Integration with the Holistic Intelligence Model:

- **Creativity Intelligence (CrQ):** Nurtures inventive thinking.
- **Practical Intelligence (PQ):** Applies innovative ideas effectively.
- **Emotional Resilience (ER):** Manages uncertainty inherent in experimentation.

Practical Strategies:

- **Hackathons or Innovation Days:** Organize events focused on generating new ideas.
- **Idea Incubators:** Provide resources to develop and test innovative concepts.

Remaining Open to Feedback and Critique: Embracing Constructive Criticism

Leaders with a growth mindset are receptive to feedback, recognizing it as a catalyst for growth.

- **Active Listening:** Genuinely consider input from all levels within the organization.
- **Feedback Systems:** Implement structured processes for regular feedback.

Integration with the Holistic Intelligence Model:

Interpersonal Intelligence: Enhances communication and relationship-building.

- **Intrapersonal Intelligence:** Promotes self-awareness and personal development.
- **Ethical Intelligence:** Values honesty and transparency.

Practical Strategies:

- **Anonymous Feedback Channels:** Encourage honest input without fear of repercussions.
- **Regular Review Meetings:** Schedule times to discuss feedback and action plans.

Cultivating a Global Perspective: Embracing Diversity and Inclusion

In an interconnected world, leaders with a growth mindset recognize the importance of understanding global perspectives.

- **Cross-Cultural Learning:** Engage with diverse cultures to broaden understanding.
- **Inclusive Practices:** Ensure that diverse voices are heard and valued.

Integration with the Holistic Intelligence Model:

- **Cultural Intelligence (CQ):** Essential for navigating global dynamics.
- **Ethical Intelligence:** Upholds principles of fairness and respect.
- **Creativity Intelligence (CrQ):** Leverages diverse perspectives for innovation.

Case Example:

Sundar Pichai, CEO of Google, emphasizes diversity and inclusion as drivers of innovation and growth in the global market.

Leveraging Technology for Learning: Harnessing Digital Tools

In today's digital age, technology provides unprecedented access to learning resources.

- **E-Learning Platforms:** Utilize online courses and webinars.
- **Knowledge Management Systems:** Implement tools to store and share information.

Integration with the Holistic Intelligence Model:

- **Practical Intelligence (PQ):** Efficient use of technology enhances productivity.

- **Analytical Intelligence (AQ):** Analyzes data to inform learning strategies.
- **Creativity Intelligence (CrQ):** Encourages innovative use of technology.

Practical Strategies:

- **Virtual Training Programs:** Offer flexible learning opportunities.
- **Collaboration Tools:** Use platforms like Slack or Microsoft Teams to facilitate communication.

Inspiring a Hunger for Knowledge: Leading by Example

Leaders with a growth mindset inspire a hunger for knowledge within their teams.

- **Sharing Learnings:** Regularly discuss new insights and encourage others to do the same.
- **Setting Challenges:** Motivate team members to expand their skills.

Integration with the Holistic Intelligence Model:

- **Intrapersonal Intelligence:** Self-motivation influences others.
- **Interpersonal Intelligence:** Engages team members in shared learning.
- **Ethical Intelligence:** Promotes a culture of integrity in knowledge pursuit.

Practical Strategies:

- **Book Clubs or Study Groups:** Facilitate group learning experiences.
- **Recognition Programs:** Acknowledge and reward commitment to learning.

Remaining Humble and Curious: Embracing a Beginner's Mind

A growth mindset is characterized by humility and curiosity.

- **Acknowledging Limitations:** Recognize that there is always more to learn.
- **Asking Questions:** Encourage inquiry over assumption.

Integration with the Holistic Intelligence Model:

- **Intrapersonal Intelligence:** Humility stems from self-awareness.
- **Analytical Intelligence (AQ):** Curiosity drives critical thinking.
- **Interpersonal Intelligence:** Builds stronger connections through genuine interest.

Case Example:

Warren Buffett, despite his vast success, continues to spend significant time reading and learning, embodying humility and curiosity.

Embodying Resilience in the Face of Change: Inspiring Confidence Through Stability

Embracing change requires resilience, and leaders with a growth mindset embody this trait.

- **Navigating Uncertainties:** Approach challenges with purpose and determination.
- **Inspiring Others:** Their ability to remain steadfast in the face of change instills confidence in their teams.

Integration with the Holistic Intelligence Model:

- **Emotional Resilience (ER):** Core to managing change effectively.
- **Intrapersonal Intelligence:** Self-regulation during turbulent times.
- **Interpersonal Intelligence:** Provides support and guidance to others.

Practical Strategies:

- **Change Management Training:** Equip leaders and teams with skills to handle change.
- **Resilience Workshops:** Develop techniques to strengthen emotional resilience.

—

Embracing change and continuous learning are essential keys to developing and sustaining a growth mindset in leadership. By integrating these principles with the Holistic Intelligence Model, leaders can enhance their ability to adapt, innovate, and inspire their teams. This approach not only drives personal and organizational success but also fosters a culture of resilience, curiosity, and continuous improvement.

Reflection Questions

1. Adaptability: How do you currently respond to change? What steps can you take to become more adaptable?

2. Continuous Learning: In what ways are you actively pursuing new knowledge? How can you encourage your team to do the same?

3. Embracing Failure: How do you perceive and handle failures? What can you learn from recent setbacks?

Action Plan

1. Set Learning Goals: Identify areas for personal and professional development.

2. Develop Adaptability Strategies: Implement practices to enhance flexibility in leadership.

3. Foster a Learning Culture: Create initiatives that promote continuous learning within your team.

4. Embrace Feedback: Establish regular channels for giving and receiving constructive feedback.

Overcoming Fixed Mindset Traps: Navigating Challenges to Growth

Core Reading

Leadership effectiveness is often hindered by fixed mindset traps, which can limit potential and impede progress. Recognizing and overcoming these traps is essential for fostering a culture of growth and continuous improvement within an organization.

In a fixed mindset, challenges are viewed as threats to competence. Leaders with a growth mindset, however, see challenges as opportunities for development. They actively seek out situations that push their boundaries, recognizing that it is through challenges that true growth occurs.

Fixed mindset individuals tend to view failure as a reflection of their abilities. In contrast, leaders with a growth mindset understand that failure is a natural part of the learning process. They reframe failure as a temporary setback, a valuable source of feedback, and a catalyst for improvement.

Fixed mindset individuals often compare themselves to others and feel threatened by the success of peers or colleagues. Leaders with a growth mindset focus on their own progress and celebrate the achievements of others. They recognize that everyone's journey is unique and that success is not a finite resource.

Fixed mindset individuals believe that abilities are innate and static. Those with a growth mindset understand that effort and dedication lead to mastery. They value the process of learning and recognize that consistent, focused effort is the true path to excellence.

Fixed mindset individuals may be resistant to feedback, viewing it as a critique of their innate abilities. Leaders with a growth mindset welcome feedback as a means to learn and improve. They actively seek out input from peers, mentors, and team members, recognizing that it is an invaluable tool for growth.

Fixed mindset individuals tend to stay within their comfort zones, avoiding situations where they might face failure or struggle. Growth mindset leaders intentionally seek out challenges and are willing to step into the unknown. They understand that true growth occurs outside of one's comfort zone.

Fixed mindset individuals may view learning as a chore or a means to an end. Leaders with a growth mindset have a genuine love for learning. They approach new information and experiences with enthusiasm and curiosity, seeking opportunities to expand their knowledge and skills.

Fixed mindset individuals may become disheartened by setbacks, viewing them as indications of inadequacy. Leaders with a growth mindset see setbacks as opportunities for learning and improvement. They approach setbacks with a solution-oriented mindset, seeking to understand what can be gained from the experience.

Fixed mindset individuals may be quick to judge themselves and others based on perceived abilities. Leaders with a growth mindset cultivate curiosity instead of judgment. They ask questions, seek to understand, and approach situations with an open and non-judgmental attitude.

Fixed mindset individuals often view situations in black and white terms – either success or failure. Leaders with a growth mindset understand that progress is a continuum. They acknowledge incremental successes and view setbacks as part of the journey towards long-term growth.

Fixed mindset environments can discourage risk-taking due to a fear of failure. Leaders with a growth mindset create a safe space for risk-taking and experimentation. They encourage their teams to take calculated risks, knowing that innovation and progress often require stepping into the unknown.

Fixed mindset individuals may believe that their abilities and qualities are fixed and unchangeable. Leaders with a growth mindset understand that change and growth are not only possible, but they are inherent to human potential. They view themselves and others as works in progress, capable of continuous improvement.

Fixed mindset individuals may become discouraged by slow progress or initial challenges. Leaders with a growth mindset understand that meaningful change takes time and consistent effort. They demonstrate patience in the face of obstacles, knowing that sustained dedication leads to long-term success.

Fixed mindset individuals may be quick to label themselves or others based on past performance or perceived abilities. Leaders with a growth mindset reject limiting labels and stereotypes. They recognize that individuals are capable of growth and change, and they encourage others to see their potential beyond initial impressions.

Fixed mindset individuals may overemphasize their own abilities, leading to overconfidence or arrogance. Leaders with a growth mindset strike a balance between self-confidence and humility. They acknowledge their strengths while remaining open to learning from others and recognizing areas for improvement.

Fixed mindset individuals may be hesitant to seek feedback, fearing it may reveal inadequacies. Leaders with a growth mindset actively seek out feedback from diverse sources. They view feedback as a valuable resource for personal and professional development, and they use it to refine their skills and approaches.

Leaders play a crucial role in fostering a growth mindset culture among their teams. They communicate the value of a growth mindset, provide resources for development, and lead by example. By creating an environment that supports continuous improvement, leaders empower their teams to overcome fixed mindset traps.

Leaders with a growth mindset model vulnerability by acknowledging their own areas for improvement and sharing their learning journey. They demonstrate that growth is an ongoing process, even for experienced leaders. This authenticity fosters a culture of openness and encourages others to embrace their own opportunities for growth.

Fixed mindset individuals may be focused on achieving flawless outcomes. Leaders with a growth mindset celebrate progress, recognizing that improvement is a journey with ups and downs. They acknowledge and commend the efforts and advancements made by themselves and their teams, even in the absence of perfection.

Leaders with a growth mindset encourage reflective practice among their teams. They create opportunities for individuals to assess their own growth, identify areas for improvement, and set goals for the future. This reflective process fosters self-awareness and a commitment to continuous development.

Overcoming fixed mindset traps requires a conscious shift in perspective and a commitment to ongoing self-awareness and development. By recognizing and navigating these challenges, leaders can unlock their full potential and create environments that foster growth, innovation, and success.

Understanding Fixed Mindset Traps

1. Avoiding Challenges Instead of Embracing Them

Fixed Mindset Trap: Viewing challenges as threats to competence and avoiding them to prevent failure.

Growth Mindset Approach:

- **Embrace Challenges:** See challenges as opportunities for development and learning.
- **Seek Growth:** Actively pursue situations that push boundaries and expand skill sets.

Integration with the Holistic Intelligence Model:

- **Emotional Resilience (ER):** Builds the capacity to face challenges with confidence.
- **Creativity Intelligence (CrQ):** Encourages innovative thinking when confronting obstacles.
- **Analytical Intelligence (AQ):** Applies critical thinking to navigate complex situations.

Practical Strategies:

Set Stretch Goals: Establish objectives that require stepping out of comfort zones.

Reframe Challenges: View challenges as pathways to growth rather than threats.

2. Fear of Failure Versus Learning from Failure

Fixed Mindset Trap: Perceiving failure as a reflection of personal inadequacy, leading to risk aversion.

Growth Mindset Approach:

- **Normalize Failure:** Accept that failure is a natural part of the learning process.
- **Learn from Setbacks:** Use failures as valuable feedback for improvement.

Integration with the Holistic Intelligence Model:

- **Emotional Resilience (ER):** Helps recover from setbacks and maintain motivation.
- **Intrapersonal Intelligence:** Enhances self-awareness to understand reactions to failure.
- **Practical Intelligence (PQ):** Applies lessons learned to future endeavors.

Practical Strategies:

Failure Analysis: After setbacks, conduct a constructive review to identify lessons.

Celebrate Effort: Acknowledge the effort and risks taken, regardless of the outcome.

3. Comparing to Others Instead of Focusing on Personal Growth

Fixed Mindset Trap: Feeling threatened by others' success and engaging in negative comparisons.

Growth Mindset Approach:

- **Personal Benchmarking:** Focus on personal progress and development.
- **Celebrate Others:** Recognize and appreciate the achievements of peers.

Integration with the Holistic Intelligence Model:

- **Intrapersonal Intelligence:** Promotes self-awareness and personal goal setting.

- **Interpersonal Intelligence:** Fosters positive relationships and collaboration.
- **Ethical Intelligence:** Encourages integrity and fairness in interactions.

Practical Strategies:

Set Personal Goals: Define success based on individual aspirations and progress.

Practice Gratitude: Regularly acknowledge and appreciate others' contributions.

4. Believing Abilities are Fixed Rather than Developed

Fixed Mindset Trap: Assuming talents and intelligence are innate and unchangeable.

Growth Mindset Approach:

- **Emphasize Effort:** Recognize that abilities can be developed through dedication and hard work.
- **Pursue Mastery:** Commit to continuous learning and skill enhancement.

Integration with the Holistic Intelligence Model:

- **Intrapersonal Intelligence:** Encourages self-improvement and personal growth.
- **Analytical Intelligence (AQ):** Supports the pursuit of knowledge and skill development.
- **Creativity Intelligence (CrQ):** Inspires innovative approaches to learning.

Practical Strategies:

Lifelong Learning: Engage in ongoing education and skill development.

Skill Development Plans: Create actionable plans to enhance specific abilities.

5. Resisting Feedback Instead of Embracing It

Fixed Mindset Trap: Viewing feedback as criticism and a threat to self-esteem.

Growth Mindset Approach:

- **Seek Feedback:** Actively pursue input to identify areas for improvement.
- **Use Feedback Constructively:** Apply insights from feedback to enhance performance.

Integration with the Holistic Intelligence Model:

- **Interpersonal Intelligence:** Enhances communication and openness to others' perspectives.
- **Intrapersonal Intelligence:** Utilizes feedback for self-improvement.
- **Ethical Intelligence:** Values honesty and transparency in interactions.

Practical Strategies:

Feedback Sessions: Schedule regular times for receiving and discussing feedback.

Active Listening: Approach feedback conversations with an open mind.

6. Staying in Comfort Zones Instead of Exploring New Frontiers

Fixed Mindset Trap: Avoiding unfamiliar situations to prevent discomfort or failure.

Growth Mindset Approach:

- **Expand Horizons:** Deliberately seek new experiences and challenges.
- **Embrace Uncertainty:** Recognize that growth occurs outside of comfort zones.

Integration with the Holistic Intelligence Model:

- **Cultural Intelligence (CQ):** Adapts to new environments and diverse perspectives.
- **Emotional Resilience (ER):** Manages anxiety associated with new experiences.
- **Practical Intelligence (PQ):** Applies knowledge in varied contexts.

Practical Strategies:

Try New Roles: Take on projects or roles that require new skills.

Cross-Functional Collaboration: Work with different teams to gain diverse experiences.

Fostering a Growth Mindset Culture

1. Encouraging Safe Risk-Taking

Fixed Mindset Environment: Discourages risk due to fear of failure and negative repercussions.

Growth Mindset Culture:

- **Promote Experimentation:** Encourage teams to innovate and try new approaches.
- **Accept Mistakes:** Understand that errors are part of the innovation process.

Integration with the Holistic Intelligence Model:

- **Creativity Intelligence (CrQ):** Fosters an environment where creativity is valued.
- **Emotional Resilience (ER):** Supports team members in handling setbacks.
- **Ethical Intelligence:** Ensures that risk-taking aligns with ethical standards.

Practical Strategies:

Innovation Incentives: Reward creative ideas and initiatives.

Learning Sessions: Share lessons learned from experiments, regardless of outcome.

2. Modeling Vulnerability and Continuous Growth

Fixed Mindset Leadership: Projects an image of infallibility, discouraging openness.

Growth Mindset Leadership:

- **Demonstrate Learning:** Share personal development experiences and lessons.
- **Acknowledge Limitations:** Be honest about areas for improvement.

Integration with the Holistic Intelligence Model:

- **Intrapersonal Intelligence:** Reflects self-awareness and authenticity.
- **Interpersonal Intelligence:** Builds trust through transparency.
- **Ethical Intelligence:** Upholds integrity in leadership.

Practical Strategies:

Share Stories: Discuss personal challenges and growth experiences with the team.

Mentorship Programs: Engage in mutual learning opportunities with team members.

3. Celebrating Progress and Effort

Fixed Mindset Focus: Emphasizes perfection and end results over the learning process.

Growth Mindset Focus:

- **Value Effort:** Recognize hard work and dedication, not just outcomes.
- **Celebrate Milestones:** Acknowledge incremental progress toward goals.

Integration with the Holistic Intelligence Model:

- **Emotional Resilience (ER):** Reinforces motivation and perseverance.
- **Interpersonal Intelligence:** Strengthens team cohesion through shared recognition.
- **Practical Intelligence (PQ):** Encourages consistent effort toward improvement.

Practical Strategies:

Recognition Programs: Implement systems to acknowledge effort and progress.

Regular Check-Ins: Provide positive feedback throughout projects.

4. Encouraging Reflective Practice

Fixed Mindset Limitation: Neglects self-assessment and opportunities for growth.

Growth Mindset Practice:

- **Promote Self-Reflection:** Encourage team members to evaluate their own development.
- **Set Development Goals:** Assist in creating plans for personal and professional growth.

Integration with the Holistic Intelligence Model:

- **Intrapersonal Intelligence:** Enhances self-awareness and self-regulation.

- **Analytical Intelligence (AQ):** Supports critical evaluation of personal performance.
- **Ethical Intelligence:** Encourages honest self-assessment.

Practical Strategies:

Reflection Sessions: Schedule time for individuals to reflect on their experiences.

Personal Development Plans: Collaborate on setting and reviewing growth objectives.

Overcoming Fixed Mindset Traps Individually

1. Shifting from Judgment to Curiosity

Fixed Mindset: Quick to judge abilities, leading to negative self-talk and limiting beliefs.

Growth Mindset: Cultivate curiosity about one's abilities and potential.

Strategies:

- **Ask Questions:** Replace judgments with inquiries like "What can I learn from this?"
- **Adopt a Learning Attitude:** Approach situations as opportunities to gain knowledge.

2. Balancing Confidence with Humility

Fixed Mindset: Overemphasis on abilities can lead to arrogance.

Growth Mindset: Balance self-confidence with openness to learning from others.

Strategies:

- **Seek Diverse Perspectives:** Engage with people who have different viewpoints.
- **Acknowledge Others' Contributions:** Recognize the value others bring to the table.

3. Avoiding Labels and Stereotypes

Fixed Mindset: Assigning fixed labels to oneself or others limits potential.

Growth Mindset: See abilities as fluid and developable.

Strategies:
- Use Growth-Oriented Language: Replace "I'm not good at this" with "I'm learning how to improve."
- Encourage Potential: Focus on possibilities rather than limitations.

By overcoming fixed mindset traps, leaders can enhance their effectiveness across the 8 Pillars of the Holistic Intelligence Model:

1. Emotional Resilience (ER): Builds the strength to face challenges and learn from failures.

2. Creativity Intelligence (CrQ): Opens the mind to innovative ideas and approaches.

3. Practical Intelligence (PQ): Applies new skills and knowledge effectively.

4. Cultural Intelligence (CQ): Adapts to diverse environments and embraces different perspectives.

5. Intrapersonal Intelligence: Enhances self-awareness and personal growth.

6. Interpersonal Intelligence: Fosters strong relationships and collaborative cultures.

7. Ethical Intelligence: Upholds integrity and ethical standards in all actions.

8. Analytical Intelligence (AQ): Encourages critical thinking and problem-solving.

—

Overcoming fixed mindset traps requires a conscious shift in perspective and a commitment to ongoing self-awareness and development. By recognizing and navigating these challenges, leaders can unlock their full potential and create environments that foster growth, innovation, and success. Integrating the principles of the Holistic Intelligence Model, leaders can develop a well-rounded approach to leadership that empowers themselves and their teams.

Reflection Questions

1. Personal Traps: What fixed mindset traps have you encountered in your leadership journey?

2. Strategies for Change: Which strategies can you implement to shift toward a growth mindset?

3. Team Dynamics: How can you foster a growth mindset culture within your team or organization?

Action Plan

1. Self-Assessment: Identify areas where fixed mindset tendencies may exist.

2. Set Growth Goals: Define specific objectives to cultivate a growth mindset.

3. Implement Strategies: Apply practical steps outlined to overcome fixed mindset traps.

4. Monitor Progress: Regularly review your development and adjust your approach as needed.

Fostering a Positive Attitude in Leadership

Core Reading

A positive attitude is a cornerstone of effective leadership. It sets the tone for the entire organization, influencing culture, morale, and productivity. Leaders who cultivate a positive attitude not only inspire their teams but also navigate challenges with resilience and grace.

A positive attitude starts at the top. Leaders must embody the behavior they wish to see in their teams. By consistently demonstrating positivity, whether in the face of adversity or during moments of triumph, leaders set the standard for the entire organization.

Recognizing and appreciating the efforts of team members is a powerful way to foster positivity. Expressing gratitude for a job well done, a creative solution, or a collaborative effort not only boosts morale but also reinforces a culture of appreciation.

A positive attitude thrives in an environment of open, honest, and respectful communication. Leaders should create spaces where team members feel comfortable sharing their thoughts, concerns, and ideas. This fosters trust and allows for the free flow of positive energy.

While realism is important, leaders with a positive attitude also cultivate optimism. They approach challenges with the belief that there is a solution and that setbacks are temporary. This mindset not only instills confidence in the team but also paves the way for innovative problem-solving.

Rather than dwelling on problems, leaders with a positive attitude focus on finding solutions. They empower their teams to adopt a similar mindset, encouraging them to approach challenges with creativity and a belief that there is a way forward.

A positive attitude is closely tied to emotional resilience. Leaders who navigate ups and downs with composure and grace inspire confidence and stability in their teams. They demonstrate that challenges are a natural part of any endeavor and can be overcome.

Leaders should actively work to infuse positivity into the organizational culture. This can be achieved through various means, such as regular team-building activities, recognition programs, and even simple gestures like a kind word or a smile in passing.

A positive attitude flourishes in an environment where team members feel a sense of belonging and camaraderie. Leaders should actively work to create a culture of inclusivity and support, where everyone feels valued and part of a larger purpose.

Recognizing and celebrating achievements, whether they are major milestones or small wins, reinforces a positive attitude.

Leaders should take the time to acknowledge and commend the efforts and accomplishments of their teams.

A positive attitude in leadership is forward-thinking. It involves a focus on what can be achieved rather than dwelling on past mistakes or setbacks. Leaders should inspire their teams to look ahead, set goals, and work towards a brighter future.

Leaders with a positive attitude prioritize the growth and development of their team members. They provide opportunities for learning, mentorship, and skill-building, empowering individuals to reach their full potential.

While a positive attitude is vital, it must be balanced with a realistic understanding of challenges and limitations. Leaders should acknowledge difficulties while maintaining confidence in the ability to overcome them.

Leaders foster a positive attitude by empowering their teams to take ownership of their work and make decisions. This sense of autonomy instills a feeling of responsibility and pride, leading to a more positive and motivated workforce.

Even in moments of correction or feedback, leaders can maintain a positive attitude. They should deliver constructive feedback in a supportive and encouraging manner, focusing on growth and improvement rather than blame.

A positive attitude is closely linked to adaptability. Leaders who are open to change and flexible in their approach inspire confidence and resilience in their teams. They demonstrate that challenges are opportunities for growth and adaptation.

The way leaders communicate greatly influences the overall attitude of the organization. Positive leaders choose their words carefully, using language that uplifts and motivates rather than demoralizes.

Leaders with a positive attitude show genuine care for the well-being of their team members. They take the time to understand individual needs, provide support in times of difficulty, and celebrate personal milestones.

A well-placed dose of humor can be a powerful tool for fostering positivity. Leaders who inject humor into the workplace create an atmosphere of levity and camaraderie, helping to ease tension and build connections.

A positive attitude extends to recognizing the importance of work-life balance. Leaders who prioritize the well-being and happiness of their team members inspire loyalty and a positive outlook on both work and life.

A positive attitude doesn't waver in the face of adversity. Instead, it remains resolute and unwavering, inspiring confidence and determination in the team. Leaders who stand strong in difficult times serve as a beacon of positivity.

Leaders with a positive attitude inspire their teams by painting a vivid picture of the future. They communicate a compelling vision that instills a sense of purpose and direction, motivating individuals to work towards a common goal.

Fostering a positive attitude in leadership is a transformative endeavor. It sets the stage for a thriving organizational culture, resilient teams, and a forward-thinking approach to challenges. By embodying positivity and implementing these strategies, leaders can unleash the full potential of themselves and their teams, ultimately driving success and achievement.

The Importance of a Positive Attitude in Leadership

Impact on Organizational Culture

- **Influences Morale:** A leader's attitude directly affects team morale. A positive leader uplifts and motivates, while negativity can demoralize and hinder performance.
- **Drives Productivity:** Positivity fosters an environment where employees feel valued and engaged, leading to increased productivity.
- **Enhances Resilience:** Teams led by positive leaders are better equipped to handle adversity and change.

Integration with the Holistic Intelligence Model:

- **Emotional Resilience (ER):** A positive attitude strengthens emotional resilience, enabling leaders and teams to bounce back from setbacks.
- **Interpersonal Intelligence:** Facilitates stronger relationships and effective communication.
- **Intrapersonal Intelligence:** Promotes self-awareness and self-regulation in maintaining a positive outlook.

Leading by Example: Embodying Positivity

A positive attitude starts at the top. Leaders must embody the behavior they wish to see in their teams. By consistently demonstrating positivity, whether in the face of adversity or during moments of triumph, leaders set the standard for the entire organization.

Integration with the Holistic Intelligence Model:

- **Intrapersonal Intelligence:** Self-awareness enables leaders to monitor and adjust their attitude.
- **Interpersonal Intelligence:** Influences others through positive interactions.
- **Ethical Intelligence:** Upholds integrity and authenticity in actions.

Practical Strategies:

Self-Reflection: Regularly assess your attitude and its impact on others.

Positive Language: Use encouraging and affirming language in communications.

Visible Enthusiasm: Show genuine excitement and commitment to goals.

Case Example:

Richard Branson, founder of Virgin Group, is known for his enthusiastic and positive leadership style, which has been instrumental in building a strong company culture.

Practicing Gratitude: Cultivating Appreciation

Recognizing and appreciating the efforts of team members is a powerful way to foster positivity. Expressing gratitude for a job well done, a creative solution, or a collaborative effort boosts morale and reinforces a culture of appreciation.

Integration with the Holistic Intelligence Model:

- **Interpersonal Intelligence:** Strengthens relationships through appreciation.
- **Emotional Resilience (ER):** Enhances emotional well-being for both giver and receiver.
- **Ethical Intelligence:** Encourages fairness and recognition.

Practical Strategies:

Personal Acknowledgment: Write personalized thank-you notes or messages.

Public Recognition: Acknowledge achievements in meetings or company communications.

Gratitude Rituals: Implement regular practices, such as sharing appreciations at the start of meetings.

Case Example:

Tony Hsieh, former CEO of Zappos, emphasized gratitude as a core component of company culture, contributing to high employee satisfaction.

Encouraging Open Communication: Building Trust and Transparency

A positive attitude thrives in an environment of open, honest, and respectful communication. Leaders should create spaces where team members feel comfortable sharing their thoughts, concerns, and ideas.

Integration with the Holistic Intelligence Model:

- **Interpersonal Intelligence:** Enhances communication skills and empathetic listening.
- **Cultural Intelligence (CQ):** Respects and values diverse perspectives.
- **Ethical Intelligence:** Upholds honesty and integrity in interactions.

Practical Strategies:

Open-Door Policy: Make yourself accessible to team members.

Regular Check-Ins: Schedule one-on-one meetings to discuss concerns and feedback.

Active Listening: Practice attentive listening without judgment.

Case Example:

Satya Nadella, CEO of Microsoft, transformed the company's culture by promoting open communication and collaboration.

Cultivating Optimism: Inspiring Confidence

While realism is important, leaders with a positive attitude also cultivate optimism. They approach challenges with the belief that there is a solution and that setbacks are temporary.

Integration with the Holistic Intelligence Model:

- **Emotional Resilience (ER):** Maintains a hopeful outlook during adversity.
- **Analytical Intelligence (AQ):** Strategizes solutions with a positive perspective.
- **Intrapersonal Intelligence:** Regulates emotions to sustain optimism.

Practical Strategies:

Positive Framing: Present challenges as opportunities.

Solution-Focused Dialogue: Guide conversations toward finding answers.

Celebrate Small Wins: Recognize progress to build momentum.

Nurturing a Solutions-Oriented Mindset: Empowering Teams to Overcome Challenges

Rather than dwelling on problems, leaders with a positive attitude focus on finding solutions. They empower their teams to adopt a similar mindset.

Integration with the Holistic Intelligence Model:

- **Practical Intelligence (PQ):** Applies knowledge effectively to solve problems.
- **Creativity Intelligence (CrQ):** Encourages innovative thinking.
- **Interpersonal Intelligence:** Facilitates collaborative problem-solving.

Practical Strategies:

Brainstorming Sessions: Foster creative solutions through group discussions.

Resource Provision: Provide tools and support needed to address issues.

Encourage Autonomy: Allow team members to take ownership of solutions.

Maintaining Emotional Resilience: Navigating Ups and Downs with Grace

A positive attitude is closely tied to emotional resilience. Leaders who navigate ups and downs with composure inspire confidence and stability in their teams.

Integration with the Holistic Intelligence Model:

- **Emotional Resilience (ER):** Core to maintaining positivity under pressure.
- **Intrapersonal Intelligence:** Self-regulation of emotions.
- **Interpersonal Intelligence:** Demonstrates reliability and steadiness.

Practical Strategies:

Stress Management Techniques: Practice mindfulness, meditation, or exercise.

Mindset Shifts: Reframe negative situations to find the positive aspects.

Support Networks: Build relationships that provide encouragement and advice.

Promoting a Culture of Positivity: Embedding Positivity into Organizational DNA

Leaders should actively work to infuse positivity into the organizational culture through various means.

Integration with the Holistic Intelligence Model:

- **Cultural Intelligence (CQ):** Shapes a positive organizational culture.
- **Ethical Intelligence:** Ensures that positivity aligns with core values.
- **Interpersonal Intelligence:** Strengthens community within the organization.

Practical Strategies:

Team-Building Activities: Organize events that foster camaraderie.

Recognition Programs: Implement systems to reward positive behaviors.

Positive Environment: Create a welcoming physical and virtual workspace.

Fostering a Sense of Belonging: Creating Inclusive and Supportive Teams

A positive attitude flourishes where team members feel a sense of belonging and camaraderie.

Integration with the Holistic Intelligence Model:

- **Cultural Intelligence (CQ):** Embraces diversity and inclusion.
- **Interpersonal Intelligence:** Builds strong, supportive relationships.
- **Ethical Intelligence:** Promotes fairness and respect.

Practical Strategies:

Inclusive Practices: Ensure all voices are heard and valued.

Mentorship Programs: Pair team members to support growth and connection.

Community Building: Encourage collaboration across departments.

Celebrating Successes, Big and Small: Reinforcing Achievements

Recognizing and celebrating achievements, whether major milestones or small wins, reinforces a positive attitude.

Integration with the Holistic Intelligence Model:

- **Emotional Resilience (ER):** Boosts morale and motivation.
- **Interpersonal Intelligence:** Strengthens team cohesion.
- **Ethical Intelligence:** Fairly acknowledges contributions.

Practical Strategies:

Public Acknowledgment: Share successes in company meetings or newsletters.

Rewards and Incentives: Offer bonuses, promotions, or other incentives.

Personal Celebrations: Mark personal milestones like birthdays or anniversaries.

Encouraging Personal Growth and Development: Empowering Team Members

Leaders with a positive attitude prioritize the growth and development of their team members.

Integration with the Holistic Intelligence Model:

- **Intrapersonal Intelligence:** Supports personal development.
- **Practical Intelligence (PQ):** Enhances skills and competencies.
- **Creativity Intelligence (CrQ):** Fosters innovation through new learning.

Practical Strategies:

Professional Development Opportunities: Provide access to training and education.

Career Pathing: Work with team members to map out career progression.

Feedback and Coaching: Offer regular, constructive feedback for improvement.

Balancing Positivity with Realism: Maintaining Credibility

While positivity is vital, it must be balanced with a realistic understanding of challenges.

Integration with the Holistic Intelligence Model:

- **Analytical Intelligence (AQ):** Assesses situations accurately.
- **Ethical Intelligence:** Communicates honestly without false optimism.
- **Emotional Resilience (ER):** Manages emotions while confronting realities.

Practical Strategies:

Transparent Communication: Share both successes and challenges openly.

Realistic Goal Setting: Set achievable objectives with a positive outlook.

Empathetic Leadership: Understand and acknowledge team concerns.

Empowering Autonomy and Ownership: Building Confidence and Motivation

Leaders foster a positive attitude by empowering their teams to take ownership of their work.

Integration with the Holistic Intelligence Model:

- **Practical Intelligence (PQ):** Encourages effective decision-making.
- **Interpersonal Intelligence:** Builds trust and respect.
- **Ethical Intelligence:** Respects individual autonomy.

Practical Strategies:

Delegate Meaningfully: Assign tasks that challenge and develop skills.

Encourage Decision-Making: Allow team members to make choices in their roles.

Provide Support: Be available to guide without micromanaging.

Providing Constructive Feedback with Positivity: Focusing on Growth

Even in moments of correction, leaders can maintain a positive attitude.

Integration with the Holistic Intelligence Model:

- **Interpersonal Intelligence:** Communicates feedback effectively.
- **Intrapersonal Intelligence:** Reflects on the best approach to feedback.
- **Ethical Intelligence:** Ensures fairness and respect.

Practical Strategies:

Use the "Sandwich" Method: Begin and end with positive remarks around constructive feedback.

Focus on Behaviors: Address specific actions rather than personal attributes.

Set Improvement Goals: Collaboratively establish objectives for growth.

Remaining Adaptable and Flexible: Inspiring Confidence Through Change

A positive attitude is closely linked to adaptability. Leaders who are open to change inspire resilience in their teams.

Integration with the Holistic Intelligence Model:

- **Emotional Resilience (ER):** Handles change with composure.
- **Cultural Intelligence (CQ):** Adapts to diverse situations.
- **Creativity Intelligence (CrQ):** Innovates in response to new challenges.

Practical Strategies:

Flexible Policies: Implement adaptable work arrangements when possible.

Encourage Innovation: Be open to new ideas and approaches.

Lead by Example: Demonstrate flexibility in your actions.

Demonstrating Empathy and Compassion: Building Strong Relationships

Leaders with a positive attitude show genuine care for the well-being of their team members.

Integration with the Holistic Intelligence Model:

- **Interpersonal Intelligence:** Deepens connections through understanding.
- **Intrapersonal Intelligence:** Recognizes one's own emotions to relate to others.
- **Ethical Intelligence:** Acts with kindness and respect.

Practical Strategies:

Active Empathy: Listen attentively to team members' concerns.

Supportive Actions: Offer assistance during personal or professional difficulties.

Celebrate Personal Milestones: Acknowledge birthdays, anniversaries, or achievements.

Encouraging Work-Life Balance: Prioritizing Well-Being

A positive attitude extends to recognizing the importance of work-life balance.

Integration with the Holistic Intelligence Model:

- **Intrapersonal Intelligence:** Understands the need for personal time.
- **Ethical Intelligence:** Respects individual boundaries and needs.
- **Emotional Resilience (ER):** Supports overall well-being.

Practical Strategies:

Flexible Scheduling: Allow for varied work hours when possible.

Promote Time Off: Encourage the use of vacation days and personal time.

Wellness Programs: Implement initiatives that support health and wellness.

Fostering a positive attitude in leadership is a transformative endeavor. It sets the stage for a thriving organizational culture, resilient teams, and a forward-thinking approach to challenges. By embodying positivity and implementing these strategies—integrated with the Holistic Intelligence Model—leaders can unleash the full potential of themselves and their teams, ultimately driving success and achievement.

Reflection Questions

1. Self-Assessment: How does your current attitude influence your team's morale and productivity?

2. Areas for Growth: In which aspects of fostering a positive attitude can you improve?

3. Team Culture: What steps can you take to promote a culture of positivity within your organization?

Action Plan

1. Identify Key Areas: Pinpoint specific strategies to implement in your leadership practice.

2. Set Measurable Goals: Establish clear objectives for fostering positivity.

3. Engage Your Team: Involve team members in creating a positive work environment.

4. Monitor and Adjust: Regularly assess the impact of your efforts and make necessary adjustments.

The Ripple Effect of Positivity: How Attitude Shapes Organizational Culture

Core Reading

The attitude of a leader serves as the nucleus from which the culture of an organization radiates. It creates a ripple effect that permeates every corner, influencing the behaviors, beliefs, and interactions of every member. Understanding this dynamic is paramount for leaders who aspire to cultivate a thriving, positive organizational culture.

A positive attitude from leadership cultivates a culture of trust and transparency. When team members witness leaders who approach challenges with confidence and a constructive mindset, they are more inclined to trust the direction in which the organization is headed. This trust becomes the bedrock upon which a culture of transparency is built, as open communication flourishes in an atmosphere of mutual respect and confidence.

Positivity fosters a sense of belonging and camaraderie among team members. When leaders exude a positive attitude, they create an environment where individuals feel valued and appreciated. This sense of belonging is vital for building strong, cohesive teams that work collaboratively towards shared goals. It fosters a culture where each member feels that their contributions are integral to the collective success.

In a culture influenced by positivity, innovation thrives. Team members are more inclined to think creatively and take risks when they feel supported by leaders who encourage experimentation and value fresh perspectives. This dynamic empowers employees to explore new ideas, driving innovation and propelling the organization forward in a rapidly evolving landscape.

A positive attitude also serves as a catalyst for resilience. In an era marked by constant change and uncertainty, resilience is a cornerstone of organizational success. When leaders approach challenges with a positive mindset, they model resilience for their teams, demonstrating that setbacks are not insurmountable obstacles but rather opportunities for growth and learning.

A culture of positivity encourages a solutions-oriented mindset. When faced with difficulties, team members are more likely to approach problems with creativity and resourcefulness if they are guided by leaders who emphasize finding solutions rather than dwelling on issues. This proactive approach not only resolves immediate challenges but also cultivates a culture of continuous improvement.

Positivity is contagious. When leaders radiate positivity, it inspires team members to adopt a similar outlook. This collective attitude shift has a domino effect, creating a self-reinforcing cycle of positivity within the organization. As team members feed off one another's positive energy, it elevates the overall morale and productivity of the entire workforce.

A culture of positivity significantly impacts employee well-being. Research has consistently shown that a positive work environment leads to reduced stress levels, increased job satisfaction, and improved mental and physical health among employees. Leaders who prioritize a positive attitude contribute to a workplace where individuals feel supported, valued, and motivated.

A positive attitude also enhances adaptability and change readiness within an organization. In today's fast-paced business landscape, the ability to adapt to change is crucial. When leaders approach change with a positive mindset, they inspire their teams to embrace it as an opportunity for growth rather than a threat. This adaptability becomes a hallmark of the organizational culture, ensuring its resilience in the face of evolving circumstances.

A positive attitude from leadership promotes a culture of accountability and ownership. When leaders model accountability, it sets the standard for the entire organization. Team members are more likely to take ownership of their work and its outcomes when they see leaders who are accountable for their decisions and actions.

A culture of positivity also fosters a greater sense of customer focus and service excellence. When team members are motivated by a positive attitude, they are more likely to go above and beyond to meet customer needs and exceed expectations. This commitment to exceptional service becomes a defining characteristic of the organizational culture.

A positive culture attracts and retains top talent. In a competitive job market, organizations that prioritize a positive work environment are more likely to attract high-caliber employees. Furthermore, a positive culture serves as a powerful retention tool, as employees are more likely to stay with an organization where they feel valued and supported.

A positive attitude in leadership has a profound impact on the ethical climate of an organization. Leaders who prioritize integrity, honesty, and ethical behavior create a culture where ethical considerations are central to decision-making. This ethical foundation becomes a guiding principle for the entire organization, influencing the behavior of every member.

A culture of positivity enhances organizational agility. When leaders approach change with a positive attitude, they create an environment where teams are more willing to adapt and respond quickly to evolving circumstances. This agility becomes a competitive advantage in a rapidly changing business landscape.

A positive culture also leads to improved organizational performance and productivity. When team members work in an environment characterized by positivity, they are more engaged, motivated, and productive. This heightened performance translates into tangible results and contributes to the overall success of the organization.

The ripple effect of positivity on organizational culture is profound and far-reaching. Leaders who prioritize a positive attitude create a fertile ground for trust, transparency, innovation, and resilience to flourish. This culture, in turn, leads to improved well-being, adaptability, accountability, customer focus, talent attraction, ethical behavior, agility, and organizational performance. It is a transformative force that shapes the very essence of an organization, driving it towards sustained success.

Cultivating Trust and Transparency: Building the Foundation of Organizational Culture

A positive attitude from leadership fosters a culture of trust and transparency. When team members witness leaders who approach challenges with confidence and a constructive mindset, they are more inclined to trust the organization's direction. This trust becomes the bedrock upon which transparency is built, as open communication flourishes in an atmosphere of mutual respect and confidence.

Integration with the Holistic Intelligence Model:

- **Ethical Intelligence:** Leaders demonstrate integrity and honesty, reinforcing ethical standards.
- **Interpersonal Intelligence:** Positive interactions enhance relationships and communication.
- **Intrapersonal Intelligence:** Self-awareness helps leaders model trustworthiness and authenticity.

Practical Strategies:

Open Communication Channels: Implement regular updates and forums where employees can voice concerns and ideas.

Transparent Decision-Making: Share the rationale behind decisions to foster understanding and trust.

Lead by Example: Demonstrate honesty and integrity in all actions.

Case Example:

Howard Schultz, former CEO of Starbucks, emphasized trust and transparency by openly communicating with employees during challenging times, reinforcing a positive organizational culture.

Fostering a Sense of Belonging and Camaraderie: Building Strong, Cohesive Teams

When leaders exude a positive attitude, they create an environment where individuals feel valued and appreciated. This sense of belonging is vital for building strong, cohesive teams that work collaboratively towards shared goals. It fosters a culture where each member feels their contributions are integral to the collective success.

Integration with the Holistic Intelligence Model:

- **Cultural Intelligence (CQ):** Appreciating diversity and fostering inclusivity.
- **Interpersonal Intelligence:** Building strong relationships within the team.
- **Emotional Resilience (ER):** Supporting team members emotionally to strengthen bonds.

Practical Strategies:

Team-Building Activities: Organize events that encourage collaboration and relationship-building.

Recognition Programs: Acknowledge individual and team contributions regularly.

Inclusive Practices: Ensure all team members feel heard and valued.

Case Example:

Mary Barra, CEO of General Motors, promotes a culture of inclusivity and belonging, leading to stronger team cohesion and performance.

Inspiring Innovation and Creativity: Creating an Environment Where Ideas Flourish

In a culture influenced by positivity, innovation thrives. Team members are more inclined to think creatively and take risks when they feel supported by leaders who encourage experimentation and value fresh perspectives. This dynamic empowers employees to explore new ideas, driving innovation and propelling the organization forward.

Integration with the Holistic Intelligence Model:

- **Creativity Intelligence (CrQ):** Encouraging innovative thinking and problem-solving.
- **Emotional Resilience (ER):** Providing support during the trial-and-error process inherent in innovation.
- **Practical Intelligence (PQ):** Applying creative ideas effectively.

Practical Strategies:

Innovation Labs: Establish spaces or times dedicated to creative thinking.

Encourage Experimentation: Support calculated risk-taking without fear of negative repercussions.

Celebrate Innovative Efforts: Recognize and reward creative contributions.

Case Example:

Google's 20% Time: Google encourages employees to spend 20% of their time on projects they are passionate about, fostering innovation and leading to products like Gmail and Google Maps.

Enhancing Resilience and Adaptability: Building Strength Through Positivity

A positive attitude serves as a catalyst for resilience. In an era marked by constant change and uncertainty, resilience is a cornerstone of organizational success. When leaders approach challenges with a positive mindset, they model resilience for their teams, demonstrating that setbacks are opportunities for growth and learning.

Integration with the Holistic Intelligence Model:

- **Emotional Resilience (ER):** Strengthening the ability to cope with and adapt to adversity.

- **Intrapersonal Intelligence:** Self-regulation during challenging times.
- Analytical Intelligence (AQ): Strategizing effectively under pressure.

Practical Strategies:

Resilience Training: Offer programs to develop coping strategies.

Positive Reinforcement: Highlight lessons learned from setbacks.

Lead by Example: Demonstrate calm and constructive responses to challenges.

Case Example:

Airbnb's Response to COVID-19: CEO Brian Chesky maintained a positive and empathetic attitude, leading the company through significant challenges while preserving its core values and culture.

Encouraging a Solutions-Oriented Mindset: Focusing on Progress Over Problems

A culture of positivity encourages a solutions-oriented mindset. When faced with difficulties, team members are more likely to approach problems with creativity and resourcefulness if guided by leaders who emphasize finding solutions rather than dwelling on issues.

Integration with the Holistic Intelligence Model:

- **Practical Intelligence (PQ):** Efficiently addressing challenges.
- **Analytical Intelligence (AQ):** Critical thinking to develop effective solutions.
- **Creativity Intelligence (CrQ):** Innovative approaches to problem-solving.

Practical Strategies:

Solution-Focused Meetings: Encourage discussions that prioritize actionable solutions.

Empower Teams: Delegate authority to make decisions and implement solutions.

Recognize Problem-Solving Efforts: Acknowledge and reward effective resolution of challenges.

Enhancing Employee Well-being and Engagement: Creating a Supportive Work Environment

A culture of positivity significantly impacts employee well-being. Research consistently shows that a positive work environment leads to reduced stress levels, increased job satisfaction, and improved mental and physical health among employees.

Integration with the Holistic Intelligence Model:

- **Intrapersonal Intelligence:** Promoting self-care and personal well-being.
- **Interpersonal Intelligence:** Fostering supportive relationships.
- **Ethical Intelligence:** Ensuring fair treatment and respect for all employees.

Practical Strategies:

Wellness Programs: Implement initiatives that support mental and physical health.

Work-Life Balance: Encourage practices that promote personal time and rest.

Employee Assistance Programs: Provide resources for personal and professional challenges.

Case Example:

Salesforce's Ohana Culture: Emphasizes family values and well-being, leading to high employee satisfaction and retention.

Promoting Accountability and Ownership: Building a Culture of Responsibility

A positive attitude from leadership promotes a culture of accountability and ownership. When leaders model accountability, it sets the standard for the entire organization. Team members are more likely to take ownership of their work and its outcomes when they see leaders who are accountable for their decisions and actions.

Integration with the Holistic Intelligence Model:

- **Ethical Intelligence:** Upholding integrity and responsibility.
- **Intrapersonal Intelligence:** Self-awareness of one's impact and responsibilities.
- **Interpersonal Intelligence:** Encouraging mutual accountability within teams.

Practical Strategies:

Set Clear Expectations: Define roles and responsibilities transparently.

Model Accountability: Admit mistakes and take corrective actions openly.

Provide Feedback: Offer constructive feedback to support growth and accountability.

Enhancing Customer Focus and Service Excellence: Elevating Organizational Performance

A culture of positivity fosters a greater sense of customer focus and service excellence. Motivated by a positive attitude, team members are more likely to go above and beyond to meet customer needs and exceed expectations.

Integration with the Holistic Intelligence Model:

- **Practical Intelligence (PQ):** Delivering high-quality services and products.
- **Ethical Intelligence:** Ensuring honesty and integrity in customer interactions.
- **Interpersonal Intelligence:** Building strong relationships with customers.

Practical Strategies:

Customer Service Training: Equip employees with skills to provide exceptional service.

Empower Employees: Allow team members to make decisions that benefit customers.

Collect Feedback: Use customer insights to improve services continuously.

Case Example:

Ritz-Carlton's Empowerment Policy: Employees are empowered to spend up to $2,000 per guest to resolve issues, demonstrating a deep commitment to service excellence.

Attracting and Retaining Top Talent: Creating a Magnet for Excellence

A positive culture attracts and retains top talent. In a competitive job market, organizations that prioritize a positive work environment are more likely to attract high-caliber employees. Furthermore, a positive culture serves as a powerful retention tool.

Integration with the Holistic Intelligence Model:

- **Cultural Intelligence (CQ):** Embracing diversity enhances the talent pool.
- **Ethical Intelligence:** An ethical culture appeals to values-driven professionals.
- **Emotional Resilience (ER):** A supportive environment reduces burnout and turnover.

Practical Strategies:

Employer Branding: Promote the organization's positive culture externally.

Talent Development Programs: Invest in employee growth and career advancement.

Competitive Benefits: Offer attractive compensation and benefits packages.

Case Example:

Google's Workplace Culture: Known for its positive and innovative culture, Google attracts top talent globally.

Strengthening Ethical Climate: Embedding Integrity into Organizational DNA

A positive attitude in leadership has a profound impact on the ethical climate of an organization. Leaders who prioritize integrity, honesty, and ethical behavior create a culture where ethical considerations are central to decision-making.

Integration with the Holistic Intelligence Model:

- **Ethical Intelligence:** The cornerstone of ethical organizational culture.
- **Intrapersonal Intelligence:** Leaders' self-awareness of their moral compass.
- **Interpersonal Intelligence:** Promoting ethical interactions and relationships.

Practical Strategies:

Code of Ethics: Establish clear ethical guidelines and expectations.

Ethics Training: Provide regular training on ethical issues and decision-making.

Lead by Example: Demonstrate ethical behavior consistently.

Enhancing Organizational Agility: Responding Effectively to Change

A culture of positivity enhances organizational agility. When leaders approach change with a positive attitude, they create an environment where teams are more willing to adapt and respond quickly to evolving circumstances.

Integration with the Holistic Intelligence Model:

- **Emotional Resilience (ER):** Supports adaptability during transitions.
- **Analytical Intelligence (AQ):** Facilitates strategic thinking in dynamic environments.
- **Practical Intelligence (PQ):** Implements changes efficiently.

Practical Strategies:

Agile Methodologies: Adopt flexible frameworks for project management.

Continuous Improvement: Encourage regular assessment and refinement of processes.

Empower Decision-Making: Allow teams to make swift decisions when needed.

Driving Organizational Performance and Productivity: Achieving Excellence Through Positivity

A positive culture leads to improved organizational performance and productivity. When team members work in an environment characterized by positivity, they are more engaged, motivated, and productive.

Integration with the Holistic Intelligence Model:

- **Intrapersonal Intelligence:** Enhances individual motivation and goal-setting.

- **Interpersonal Intelligence:** Improves teamwork and collaboration.
- **Practical Intelligence (PQ):** Increases efficiency and effectiveness.

Practical Strategies:

Set Clear Goals: Align team efforts with organizational objectives.

Monitor Progress: Use performance metrics to track and encourage productivity.

Provide Resources: Ensure teams have the tools they need to succeed.

Case Example:

Southwest Airlines: Known for its positive culture, resulting in high employee engagement and consistent profitability.

—

The ripple effect of positivity on organizational culture is profound and far-reaching. Leaders who prioritize a positive attitude create fertile ground for trust, transparency, innovation, and resilience to flourish. This culture, in turn, leads to improved well-being, adaptability, accountability, customer focus, talent attraction, ethical behavior, agility, and organizational performance. It is a transformative force that shapes the very essence of an organization, driving it towards sustained success and excellence.

Reflection Questions

1. Leadership Influence: How does your attitude currently impact your organization's culture?

2. Cultural Development: What aspects of your organizational culture could benefit from a more positive influence?

3. Action Steps: What specific actions can you take to enhance positivity within your organization?

Action Plan

1. Assess Current Culture: Conduct surveys or assessments to understand the existing cultural climate.

2. Set Cultural Goals: Define clear objectives for the desired organizational culture.

3. Develop Strategies: Implement the practical strategies outlined to foster positivity.

4. Engage the Team: Involve employees at all levels in cultural initiatives.

5. Monitor and Adapt: Regularly review progress and make adjustments as needed.

Strategies for Cultivating a Positive Attitude in Leadership Roles

Core Reading

Cultivating a positive attitude is not merely a disposition; it is a skill that can be honed and developed over time. Leaders who intentionally work towards fostering positivity in themselves set the stage for a transformative influence on their teams and organizational culture.

First and foremost, self-awareness forms the foundation of a positive attitude in leadership. Leaders must take the time for introspection, recognizing their own thought patterns, reactions, and emotional responses. This self-awareness enables them to identify areas where a more positive outlook can be cultivated.

A crucial component of cultivating a positive attitude is embracing a growth mindset. This perspective, championed by psychologist Carol Dweck, posits that abilities and intelligence can be developed with dedication and hard work. Leaders with a growth mindset view challenges as opportunities for learning and improvement, rather than insurmountable obstacles.

Practicing gratitude is a powerful tool in fostering positivity. Leaders who regularly reflect on and express gratitude for the accomplishments and contributions of their team members create an environment where appreciation is valued. This not only boosts morale but also reinforces a positive, appreciative culture.

Maintaining a healthy work-life balance is essential for sustaining a positive attitude. Leaders who prioritize their own well-being and model this behavior for their teams demonstrate that self-care is a fundamental aspect of success. This balance not only rejuvenates leaders but also sets an example for the entire organization.

Effective communication is paramount in cultivating a positive attitude within leadership roles. Clear, transparent, and empathetic communication fosters an environment of trust and mutual respect. When leaders communicate openly, it establishes a culture where team members feel valued and heard, contributing to a positive overall atmosphere.

Practicing mindfulness is a valuable strategy for cultivating a positive attitude. Mindfulness involves being present in the moment, fully engaged with one's thoughts and surroundings. Leaders who practice mindfulness are better equipped to navigate challenges with clarity and composure, ultimately fostering a more positive outlook.

Setting clear and achievable goals is another pivotal strategy. When leaders provide their teams with a clear sense of direction and purpose, it instills a sense of accomplishment and progress. Celebrating small victories along the way reinforces a positive attitude and motivates team members to continue their efforts.

Embracing failures and setbacks as learning opportunities is a hallmark of leaders with a positive attitude. Instead of dwelling on missteps, they approach them with a constructive mindset, extracting lessons and using them to drive future success. This resilience in the face of adversity models a positive approach to challenges.

Practicing empathy is a cornerstone of cultivating a positive attitude. Leaders who seek to understand the perspectives, emotions, and needs of their team members create a culture of compassion and support. This empathetic approach fosters a sense of belonging and trust within the team.

Encouraging autonomy and decision-making among team members is a powerful strategy for cultivating positivity. When leaders empower their teams to take ownership of their work and make decisions, it instills a sense of pride and accomplishment. This autonomy contributes to a positive, empowered culture.

Leading by example is perhaps the most impactful strategy for cultivating a positive attitude. When leaders consistently model a positive outlook, it sets the standard for the entire organization. Team members look to their leaders for guidance and inspiration, making the leader's attitude a powerful force in shaping the overall culture.

Engaging in ongoing learning and development is crucial for leaders seeking to cultivate a positive attitude. Staying curious and open to new ideas fosters a mindset of growth and adaptability. This continuous learning not only benefits the leader personally but also sets an example for the entire organization.

Fostering a culture of celebration and recognition is instrumental in cultivating positivity. Leaders who regularly acknowledge and celebrate the achievements, big or small, of their team members create an environment where accomplishments are valued and appreciated. This recognition reinforces a positive, motivated culture.

Encouraging creativity and innovation is a strategy that nurtures a positive attitude in leadership. When leaders create a space where team members feel empowered to think outside the box and explore new ideas, it fosters a culture of forward-thinking and optimism. This innovative spirit contributes to a positive, dynamic environment.

Maintaining a solution-oriented mindset is paramount in cultivating a positive attitude. When faced with challenges, leaders who focus on finding solutions rather than dwelling on problems create a culture of proactive problem-solving. This approach not only resolves immediate issues but also reinforces a positive, can-do attitude.

Building and nurturing strong relationships with team members is a fundamental strategy for cultivating a positive attitude. Leaders who invest time in getting to know their team members on a personal level create a sense of camaraderie and trust. This strong interpersonal connection contributes to a positive, supportive culture.

Promoting a culture of inclusivity and diversity is essential in fostering a positive attitude. When leaders prioritize diversity of thought, backgrounds, and perspectives, it creates an environment where every voice is valued. This inclusivity not only enriches the organization's collective intelligence but also contributes to a positive, inclusive culture.

Encouraging a sense of purpose and meaning in work is a powerful strategy for cultivating a positive attitude. When leaders help team members connect their individual roles to the broader mission and vision of the organization, it instills a sense of fulfillment and motivation. This sense of purpose contributes to a positive, engaged culture.

Providing opportunities for skill development and growth is a strategy that fosters a positive attitude. When leaders invest in the professional development of their team members, it demonstrates a commitment to their growth and success. This investment not only enhances individual capabilities but also reinforces a positive, forward-thinking culture.

Creating a culture of transparency and open communication is crucial in cultivating a positive attitude. When leaders are honest, authentic, and forthcoming in their interactions, it builds a culture of trust and mutual respect. This transparency fosters a positive, collaborative environment where team members feel valued and heard.

Incorporating play and creativity into the work environment is a strategy that promotes a positive attitude. When leaders encourage a playful, creative approach to tasks and projects, it fosters a culture of innovation and enjoyment. This lighthearted approach contributes to a positive, energized work atmosphere.

The cultivation of a positive attitude is a multifaceted endeavor that requires intentional effort and commitment from leaders. By incorporating these strategies into their leadership approach, leaders can create an environment where positivity flourishes, ultimately shaping a vibrant, empowered organizational culture. This positive attitude, in turn, becomes a catalyst for organizational success and growth.

Developing Self-Awareness

Self-awareness is the cornerstone of a positive attitude in leadership. By understanding their own thought patterns, reactions, and emotional responses, leaders can identify areas where a more positive outlook can be cultivated.

Integration with the Holistic Intelligence Model:

Intrapersonal Intelligence: Enhances self-understanding and emotional regulation.

Emotional Resilience (ER): Builds the capacity to manage emotions effectively.

Practical Strategies:

Reflective Journaling: Regularly document thoughts and feelings to identify patterns.

Mindfulness Practices: Engage in meditation or mindfulness exercises to stay present.

Seek Feedback: Encourage input from trusted colleagues to gain external perspectives.

Case Example:

Ray Dalio, founder of Bridgewater Associates, emphasizes radical transparency and self-reflection, fostering a culture of continuous self-improvement.

Transforming Challenges into Opportunities

Adopting a growth mindset enables leaders to view challenges as opportunities for learning and improvement rather than insurmountable obstacles.

Integration with the Holistic Intelligence Model:

Analytical Intelligence (AQ): Encourages critical thinking and problem-solving.

Creativity Intelligence (CrQ): Fosters innovative approaches to challenges.

Practical Strategies:

Reframe Challenges: View obstacles as learning experiences.

Encourage Learning: Promote professional development for yourself and your team.

Set Stretch Goals: Establish ambitious objectives to stimulate growth.

Case Example:

Carol Dweck's Research: Demonstrates how a growth mindset leads to higher achievement and resilience.

Cultivating Appreciation and Positivity

Regularly expressing gratitude enhances a positive atmosphere and reinforces a culture of appreciation within the organization.

Integration with the Holistic Intelligence Model:

Interpersonal Intelligence: Strengthens relationships through appreciation.

Ethical Intelligence: Promotes fairness and recognition.

Practical Strategies:

Gratitude Journals: Keep a personal log of things you're thankful for.

Public Acknowledgment: Recognize team members' contributions openly.

Gratitude Rituals: Start meetings by sharing successes or appreciations.

Sustaining Positivity Through Well-Being

Prioritizing personal well-being is essential for sustaining a positive attitude. Leaders who model this behavior demonstrate that self-care is fundamental to success.

Integration with the Holistic Intelligence Model:

Intrapersonal Intelligence: Recognizes personal needs and sets boundaries.

Emotional Resilience (ER): Prevents burnout and maintains energy levels.

Practical Strategies:

Set Boundaries: Define clear work hours and personal time.

Promote Wellness: Encourage healthy habits within the team.

Lead by Example: Take vacations and disconnect when necessary.

Case Example:

Arianna Huffington, founder of Thrive Global, advocates for work-life balance and well-being in leadership.

Fostering Trust and Understanding

Effective communication is paramount in cultivating a positive attitude. Clear, transparent, and empathetic communication fosters an environment of trust and mutual respect.

Integration with the Holistic Intelligence Model:

Interpersonal Intelligence: Improves understanding and connection.

Cultural Intelligence (CQ): Navigates diverse communication styles.

Practical Strategies:

Active Listening: Fully engage with team members during conversations.

Open Dialogue: Encourage questions and discussions.

Transparent Messaging: Communicate intentions and decisions clearly.

Enhancing Presence and Composure

Mindfulness involves being present and fully engaged, allowing leaders to navigate challenges with clarity and composure.

Integration with the Holistic Intelligence Model:

- Intrapersonal Intelligence: Heightens self-awareness.
- Emotional Resilience (ER): Reduces stress and enhances emotional regulation.

Practical Strategies:
- Mindful Breathing: Incorporate breathing exercises into your routine.

- Mindful Meetings: Begin meetings with a moment of mindfulness.
- Mindfulness Training: Offer workshops for the team.

Instilling Purpose and Motivation

Providing clear direction and purpose instills a sense of accomplishment and progress, reinforcing a positive attitude.

Integration with the Holistic Intelligence Model:

- Analytical Intelligence (AQ): Enables strategic planning.
- Practical Intelligence (PQ): Facilitates effective execution.

Practical Strategies:
- WISE Goals—standing for Well-Defined, Inspiring, Sustainable, and Empowering—is a modern approach to goal-setting that emphasizes clarity, motivation, longevity, and personal growth. It is designed to guide individuals on their leadership and personal development journeys by aligning goals with their core values and long-term aspirations.
- Regular Check-Ins: Monitor progress and adjust as needed.
- Celebrate Milestones: Recognize achievements along the way.

For a complete discussion of WISE and GROW, see "Thriving Amidst Flux: Navigating Change and Uncertainty" by William Stanek.

Cultivating Resilience and Growth

Leaders with a positive attitude approach failures with a constructive mindset, extracting lessons to drive future success.

Integration with the Holistic Intelligence Model:

- Emotional Resilience (ER): Bounces back from setbacks.
- Analytical Intelligence (AQ): Analyzes failures to inform improvement.

Practical Strategies:
- Failure Analysis: Conduct debriefs to understand what went wrong.
- Share Lessons Learned: Promote a culture of transparency regarding mistakes.
- Encourage Risk-Taking: Support innovative efforts, even if they fail.

Building Compassionate Connections

Leaders who understand and relate to their team members' perspectives create a culture of compassion and support.

Integration with the Holistic Intelligence Model:

- Interpersonal Intelligence: Enhances relationships through empathy.
- Cultural Intelligence (CQ): Respects diverse backgrounds and experiences.

Practical Strategies:
- One-on-One Meetings: Take time to understand individual team members.
- Active Listening: Validate feelings and concerns.
- Empathy Training: Provide resources to develop empathetic skills.

Fostering Ownership and Confidence

Empowering team members to make decisions and take ownership instills pride and accomplishment.

Integration with the Holistic Intelligence Model:

- Practical Intelligence (PQ): Develops problem-solving skills.
- Ethical Intelligence: Respects individual autonomy.

Practical Strategies:
- Delegate Meaningfully: Assign responsibilities that challenge and engage.
- Support Decision-Making: Provide guidance without micromanaging.
- Recognize Initiative: Acknowledge proactive efforts.

Modeling Positivity and Integrity

Consistently modeling a positive outlook sets the standard for the organization.

Integration with the Holistic Intelligence Model:

- Intrapersonal Intelligence: Self-regulates to maintain positivity.

- Ethical Intelligence: Demonstrates integrity and consistency.

Practical Strategies:
- Consistent Behavior: Align actions with words.
- Positive Demeanor: Maintain an optimistic attitude, even in tough times.
- Share Successes: Highlight positive outcomes and contributions.

Fostering Growth and Adaptability

Staying curious and open to new ideas fosters a mindset of growth and adaptability.

Integration with the Holistic Intelligence Model:

- Analytical Intelligence (AQ): Enhances knowledge and critical thinking.
- Creativity Intelligence (CrQ): Sparks innovation through new insights.

Practical Strategies:
- Professional Development: Attend workshops, conferences, or courses.
- Learning Culture: Encourage team members to pursue learning opportunities.
- Knowledge Sharing: Share insights and encourage others to do the same.

Motivating Through Appreciation

Regularly acknowledging achievements creates an environment where accomplishments are valued.

Integration with the Holistic Intelligence Model:

- Interpersonal Intelligence: Strengthens team cohesion.
- Ethical Intelligence: Fairly recognizes contributions.

Practical Strategies:
- Recognition Programs: Implement systems to reward achievements.
- Team Celebrations: Mark significant milestones together.
- Personalized Appreciation: Tailor recognition to individual preferences.

Nurturing Forward-Thinking Mindsets

Creating space for creativity empowers team members to explore new ideas.

Integration with the Holistic Intelligence Model:

- Creativity Intelligence (CrQ): Central to fostering innovation.
- Practical Intelligence (PQ): Applies creative ideas effectively.

Practical Strategies:
- Idea Generation Sessions: Host brainstorming meetings.
- Innovation Challenges: Encourage solutions to existing problems.
- Support Experimentation: Provide resources for testing new concepts.

Focusing on Possibilities Over Problems

Leaders who focus on solutions foster a culture of proactive problem-solving.

Integration with the Holistic Intelligence Model:

- Analytical Intelligence (AQ): Identifies effective solutions.
- Practical Intelligence (PQ): Implements solutions efficiently.

Practical Strategies:
- Positive Language: Frame discussions around what can be done.
- Collaborative Problem-Solving: Involve the team in finding solutions.
- Action Plans: Develop clear steps to address challenges.

Strengthening Team Dynamics

Investing time in relationships creates a sense of camaraderie and trust.

Integration with the Holistic Intelligence Model:

- Interpersonal Intelligence: Essential for building connections.
- Cultural Intelligence (CQ): Appreciates diversity within the team.

Practical Strategies:
- Regular Check-Ins: Engage with team members beyond work tasks.
- Team Activities: Organize events to foster bonding.
- Open-Door Policy: Be accessible and approachable.

Valuing Every Voice

Prioritizing diversity of thought and background creates an environment where everyone feels valued.

Integration with the Holistic Intelligence Model:

- Cultural Intelligence (CQ): Central to embracing diversity.
- Ethical Intelligence: Ensures fairness and respect.

Practical Strategies:

- Diverse Hiring Practices: Recruit from a wide talent pool.
- Inclusive Meetings: Encourage participation from all team members.
- Cultural Celebrations: Recognize and honor diverse traditions.

Aligning Individual Roles with Organizational Goals

Helping team members connect their roles to the broader mission instills fulfillment.

Integration with the Holistic Intelligence Model:

- Ethical Intelligence: Aligns actions with core values.
- Intrapersonal Intelligence: Enhances personal motivation.

Practical Strategies:

- Mission Statements: Clearly communicate organizational purpose.
- Goal Alignment: Link individual objectives to larger goals.

- Storytelling: Share stories that highlight the impact of the team's work.

Investing in Growth

Investing in team members' professional development demonstrates commitment to their success.

Integration with the Holistic Intelligence Model:

- Practical Intelligence (PQ): Enhances skills and competencies.
- Intrapersonal Intelligence: Encourages self-improvement.

Practical Strategies:
- Training Programs: Offer workshops and courses.
- Mentorship: Facilitate relationships with experienced professionals.
- Career Pathing: Help team members plan their growth trajectories.

Building Trust and Collaboration

Honest and authentic interactions build a culture of trust and mutual respect.

Integration with the Holistic Intelligence Model:

- Interpersonal Intelligence: Enhances communication and understanding.
- Ethical Intelligence: Upholds integrity in all interactions.

Practical Strategies:

- Regular Updates: Keep the team informed about organizational changes.
- Open Forums: Provide platforms for open discussion.
- Honest Feedback: Encourage and model candid communication.

Cultivating a positive attitude is a multifaceted endeavor requiring intentional effort and commitment from leaders. By integrating these strategies with the Holistic Intelligence Model, leaders can create an environment where positivity flourishes, ultimately shaping a vibrant, empowered organizational culture. This positive attitude becomes a catalyst for organizational success and growth.

Reflection Questions

1. Self-Assessment: Which strategies for cultivating a positive attitude resonate most with you?

2. Implementation: How can you integrate these strategies into your daily leadership practices?

3. Impact: What changes do you anticipate in your team or organization as a result?

Action Plan

1. Select Key Strategies: Choose a few strategies to focus on initially.

2. Set Specific Goals: Define what success looks like for each strategy.

3. Create a Timeline: Establish a schedule for implementing changes.

4. Engage Your Team: Involve team members in your efforts to cultivate positivity.

5. Evaluate and Adjust: Regularly assess the effectiveness of your strategies and make adjustments as needed.

Navigating Challenges and Adversities: Resilience and Attitude in Leadership

Core Reading

Leadership, while immensely rewarding, is not without its share of challenges and adversities. How a leader navigates these hurdles is often a testament to their resilience and attitude. A resilient leader possesses the capacity to not only weather storms but to emerge stronger, armed with invaluable lessons. This section delves into the critical interplay between resilience, attitude, and effective leadership.

Resilience, often defined as the ability to bounce back from setbacks, is an indispensable trait for leaders. It is not about avoiding challenges, but rather about confronting them with a positive and determined mindset. Resilient leaders view difficulties as opportunities for growth and transformation, refusing to be defeated by temporary setbacks.

Attitude is the lens through which leaders perceive and respond to challenges. A positive attitude provides the foundation for resilience. Leaders who maintain an optimistic outlook are more likely to find constructive solutions to problems. They approach adversity with a sense of determination, believing that they have the capacity to overcome obstacles.

Adversity, though often viewed as an unwelcome guest, has the potential to catalyze personal and professional growth. When leaders face adversity with a resilient attitude, they emerge with newfound strength, wisdom, and experience. Each challenge becomes a stepping stone towards becoming a more capable and effective leader.

A leader's attitude towards setbacks can be the differentiator between stagnation and progress. Those with a resilient mindset view setbacks as temporary detours rather than permanent roadblocks. They learn from their experiences, adapt their strategies, and forge ahead with renewed determination.

Resilience is not an innate quality, but rather a skill that can be developed through deliberate effort. Leaders can cultivate resilience by adopting a growth mindset. This perspective fosters a belief in one's ability to learn, adapt, and grow in the face of challenges. It transforms setbacks into opportunities for learning and improvement.

Leaders who navigate challenges with resilience do not shy away from the possibility of failure. Instead, they view failure as a natural part of the learning process. This attitude liberates them from the fear of making mistakes, allowing them to take calculated risks and pursue innovative solutions.

Emotional intelligence plays a pivotal role in a leader's resilience. Leaders who are in touch with their own emotions can navigate challenges with greater self-awareness and composure. They are adept at regulating their emotions, enabling them to make sound decisions even in high-pressure situations.

A positive attitude is not only a product of resilience but also a powerful tool for developing it. Leaders who maintain a positive outlook are more likely to persevere through challenges. Their optimism serves as a beacon of hope for their teams, inspiring them to weather difficulties with fortitude.

Resilience is not solely an individual trait but a collective one that permeates the organizational culture. Leaders who prioritize resilience set the tone for the entire organization. They create an environment where challenges are met with a solution-oriented mindset, and setbacks are viewed as opportunities for growth.

Resilient leaders strike a delicate balance between acknowledging the reality of challenges and maintaining an optimistic outlook. They do not downplay the difficulties that lie ahead but approach them with a belief in their capacity to find solutions. This balance fuels their determination to navigate even the most formidable challenges.

Resilient leaders recognize the importance of a strong support network. They surround themselves with individuals who offer encouragement, insights, and different perspectives. This network serves as a source of strength and resilience, providing valuable perspectives and advice during challenging times.

Resilience is closely tied to a leader's overall well-being. Leaders who prioritize their physical and mental health are better equipped to navigate challenges. Regular exercise, healthy eating, and adequate rest contribute to increased energy levels and mental clarity, bolstering resilience in the face of adversity.

Resilient leaders approach challenges with a solution-focused mindset. Rather than dwelling on the magnitude of the problem, they channel their energy into identifying and implementing actionable solutions. This proactive approach empowers them to take control of the situation and move towards resolution.

Adversity serves as a powerful teacher for leaders with a growth mindset. They view challenges not as insurmountable obstacles, but as opportunities for learning and development. Each setback becomes a valuable lesson that propels them forward with newfound wisdom and insight.

Resilient leaders foster a culture of innovation and adaptability within their organizations. They encourage their teams to explore new approaches and embrace change as a means of overcoming challenges. This forward-thinking culture positions the organization to thrive in even the most uncertain and demanding environments.

Resilience is not a destination but a continuous journey of growth and self-discovery. Leaders commit themselves to ongoing development, recognizing that their ability to navigate challenges is an ever-evolving skill. They remain open to new experiences and perspectives, knowing that each contributes to their resilience.

The impact of a resilient leader extends far beyond the challenges of the present moment. Their legacy is one of inspiration, empowerment, and unwavering determination. Through their resilient attitude, they leave a lasting imprint on their teams, organizations, and the broader landscape of leadership.

Resilience: The Bedrock of Leadership

Resilience is the capacity to recover quickly from difficulties; it's a form of emotional and mental toughness that enables leaders to bounce back from setbacks. In leadership, resilience is indispensable. It is not about avoiding challenges but confronting them with a positive and determined mindset.

Integration with the Holistic Intelligence Model:

- **Emotional Resilience (ER):** The cornerstone of resilience, enabling leaders to manage emotions effectively during adversity.
- **Intrapersonal Intelligence:** Enhances self-awareness and self-regulation, critical for resilient behavior.
- **Interpersonal Intelligence:** Supports building strong relationships that can provide support during challenging times.

Key Characteristics of Resilient Leaders:

- **Adaptability:** Ability to adjust strategies in response to changing circumstances.

- **Perseverance:** Commitment to goals despite obstacles.
- **Optimism:** Maintaining a hopeful outlook.
- **Resourcefulness:** Finding innovative solutions to problems.

Case Example:

Nelson Mandela: Endured 27 years of imprisonment yet emerged with a vision for reconciliation and nation-building, exemplifying unparalleled resilience.

Attitude as the Lens for Perception

Attitude is the mental frame through which leaders perceive and respond to challenges. A positive attitude provides the foundation for resilience, influencing how leaders interpret setbacks and determine their responses.

Integration with the Holistic Intelligence Model:

- **Intrapersonal Intelligence:** Shapes the internal dialogue and mindset.
- **Emotional Resilience (ER):** Reinforces a positive attitude during stress.
- **Ethical Intelligence:** Guides attitudes aligned with core values and principles.

Strategies for Cultivating a Positive Attitude:

1. Reframing Challenges: View difficulties as opportunities for growth.

2. Positive Self-Talk: Replace negative thoughts with affirming ones.

3. Visualization: Envision successful outcomes to foster optimism.

4. Gratitude Practice: Regularly acknowledge and appreciate positive aspects.

Practical Application:

Mindset Shifts: Leaders can adopt a "glass-half-full" perspective, focusing on possibilities rather than limitations.

Embracing Challenges for Development

Adversity, though often unwelcome, can catalyze significant personal and professional growth. Leaders who face adversity with resilience emerge stronger, gaining invaluable insights and skills.

Integration with the Holistic Intelligence Model:

- **Analytical Intelligence (AQ):** Helps in extracting lessons from challenges.
- **Creativity Intelligence (CrQ):** Encourages innovative responses to adversity.
- **Practical Intelligence (PQ):** Applies learned lessons to real-world situations.

Benefits of Embracing Adversity:

- **Enhanced Problem-Solving Skills:** Adversity forces leaders to think critically.
- **Increased Empathy:** Personal challenges can deepen understanding of others' struggles.

- **Strengthened Character:** Overcoming difficulties builds confidence and integrity.

Case Example:

Oprah Winfrey: Overcame a challenging childhood to become a media mogul and philanthropist, using her experiences to connect with and inspire others.

Turning Setbacks into Comebacks

A leader's attitude toward setbacks can differentiate between stagnation and progress. Those with a resilient mindset view setbacks as temporary detours, learning from experiences, adapting strategies, and forging ahead.

Integration with the Holistic Intelligence Model:

- **Emotional Resilience (ER):** Manages emotional responses to setbacks.
- **Intrapersonal Intelligence:** Reflects on failures to identify growth opportunities.
- **Practical Intelligence (PQ):** Implements new approaches based on lessons learned.

Strategies for Turning Setbacks into Opportunities:

1. Reflective Analysis: Systematically evaluate what went wrong.

2. Adjust and Adapt: Modify plans and strategies accordingly.

3. Seek Feedback: Gain insights from others to enhance understanding.

4. Maintain Momentum: Keep moving forward despite obstacles.

Case Example:

Steve Jobs: After being ousted from Apple, he founded NeXT and acquired Pixar, eventually returning to Apple to lead it to unprecedented success.

Cultivating Resilience through Mindset Shifts

Resilience is not solely an innate quality but a skill that can be developed through deliberate effort. Adopting a growth mindset is pivotal in cultivating resilience.

Integration with the Holistic Intelligence Model:

- **Intrapersonal Intelligence:** Enhances self-awareness needed for mindset shifts.
- **Analytical Intelligence (AQ):** Supports critical examination of beliefs.
- **Emotional Resilience (ER):** Reinforces the ability to adapt to new perspectives.

Growth Mindset Principles:

1. Belief in Development: Recognizing that abilities can be honed.

2. Embracing Challenges: Viewing difficulties as learning opportunities.

3. Persistence: Continuing efforts despite setbacks.

4. Learning from Criticism: Using feedback constructively.

Practical Strategies:

Mindset Training: Engage in programs that promote growth-oriented thinking.

Affirmations: Use positive statements to reinforce a growth mindset.

Learning Goals over Performance Goals: Focus on acquiring skills rather than solely on outcomes.

Embracing Failure as a Stepping Stone

Leaders who navigate challenges with resilience do not shy away from failure. Instead, they view it as a natural part of the learning process, liberating them from the fear of making mistakes.

Integration with the Holistic Intelligence Model:

- **Emotional Resilience (ER):** Manages fear and disappointment associated with failure.
- **Analytical Intelligence (AQ):** Analyzes failures to derive insights.
- **Creativity Intelligence (CrQ):** Inspires innovative solutions post-failure.

Approach to Failure:

1. Normalize Failure: Accept it as a common experience.

2. Fail Fast and Learn Quickly: Rapidly iterate to find what works.

3. Share Failures Openly: Promote a culture where failures are discussed and learned from.

Case Example:

Thomas Edison: Famously remarked, "I have not failed. I've just found 10,000 ways that won't work," exemplifying the use of failure as a stepping stone.

The Role of Emotional Intelligence in Resilience

Emotional intelligence is pivotal in a leader's resilience. Leaders adept in emotional intelligence can navigate challenges with greater self-awareness and composure.

Components of Emotional Intelligence:

- **Self-Awareness:** Recognizing one's emotions.
- **Self-Regulation:** Managing emotions effectively.
- **Motivation:** Harnessing emotions to achieve goals.
- **Empathy:** Understanding others' emotions.
- **Social Skills:** Building relationships.

Practical Strategies:

Emotional Literacy: Expand vocabulary to describe emotions.

Mindfulness Practices: Increase present-moment awareness.

Empathy Exercises: Practice perspective-taking.

Case Example:

Satya Nadella, CEO of Microsoft, emphasizes empathy and emotional intelligence, transforming the company's culture and driving innovation.

Maintaining Positivity in the Face of Adversity

A positive attitude is both a product and a catalyst of resilience. Leaders who maintain a positive outlook are more likely to persevere through challenges, inspiring their teams to do the same.

Integration with the Holistic Intelligence Model:

- **Emotional Resilience (ER):** Sustains positivity under stress.
- **Intrapersonal Intelligence:** Self-regulates to maintain optimism.
- **Interpersonal Intelligence:** Influences team morale positively.

Strategies for Sustaining Positivity:

1. Positive Affirmations: Reinforce optimistic beliefs.

2. Focus on Solutions: Direct energy toward resolving issues.

3. Surround with Positivity: Engage with positive people and content.

4. Practice Gratitude: Regularly acknowledge and appreciate positives.

Case Example:

Richard Branson: Maintains an upbeat attitude, even during setbacks, motivating his teams at Virgin Group.

Fostering a Resilient Organizational Culture

Resilience extends beyond individuals to the organizational culture. Leaders who prioritize resilience create an environment where challenges are met with a solution-oriented mindset.

Integration with the Holistic Intelligence Model:

- **Cultural Intelligence (CQ):** Shapes organizational norms and values.
- **Ethical Intelligence:** Embeds resilience within ethical practices.
- **Interpersonal Intelligence:** Strengthens team dynamics.

Strategies for Building a Resilient Culture:

1. Promote Psychological Safety: Encourage open communication without fear of reprisal.

2. Develop Shared Values: Align the organization around principles that support resilience.

3. Provide Resources: Equip teams with tools and training to handle adversity.

4. Recognize Resilience: Acknowledge and reward resilient behaviors.

Practical Application:

Resilience Training Programs: Implement organizational development initiatives focused on building resilience.

Navigating Challenges with Balanced Perspective

Resilient leaders acknowledge the reality of challenges while maintaining an optimistic outlook, fueling determination to navigate formidable obstacles.

Integration with the Holistic Intelligence Model:

- **Analytical Intelligence (AQ):** Assesses situations accurately.
- **Emotional Resilience (ER):** Maintains emotional balance.
- **Ethical Intelligence:** Ensures honesty and integrity.

Strategies for Balance:

1. Reality Testing: Evaluate situations objectively.

2. Positive Framing: Identify opportunities within challenges.

3. Strategic Planning: Develop realistic action plans.

4. Communicate Transparently: Share both challenges and strategies with the team.

Case Example:

Winston Churchill's Leadership: During WWII, balanced acknowledging dire circumstances with rallying optimism.

Building a Supportive Network

Resilient leaders recognize the importance of a strong support network, surrounding themselves with individuals who offer encouragement and diverse perspectives.

Integration with the Holistic Intelligence Model:

- **Interpersonal Intelligence:** Builds and maintains strong relationships.
- **Cultural Intelligence (CQ):** Engages with a diverse network.
- **Intrapersonal Intelligence:** Understands personal needs for support.

Strategies for Network Building:

1. Mentorship Relationships: Seek guidance from experienced individuals.

2. Peer Support Groups: Engage with colleagues facing similar challenges.

3. Professional Networks: Participate in industry associations.

4. Personal Relationships: Nurture friendships and family ties.

Practical Application:

Mastermind Groups: Join or form groups focused on mutual support and problem-solving.

Cultivating Physical and Mental Well-being

Physical and mental well-being are critical for maintaining resilience. Leaders who prioritize health are better equipped to navigate challenges.

Integration with the Holistic Intelligence Model:

- **Intrapersonal Intelligence:** Recognizes the importance of self-care.
- **Emotional Resilience (ER):** Enhanced through well-being practices.
- **Ethical Intelligence:** Models responsible behavior.

Strategies for Well-being:

1. Regular Exercise: Incorporate physical activity into daily routines.

2. Healthy Nutrition: Maintain a balanced diet.

3. Adequate Rest: Prioritize sleep and relaxation.

4. Stress Management: Utilize techniques like meditation or yoga.

Case Example:

Jeff Weiner, former CEO of LinkedIn, advocates for compassionate leadership and personal well-being practices.

Adopting a Solution-Focused Mindset

Resilient leaders approach challenges with a solution-focused mindset, channeling energy into identifying and implementing actionable solutions.

Integration with the Holistic Intelligence Model:

- **Analytical Intelligence (AQ):** Critical for problem analysis.
- **Practical Intelligence (PQ):** Essential for implementing solutions.
- **Creativity Intelligence (CrQ):** Generates innovative ideas.

Strategies for a Solution-Focused Approach:

1. Define the Problem Clearly: Understand the issue in depth.

2. Brainstorm Solutions: Generate a range of possible approaches.

3. Evaluate Options: Assess the feasibility and impact.

4. Implement and Monitor: Take action and adjust as needed.

Practical Application:

Design Thinking Methodology: Employ user-centric problem-solving techniques.

Learning from Adversity: The Growth Mindset

Adversity serves as a powerful teacher for leaders with a growth mindset, transforming setbacks into valuable lessons.

Integration with the Holistic Intelligence Model:

- **Intrapersonal Intelligence:** Reflects on personal experiences.
- **Analytical Intelligence (AQ):** Derives insights from adversity.
- **Emotional Resilience (ER):** Supports the learning process.

Strategies for Learning from Adversity:

1. Reflective Practice: Regularly review experiences to extract lessons.

2. Document Insights: Keep a learning journal.

3. Apply Learnings: Integrate lessons into future actions.

4. Share Knowledge: Educate others based on your experiences.

Case Example:

Sara Blakely, founder of Spanx, credits her father's encouragement to share failures at the dinner table as key to her resilience and success.

Preparing for Future Challenges

Resilient leaders foster a culture of innovation and adaptability, positioning the organization to thrive in uncertain environments.

Integration with the Holistic Intelligence Model:

- **Creativity Intelligence (CrQ):** Central to innovation.
- **Cultural Intelligence (CQ):** Adapts to diverse markets and trends.
- **Practical Intelligence (PQ):** Implements innovative ideas effectively.

Strategies for Cultivating Innovation:

1. Encourage Experimentation: Allow teams to test new ideas.

2. Agile Methodologies: Implement flexible approaches to project management.

3. Continuous Learning: Promote ongoing education and skill development.

4. Diverse Teams: Assemble teams with varied backgrounds and perspectives.

Case Example:

Amazon's Culture: Emphasizes innovation and customer obsession, enabling rapid adaptation.

Embracing Resilience as a Continuous Journey

Resilience is not a destination but an ongoing journey of growth. Leaders remain open to new experiences and perspectives, continually enhancing their ability to navigate challenges.

Integration with the Holistic Intelligence Model:

- **Intrapersonal Intelligence:** Supports self-improvement.

- **Emotional Resilience (ER):** Evolves through experience.
- **Ethical Intelligence:** Guides continuous alignment with values.

Strategies for Continuous Resilience Development:

1. Set Personal Development Goals: Identify areas for growth.

2. Seek New Challenges: Embrace opportunities that stretch capabilities.

3. Engage in Reflective Practice: Regularly assess progress.

4. Adapt to Change: Remain flexible in the face of evolving circumstances.

Practical Application:

Lifelong Learning Plans: Develop and follow a plan for ongoing education and skill acquisition.

—

The impact of a resilient leader extends far beyond immediate challenges. Their legacy is one of inspiration, empowerment, and unwavering determination. Through resilience and a positive attitude, leaders not only overcome obstacles but also transform their organizations and the people within them.

By embodying the principles across the 8 Pillars of the Holistic Intelligence Model, resilient leaders create a well-rounded approach to leadership that is adaptable, ethical, innovative, and effective.

Final Reflection:

Self-Assessment: Consider how resilience and attitude currently influence your leadership.

Legacy Planning: Reflect on the legacy you wish to leave as a leader.

Reflection Questions

1. Personal Resilience: How do you currently respond to challenges and setbacks in your leadership role?

2. Attitude Adjustment: What steps can you take to cultivate a more positive and resilient attitude?

3. Organizational Impact: How can you foster resilience within your team or organization?

Action Plan

1. Identify Areas for Growth: Conduct a self-assessment to pinpoint areas where resilience can be enhanced.

2. Set Specific Goals: Define clear objectives for developing resilience and a positive attitude.

3. Implement Strategies: Apply the practical strategies outlined in this section.

4. Engage Support Networks: Build relationships that support your resilience journey.

5. Monitor Progress: Regularly review your development and adjust your approach as needed.

Building Resilience Through a Positive Attitude: Thriving Amidst Adversity

Core Reading

In the realm of leadership, a positive attitude is not just a desirable trait; it is a formidable tool for building resilience. A positive attitude equips leaders with the mental and emotional fortitude to not only weather storms but to thrive amidst adversity. This section unravels the profound connection between a positive attitude and resilience, illuminating how leaders can harness this potent combination to navigate even the most challenging circumstances. By integrating the principles of the Holistic Intelligence Model, leaders can deepen their capacity for resilience and inspire the same in their teams.

Positivity serves as the cornerstone of a leader's ability to build resilience. A positive attitude bolsters the belief that challenges are temporary and surmountable. It infuses leaders with a sense of hope and optimism that empowers them to face adversity with unwavering determination.

A positive attitude is characterized by a solution-oriented mindset. Rather than fixating on the problems at hand, leaders with a positive outlook channel their energy into identifying and implementing actionable solutions. This proactive approach not only expedites problem-solving but also instills a sense of agency and control.

A positive attitude exerts a profound impact on a leader's emotional well-being. It enables leaders to navigate challenges with greater emotional intelligence, allowing them to regulate their emotions and maintain composure even in high-pressure situations. This emotional resilience serves as a pillar of strength during turbulent times.

A positive attitude fuels creativity and innovation in leadership. Leaders who approach challenges with a positive outlook are more likely to explore unconventional solutions and think outside the box. This spirit of innovation positions organizations to not only overcome adversity but to emerge stronger and more agile.

Leaders with a positive attitude view setbacks as opportunities for growth and learning. They recognize that every challenge carries with it a valuable lesson. Rather than being defeated by temporary failures, they extract insights that propel them forward with renewed vigor.

A leader's attitude has a ripple effect that permeates the organizational culture. A positive leader sets the tone for the entire team, fostering an environment where challenges are met with a can-do spirit. This cultural shift cultivates a collective resilience that empowers the organization to navigate adversity as a united front.

A positive attitude emboldens leaders to take calculated risks. They approach uncertainty with a sense of optimism, believing that even in the face of potential failure, there exists an opportunity for growth and learning. This willingness to embrace risk positions them as forward-thinking leaders.

Leaders with a positive attitude serve as beacons of inspiration for their teams. Their optimism and unwavering belief in the team's collective capabilities instill a sense of confidence and motivation. This inspiration becomes a driving force for the entire organization, spurring them to confront challenges with courage.

In moments of crisis, a positive attitude becomes a lifeline for leaders. It enables them to remain calm, composed, and focused on finding solutions. This constructive outlook provides a sense of direction even in the midst of chaos, instilling confidence in the team.

A positive attitude involves a process of cognitive restructuring. It entails reframing negative or defeatist thoughts into constructive and empowering narratives. This mental shift equips leaders with the cognitive tools to navigate challenges with clarity and purpose.

A positive leader fosters a sense of unity and cohesion within the team. Their optimistic outlook creates a supportive and uplifting work environment. This camaraderie becomes a source of strength during difficult times, as team members draw inspiration and motivation from one another.

Maintaining a positive attitude necessitates self-care and self-compassion. Leaders prioritize their physical and mental well-being, recognizing that a healthy and balanced lifestyle is the foundation of resilience. Regular exercise, adequate rest, and mindfulness practices contribute to their overall positivity.

A positive attitude is reflected in a leader's communication style. They convey messages of hope, confidence, and determination, inspiring their teams to face challenges head-on. Their words become a source of encouragement, reinforcing the belief that together, they can overcome any obstacle.

Maintaining a positive attitude is not a one-time achievement, but an ongoing practice. Leaders commit themselves to cultivating positivity daily, even in the face of adversity. They recognize that it is through this consistent effort that they build and fortify their resilience.

A positive leader acknowledges and celebrates even the smallest victories. This practice serves as a reminder of progress and reinforces the belief in the team's collective ability to overcome challenges. It instills a sense of accomplishment and motivation to persevere.

A positive attitude extends beyond the present moment; it encompasses a vision for the future. Leaders with a positive outlook inspire hope for what lies ahead, assuring their teams that challenges are but temporary detours on the path to success.

A positive attitude is a reservoir of inner strength for leaders. It provides them with the resilience to weather even the most formidable storms. In moments of doubt or uncertainty, they draw upon this wellspring of positivity to press forward.

A positive attitude is not a passive disposition; it is a dynamic force that empowers leaders to thrive amidst adversity. It shapes their responses to challenges, infuses their teams with confidence, and ultimately, defines their legacy as resilient leaders. Through the deliberate cultivation of positivity, leaders unlock a wellspring of inner strength that propels them forward on their leadership journey.

Positivity as the Cornerstone of Resilient Leadership

A positive attitude bolsters the belief that challenges are temporary and surmountable. It infuses leaders with hope and optimism, empowering them to face adversity with unwavering determination.

Integration with the Holistic Intelligence Model:

- Emotional Resilience (ER): A positive attitude enhances emotional resilience by fostering a mindset that views adversity as an opportunity rather than a setback.
- Intrapersonal Intelligence: Self-awareness allows leaders to recognize and regulate their emotions, maintaining positivity even under stress.
- Interpersonal Intelligence: Positivity improves relationships, enabling leaders to support and be supported by others.

Practical Strategies:

1. Positive Affirmations: Regularly reinforce positive beliefs about one's ability to overcome challenges.

2. Gratitude Practice: Cultivate gratitude to shift focus from problems to appreciation of what is going well.

3. Optimistic Reframing: Consciously reinterpret negative events to find positive aspects or lessons.

Case Example:

Nelson Mandela maintained a positive outlook during 27 years of imprisonment, emerging as a unifying leader who transformed South Africa through reconciliation.

Channeling Energy into Actionable Solutions

Leaders with a positive attitude focus on identifying and implementing solutions rather than fixating on problems. This proactive approach instills a sense of agency and control.

Integration with the Holistic Intelligence Model:

- Analytical Intelligence (AQ): Critical thinking aids in dissecting problems and devising effective solutions.
- Practical Intelligence (PQ): Applies solutions efficiently in real-world contexts.
- Creativity Intelligence (CrQ): Encourages innovative problem-solving strategies.

Practical Strategies:

1. Root Cause Analysis: Use tools like the 5 Whys to identify underlying issues.

2. Brainstorming Sessions: Facilitate collaborative idea generation with the team.

3. Action Plans: Develop clear, step-by-step plans to address challenges.

Case Example:

Indra Nooyi, former CEO of PepsiCo, led the company through significant strategic shifts by focusing on solutions that aligned with long-term sustainability.

Enhancing Emotional Intelligence through Positivity

A positive attitude allows leaders to regulate their emotions, maintaining composure even in high-pressure situations. This emotional resilience is critical during turbulent times.

Integration with the Holistic Intelligence Model:

- Emotional Resilience (ER): Strengthens the ability to manage stress and recover from setbacks.
- Intrapersonal Intelligence: Enhances self-regulation and emotional awareness.
- Ethical Intelligence: Guides leaders to act consistently with their values, fostering trust.

Practical Strategies:

1. Mindfulness Practices: Incorporate meditation or deep-breathing exercises to manage stress.

2. Emotional Check-ins: Regularly assess and acknowledge one's emotional state.

3. Seek Support: Engage with mentors or peers for emotional guidance.

Case Example:

Arianna Huffington advocates for well-being and mindfulness in leadership, emphasizing their role in maintaining a positive attitude and resilience.

Unlocking Creativity in the Face of Adversity

Leaders who approach challenges with positivity are more likely to explore unconventional solutions and think outside the box, fueling innovation.

Integration with the Holistic Intelligence Model:

- Creativity Intelligence (CrQ): Positivity opens the mind to new ideas and perspectives.
- Practical Intelligence (PQ): Translates creative ideas into actionable strategies.
- Cultural Intelligence (CQ): Incorporates diverse perspectives to enhance innovation.

Practical Strategies:

1. Encourage Experimentation: Create a safe environment for testing new ideas.

2. Diverse Teams: Build teams with varied backgrounds to foster diverse thinking.

3. Innovation Workshops: Host sessions focused on creative problem-solving.

Case Example:

Elon Musk consistently applies a positive, solution-focused attitude to drive innovation at Tesla and SpaceX, tackling challenges deemed insurmountable by others.

Leveraging Adversity for Growth

Leaders with a positive attitude view setbacks as opportunities for learning. They extract insights that propel them forward with renewed vigor.

Integration with the Holistic Intelligence Model:

- Analytical Intelligence (AQ): Analyzes failures to gain valuable insights.
- Emotional Resilience (ER): Maintains motivation after setbacks.
- Intrapersonal Intelligence: Reflects on experiences for personal growth.

Practical Strategies:

1. Failure Analysis Meetings: Systematically review what went wrong to learn from it.

2. Growth Mindset Cultivation: Encourage the belief that abilities can improve with effort.

3. Set Learning Goals: Focus on development rather than solely on outcomes.

Case Example:

J.K. Rowling faced numerous rejections before publishing the Harry Potter series, viewing each setback as a step closer to success.

Creating a Ripple Effect of Positivity

A leader's positive attitude sets the tone for the organization, fostering an environment where challenges are met with a can-do spirit.

Integration with the Holistic Intelligence Model:

- Cultural Intelligence (CQ): Shapes an inclusive and positive organizational culture.
- Interpersonal Intelligence: Builds strong relationships that promote teamwork.
- Ethical Intelligence: Ensures that positivity aligns with organizational values.

Practical Strategies:

1. Lead by Example: Demonstrate positivity in actions and decisions.

2. Positive Communication: Use language that inspires and motivates.

3. Recognition Programs: Celebrate successes to reinforce positive behaviors.

Case Example:

Satya Nadella transformed Microsoft's culture by promoting a growth mindset and positive leadership, leading to renewed innovation.

Embracing Calculated Risks with Confidence

A positive attitude emboldens leaders to take calculated risks, approaching uncertainty with optimism.

Integration with the Holistic Intelligence Model:

- Emotional Resilience (ER): Manages fear and anxiety associated with risk.
- Analytical Intelligence (AQ): Evaluates risks effectively.
- Practical Intelligence (PQ): Implements risk strategies wisely.

Practical Strategies:

1. Risk Assessment Tools: Utilize frameworks to weigh potential outcomes.

2. Pilot Programs: Test initiatives on a small scale before full implementation.

3. Encourage Team Participation: Involve team members in the risk-taking process.

Case Example:

Reed Hastings took a significant risk transitioning Netflix from DVD rentals to streaming, leading to industry disruption.

Motivating Teams Through Optimism

Leaders with a positive attitude inspire their teams by instilling confidence and motivation, becoming a driving force for the organization.

Integration with the Holistic Intelligence Model:

- Interpersonal Intelligence: Enhances the ability to connect and inspire.
- Ethical Intelligence: Builds trust through authenticity and integrity.
- Emotional Resilience (ER): Projects stability and confidence.

Practical Strategies:

1. Storytelling: Share inspiring narratives that resonate with the team's values.

2. Vision Casting: Clearly communicate a compelling vision for the future.

3. Empowerment: Provide autonomy and encourage ownership of work.

Case Example:

Sheryl Sandberg, COO of Facebook, inspires through her advocacy for resilience and empowerment in leadership.

Providing Direction Amidst Chaos

In moments of crisis, a positive attitude enables leaders to remain calm and focused on solutions, instilling confidence in their teams.

Integration with the Holistic Intelligence Model:

- Emotional Resilience (ER): Manages stress to think clearly under pressure.
- Analytical Intelligence (AQ): Quickly assesses situations to make informed decisions.
- Practical Intelligence (PQ): Coordinates effective response strategies.

Practical Strategies:

1. Crisis Management Plans: Prepare protocols in advance.

2. Transparent Communication: Keep the team informed to reduce uncertainty.

3. Stay Accessible: Be available to address concerns and provide guidance.

Case Example:

Mary Barra, CEO of General Motors, navigated the company through recalls and restructuring with a focus on transparency and a positive vision for the future.

Reframing Thoughts to Empower Action

Cognitive restructuring involves reframing negative thoughts into constructive narratives, equipping leaders to navigate challenges with clarity.

Integration with the Holistic Intelligence Model:

- Intrapersonal Intelligence: Recognizes and adjusts thought patterns.
- Emotional Resilience (ER): Reduces negative emotional responses.
- Analytical Intelligence (AQ): Applies logical reasoning to thought processes.

Practical Strategies:

1. Identify Negative Thoughts: Be aware of unhelpful thinking patterns.

2. Challenge and Replace: Question the validity of negative thoughts and replace them with positive alternatives.

3. Affirmations: Use positive statements to reinforce constructive beliefs.

Building a Supportive and Uplifting Environment

A positive leader fosters unity and cohesion, creating a supportive work environment that becomes a source of strength during difficult times.

Integration with the Holistic Intelligence Model:

- Interpersonal Intelligence: Enhances team dynamics and cooperation.
- Cultural Intelligence (CQ): Respects and values diversity within the team.
- Ethical Intelligence: Promotes fairness and respect.

Practical Strategies:

1. Team-Building Activities: Organize events to strengthen relationships.

2. Open Communication: Encourage sharing of ideas and concerns.

3. Collective Problem-Solving: Involve the team in addressing challenges.

Prioritizing Well-being to Sustain Positivity

Leaders recognize that a healthy and balanced lifestyle is the foundation of resilience and positivity.

Integration with the Holistic Intelligence Model:

- Intrapersonal Intelligence: Acknowledges personal needs and well-being.
- Emotional Resilience (ER): Supports sustained energy and mood.
- Ethical Intelligence: Models responsible self-care practices.

Practical Strategies:

1. Regular Exercise: Incorporate physical activity into daily routines.

2. Mindfulness and Relaxation: Practice meditation or yoga to reduce stress.

3. Healthy Habits: Maintain a balanced diet and adequate sleep.

Using Language to Motivate and Encourage

A positive attitude is reflected in a leader's communication style, which becomes a source of encouragement for their teams.

Integration with the Holistic Intelligence Model:

- Interpersonal Intelligence: Enhances effective and empathetic communication.
- Ethical Intelligence: Ensures honesty and integrity in messaging.
- Emotional Resilience (ER): Conveys steadiness and assurance.

Practical Strategies:

1. Positive Language: Choose words that uplift and motivate.

2. Active Listening: Show genuine interest in team members' perspectives.

3. Regular Updates: Keep the team informed to build trust and confidence.

Positivity as a Continuous Practice

Maintaining a positive attitude requires consistent effort and practice.

Integration with the Holistic Intelligence Model:

- Intrapersonal Intelligence: Develops habits that reinforce positivity.
- Emotional Resilience (ER): Strengthens over time with practice.
- Ethical Intelligence: Aligns daily actions with core values.

Practical Strategies:

1. Daily Reflections: Spend time each day reviewing positive experiences.

2. Set Intentions: Begin each day with a positive focus or goal.

3. Continuous Learning: Seek out resources that promote positive thinking.

Acknowledging Progress to Maintain Momentum

Recognizing and celebrating even small victories reinforces a positive attitude and motivates the team to persevere.

Integration with the Holistic Intelligence Model:

- Interpersonal Intelligence: Strengthens team relationships through shared success.
- Emotional Resilience (ER): Boosts morale and confidence.

- Practical Intelligence (PQ): Highlights effective strategies and practices.

Practical Strategies:

1. Regular Recognition: Implement systems to acknowledge achievements.

2. Share Success Stories: Communicate wins to the broader organization.

3. Encourage Peer Recognition: Foster a culture where team members celebrate each other.

Visionary Leadership through Positivity

Leaders with a positive outlook inspire hope for the future, assuring their teams that challenges are temporary detours on the path to success.

Integration with the Holistic Intelligence Model:

- Ethical Intelligence: Aligns vision with values and purpose.
- Interpersonal Intelligence: Communicates vision effectively.
- Analytical Intelligence (AQ): Develops strategic plans to achieve the vision.

Practical Strategies:

1. Vision Casting Events: Host sessions to share and refine the organization's future direction.

2. Long-Term Goals: Set and communicate clear objectives for the future.

3. Empowerment: Involve the team in shaping the vision and their role in achieving it.

Drawing on Positivity for Resilience

A positive attitude serves as an internal reservoir of strength, enabling leaders to press forward even in the most formidable storms.

Integration with the Holistic Intelligence Model:

- Intrapersonal Intelligence: Harnesses inner resources and self-belief.
- Emotional Resilience (ER): Sustains endurance over time.
- Ethical Intelligence: Keeps actions aligned with personal and organizational values.

Practical Strategies:

1. Self-Affirmation Techniques: Reinforce self-belief and confidence.

2. Resilience Training: Engage in programs that build mental toughness.

3. The Power of Positivity in Resilience

Personal Mission Statement: Define and regularly revisit your purpose as a leader.

A positive attitude is not a passive disposition but a dynamic force that empowers leaders to thrive amidst adversity. It shapes responses to challenges, infuses teams with confidence, and ultimately defines a leader's legacy. Through the deliberate cultivation of positivity—integrated with the Holistic Intelligence Model—leaders unlock a wellspring of inner strength that propels them forward on their leadership journey. This positive resilience becomes contagious, fostering a culture where the entire organization thrives, even in the face of challenges.

Reflection Questions

1. Personal Practice: How can you incorporate daily practices to cultivate and maintain a positive attitude?

2. Team Influence: In what ways can your positive attitude enhance the resilience of your team?

3. Organizational Impact: How can fostering positivity contribute to your organization's ability to navigate adversity?

Action Plan

1. Self-Assessment: Evaluate your current attitude and its impact on your resilience.

2. Set Intentional Goals: Identify specific areas where you can enhance positivity in your leadership.

3. Implement Strategies: Choose practical strategies from this section to integrate into your daily routine.

4. Engage Your Team: Encourage and model positivity within your team to build collective resilience.

5. Monitor Progress: Regularly reflect on the effects of these changes and adjust as needed.

Emotional Intelligence and Its Role in Maintaining a Resilient Attitude

In the crucible of leadership, Emotional Intelligence (EI) and Emotional Resilience (ER) emerge as pivotal attributes that significantly influence a leader's effectiveness and longevity. While EI focuses on the understanding and management of one's own emotions and those of others, ER provides the foundational strength to navigate adversity, recover from setbacks, and maintain a balanced outlook. This section delves deep into the intricate relationship between EI and ER, elucidating how leaders can harness both to foster resilience, adaptability, and unwavering determination. By integrating these concepts with the Holistic Intelligence Model, leaders can achieve a comprehensive approach to personal and professional development, ensuring sustained success and influence.

Emotional Resilience (ER): The Foundation of Strength

Emotional Resilience (ER) is the keystone pillar of leadership strength, equipping individuals to handle adversity, bounce back from setbacks, and maintain a balanced outlook. It forms the emotional bedrock for navigating personal challenges and professional pressures, fostering stability and perseverance in every aspect of life.

Understanding the distinction between ER and EI is crucial for leaders aiming to develop a comprehensive emotional framework.

Emotional Resilience (ER)

Definition: The capacity to navigate and bounce back from adversity, maintaining composure and effectiveness in high-pressure situations.

Attributes:
- **Adaptability and Flexibility:** Ability to adjust to changing circumstances and recover from setbacks.
- **Stress Management:** Employing techniques to channel stress into productive energy.
- **Problem-Solving Under Pressure:** Maintaining clarity and effectiveness in decision-making during crises.
- **Positive Outlook and Optimism:** Sustaining hope and confidence despite challenges.
- **Perseverance and Determination:** Commitment to goals despite obstacles.
- **Emotional Regulation and Control:** Managing emotions to maintain composure and rationality.
- **Healthy Coping Mechanisms:** Utilizing constructive strategies to handle stress and emotions.
- **Empathy and Understanding of Others:** Navigating interpersonal dynamics effectively, especially in stressful environments.
- **Proactive Growth and Learning:** Viewing adversity as an opportunity for development.
- **Maintaining Composure in Crisis:** Providing stability and leadership during emergencies.

- **Effective Communication Under Pressure:** Conveying messages clearly and inspiring confidence in others.
- **Balancing Emotions with Practical Considerations:** Aligning emotional responses with goals and values.

Emotional Intelligence (EI)

Definition: The ability to recognize, understand, and manage one's own emotions, as well as the ability to recognize and influence the emotions of others.

Attributes:
- **Self-Awareness:** Recognizing one's emotions and their impact.
- **Self-Regulation:** Managing disruptive emotions and adapting to changing circumstances.
- **Empathy:** Understanding and sharing the feelings of others.
- **Effective Communication:** Conveying information clearly and fostering positive interactions.
- **Relationship Management:** Building and maintaining healthy relationships through trust and respect.

ER vs. EI: Understanding the Distinction

Aspect	Emotional Resilience (ER)	Emotional Intelligence (EI)
Scope of Application	Encompasses adaptability, problem-	Focuses on understanding and managing

	solving, and decision-making under stress.	emotions within oneself and in interpersonal interactions.
Adaptability in Adversity	Addresses how individuals respond to adversity and pressure, maintaining effectiveness and composure.	Recognizes and manages emotions in various contexts, emphasizing interpersonal relationships.
Cognitive Processes	Involves understanding and interpreting emotions in complex, demanding situations, aiding in decision-making.	Centers on recognizing, understanding, and managing emotions at an individual level.
Interaction with Other Intelligences	Integrates with analytical, interpersonal, and practical intelligences for comprehensive resilience.	Primarily operates within the emotional and interpersonal domains, with less emphasis on

		integrating other intelligences.
Thriving in Adversity	Emphasizes growth, learning, and excellence in the face of challenges.	Provides tools for managing emotions, which may not inherently include a growth orientation.
Depth of Response	Addresses a wide range of emotional responses, from everyday stressors to significant crises.	Focuses on emotional responses broadly but may lack depth in high-pressure scenarios.
Proactive Growth Orientation	Encourages viewing adversity as an opportunity for development and actively pursuing growth.	While valuable, does not inherently emphasize proactive growth in the face of adversity.

In essence, Emotional Resilience is a broader and more comprehensive intelligence that encompasses elements of Emotional Intelligence. While EI is crucial for managing emotions and fostering interpersonal relationships, ER extends beyond by incorporating adaptability, problem-solving, and a proactive approach to growth in the face of adversity. Together, they form critical cornerstones of an individual's emotional and psychological well-being, each contributing uniquely to personal and professional success.

A More Comprehensive Look at Resilience

Building upon the foundational aspects of ER, we explore its advanced characteristics:

- **Self-Awareness and Emotional Insight:** Deep understanding of one's own emotions, including triggers and patterns.
- **Adaptability and Flexibility:** Ability to adjust to changing circumstances and recover from setbacks.
- **Positive Outlook and Optimism:** Maintaining hope and confidence despite challenges.
- **Effective Stress Management:** Employing robust techniques to channel stress productively.
- **Problem-Solving and Decision-Making Under Stress:** Making sound decisions and solving complex problems in high-pressure situations.
- **Emotional Regulation and Control:** Managing emotions to maintain composure and rationality.
- **Healthy Coping Mechanisms:** Utilizing constructive strategies to handle stress and emotions.

- **Perseverance and Determination:** Staying committed to goals despite obstacles.
- **Empathy and Understanding of Others:** Navigating interpersonal dynamics effectively, especially in stressful environments.
- **Proactive Growth and Learning:** Viewing adversity as an opportunity for development.
- **Maintaining Composure in Crisis:** Providing stability and leadership during emergencies.
- **Effective Communication Under Pressure:** Conveying messages clearly and inspiring confidence in others.
- **Balancing Emotions with Practical Considerations:** Aligning emotional responses with goals and values.

Synergy between Emotional Resilience and Emotional Intelligence

While ER and EI are distinct, their synergy creates a powerful combination that enhances overall leadership effectiveness:

1. Enhanced Decision-Making:

- EI equips leaders to make emotionally informed decisions and navigate social interactions effectively.
- ER provides the fortitude to make tough decisions under pressure, maintaining effectiveness and composure.

2. Navigating Complex Relationships:

- EI is crucial for building and maintaining positive relationships.
- ER offers the strength to weather conflicts and challenges, ensuring sustained interpersonal dynamics.

3. Coping with Change and Uncertainty:

- ER is instrumental in adapting to significant changes and uncertainties.
- EI facilitates understanding and processing the emotions associated with change, smoothing transitions.

4. Leadership Effectiveness:

- EI inspires and motivates teams.
- ER ensures leaders remain effective in high-pressure situations, guiding teams with grace and determination.

5. Fostering a Growth Mindset:

- ER encourages viewing challenges as opportunities for learning and development.
- EI provides tools to understand and regulate emotions in the face of challenges, creating a positive feedback loop.

6. Adaptability and Innovation:

- EI aids in understanding the needs and emotions of others.
- ER fosters adaptability and innovative thinking, essential in rapidly changing environments.

By recognizing the interplay between Emotional Resilience and Emotional Intelligence, leaders can cultivate a balanced and robust emotional framework. This integrated approach empowers individuals to navigate complex situations with both emotional insight and resilience, enhancing their capacity for growth and success.

Integrating Emotional Intelligence and Emotional Resilience with the Holistic Intelligence Model

The Holistic Intelligence Model encompasses eight pillars of intelligence that collectively contribute to a leader's effectiveness. Integrating EI and ER within this model provides definitive strategies for enhancing leadership capabilities.

1. Emotional Resilience (ER): Strengthening the Foundation

Definitive Advice:

Stress Management Techniques: Implement regular practices such as mindfulness meditation, physical exercise, and time management to build resilience against stress.

Adaptability Training: Engage in workshops that focus on developing flexibility and adaptability in changing environments.

Problem-Solving Under Pressure: Participate in scenario-based training to enhance decision-making skills during crises.

Integration with the Holistic Intelligence Model:

Emotional Resilience (ER): Enables leaders to manage stress, recover from setbacks, and maintain composure.

Creativity Intelligence (CrQ): Encourages innovative solutions during adversity.

Practical Intelligence (PQ): Ensures effective application of resilience strategies in real-world situations.

2. Emotional Intelligence (EI): Enhancing Emotional Insight

Definitive Advice:

Self-Awareness Exercises: Utilize tools like emotional journaling and personality assessments to deepen self-understanding.

Empathy Development: Engage in active listening and perspective-taking activities to enhance empathy towards others.

Effective Communication Training: Attend workshops focused on clear, compassionate, and assertive communication techniques.

Integration with the Holistic Intelligence Model:

Emotional Intelligence (EI): Facilitates understanding and management of personal and others' emotions.

Interpersonal Intelligence: Strengthens relationships through effective emotional interactions.

Cultural Intelligence (CQ): Enhances ability to navigate diverse emotional expressions and cultural nuances.

3. Intrapersonal Intelligence: Building Self-Awareness

Definitive Advice:

Regular Self-Reflection: Allocate time for introspection to assess personal strengths and areas for growth.

Mindfulness Practices: Incorporate mindfulness into daily routines to increase present-moment awareness.

Personal Development Plans: Create and follow structured plans that align personal goals with professional aspirations.

Integration with the Holistic Intelligence Model:

Intrapersonal Intelligence: Promotes self-awareness and self-regulation, essential for both EI and ER.

Analytical Intelligence (AQ): Enhances critical thinking about personal development and emotional responses.

4. Interpersonal Intelligence: Fostering Strong Relationships

Definitive Advice:

Team-Building Activities: Organize regular activities that promote trust and collaboration among team members.

Conflict Resolution Skills: Train in mediation and negotiation to handle interpersonal conflicts constructively.

Feedback Mechanisms: Establish open channels for giving and receiving feedback within teams.

Integration with the Holistic Intelligence Model:

Interpersonal Intelligence: Essential for building and maintaining effective relationships.

Emotional Resilience (ER): Supports the ability to manage and recover from interpersonal challenges.

5. Analytical Intelligence (AQ): Enhancing Critical Thinking

Definitive Advice:

Data-Driven Decision Making: Utilize analytics tools and methodologies to inform strategic decisions.

Scenario Planning: Engage in exercises that explore various outcomes based on different decisions.

Continuous Learning: Stay updated with industry trends and best practices through ongoing education.

Integration with the Holistic Intelligence Model:

Analytical Intelligence (AQ): Supports critical evaluation and problem-solving.

Emotional Resilience (ER): Provides a stable foundation for making informed decisions under pressure.

6. Practical Intelligence (PQ): Applying Knowledge Effectively

Definitive Advice:

Project Management Skills: Develop competencies in planning, executing, and closing projects efficiently.

Resource Optimization: Learn techniques to maximize the use of available resources.

Real-World Application: Apply theoretical knowledge to practical tasks and challenges.

Integration with the Holistic Intelligence Model:

Practical Intelligence (PQ): Ensures effective implementation of strategies and solutions.

Emotional Resilience (ER): Enhances the ability to adapt and apply knowledge in dynamic environments.

7. Creativity Intelligence (CrQ): Encouraging Innovation

Definitive Advice:

Creative Thinking Workshops: Participate in sessions that stimulate out-of-the-box thinking and innovation.

Idea Generation Techniques: Use methods like brainstorming, mind mapping, and design thinking to generate new ideas.

Supportive Environment: Create a culture that encourages experimentation and tolerates failure as part of the innovation process.

Integration with the Holistic Intelligence Model:

Creativity Intelligence (CrQ): Drives innovative solutions and approaches.

Emotional Resilience (ER): Supports the ability to experiment and recover from unsuccessful attempts.

8. Cultural Intelligence (CQ): Navigating Diversity

Definitive Advice:

Cultural Competence Training: Engage in programs that increase understanding of different cultural norms and practices.

Diverse Team Collaboration: Promote interactions among team members from diverse backgrounds to enhance cultural sensitivity.

Global Awareness: Stay informed about global trends and cultural shifts that may impact the organization.

Integration with the Holistic Intelligence Model:

Cultural Intelligence (CQ): Enhances ability to work effectively in diverse environments.

Emotional Intelligence (EI): Facilitates understanding and managing emotions across cultural contexts.

Interpersonal Intelligence: Strengthens relationships through cultural sensitivity and appreciation.

9. Ethical Intelligence (EthQ): Upholding Integrity

Definitive Advice:

Ethics Training: Participate in programs that reinforce ethical standards and decision-making.

Values Alignment: Ensure personal and organizational values are clearly defined and consistently applied.

Transparent Practices: Maintain openness and honesty in all professional interactions.

Integration with the Holistic Intelligence Model:

Ethical Intelligence (EthQ): Guides leaders to act with integrity and uphold moral standards.

Emotional Intelligence (EI): Ensures ethical considerations are integrated into emotional and interpersonal interactions.

Emotional Resilience (ER): Supports maintaining ethical standards even under pressure or adversity.

The Symbiotic Relationship Between Emotional Intelligence and Resilience

The symbiotic relationship between Emotional Intelligence (EI) and Emotional Resilience (ER) is undeniable and forms a critical foundation for effective leadership. EI equips leaders with the ability to understand and manage their own emotions and those of others, fostering strong interpersonal relationships and effective communication. ER, on the other hand, provides the strength to navigate adversity, recover from setbacks, and maintain a positive and proactive outlook in the face of challenges.

By integrating both EI and ER within the Holistic Intelligence Model, leaders can achieve a balanced and comprehensive approach to personal and professional development. This integration not only enhances individual capabilities but also positively influences organizational culture, fostering an environment of continuous learning, ethical behavior, and resilient performance.

Final Thought: Leaders who cultivate both emotional intelligence and emotional resilience are better equipped to inspire their teams, drive innovation, and lead their organizations toward sustained success and adaptability in an ever-changing world.

Reflection Questions

1. Self-Assessment: How do your current levels of emotional intelligence and emotional resilience influence your leadership effectiveness?

2. Development Areas: Which aspects of emotional resilience and emotional intelligence do you find most challenging, and what steps can you take to improve them?

3. Synergy Utilization: How can you leverage the synergy between emotional intelligence and emotional resilience to enhance your leadership style and team performance?

Action Plan

1. Evaluate Current Competencies: Use emotional intelligence assessments and resilience questionnaires to identify strengths and areas for improvement.

2. Set Specific Goals: Define clear, actionable objectives for enhancing both emotional intelligence and resilience.

3. Implement Development Strategies:

- For EI: Engage in active listening exercises, empathy training, and effective communication workshops.
- For ER: Adopt stress management techniques, participate in resilience training programs, and practice adaptability in varied situations.

4. Seek Feedback: Regularly solicit input from peers, mentors, and team members to gauge progress and adjust strategies accordingly.

5. Integrate into Daily Practice: Apply learned skills in everyday leadership scenarios, ensuring continuous reinforcement and development.

6. Monitor Progress: Establish regular check-ins to assess improvements and recalibrate goals as needed.

Case Study: The Transformational Impact of Mindset and Attitude

Akio Yamamoto, a luminary in the domain of Supply Chain & Logistics, emerges as a paragon of the transformative power of mindset and attitude in leadership. Hailing from a background steeped in operational intricacies, Akio's journey to becoming the Fleet Operations Director is a testament to the indomitable spirit that defines his leadership style.

Born in Osaka, Japan, Akio's formative years were marked by an insatiable curiosity about the world of logistics. As a teenager, he immersed himself in books on supply chain dynamics, harboring a dream of streamlining operations on a global scale. This early fascination with logistics laid the groundwork for his future endeavors.

Akio's foray into the professional world began with a role in a local logistics firm. It was here that he honed his operational acumen, gaining firsthand experience in the orchestration of complex supply chains. His natural proclivity for problem-solving and his uncanny ability to navigate logistical challenges swiftly garnered the attention of industry stalwarts.

Under the mentorship of seasoned leaders, Akio ascended the ranks, consistently displaying a mindset that transcended the conventional boundaries of operational management. He approached each challenge as an opportunity for innovation, leveraging his attitude of relentless determination to effect transformative change.

One of Akio's hallmark achievements came during a critical juncture when the company faced a supply chain disruption of unprecedented magnitude. While conventional wisdom dictated a reactive approach, Akio's unwavering mindset advocated for a proactive overhaul of the existing processes. His audacious proposal, backed by meticulous research and a compelling vision, heralded a paradigm shift in the company's approach to logistics.

Akio's leadership style is distinguished by a unique blend of strategic foresight and hands-on operational involvement. He is known for immersing himself in the day-to-day workings of the fleet, forging genuine connections with team members at every level. This approachability, coupled with an attitude of humility and a genuine appreciation for the contributions of his team, forms the bedrock of his leadership philosophy.

Noteworthy among Akio's achievements is the implementation of a groundbreaking routing algorithm that optimized delivery schedules, significantly reducing transit times and costs. This innovation not only bolstered operational efficiency but also underscored Akio's unwavering belief in the potential for transformative change through innovative thinking.

Akio Yamamoto's leadership journey is emblematic of the profound impact that mindset and attitude can wield in the realm of Supply Chain & Logistics. His story serves as an inspiration to leaders across industries, illustrating that a steadfast belief in the potential for positive change, coupled with an unwavering commitment to operational excellence, can pave the way for transformative leadership.

Akio Yamamoto's narrative exemplifies the transformative potential of mindset and attitude, offering valuable insights for leaders seeking to effect meaningful change within their respective domains.

Analyzing Key Instances Demonstrating the Influence of Mindset and Attitude

Akio Yamamoto's leadership journey is a tapestry woven with threads of resilience, strategic thinking, and an unwavering positive attitude. Through a meticulous analysis of key instances in his career, we unearth valuable insights and actionable strategies that can be harnessed by leaders across diverse industries.

One pivotal instance that underscores Akio's impact revolves around a major logistical bottleneck the company encountered. Faced with a confluence of unforeseen challenges, conventional wisdom dictated a reactive stance. However, Akio's indomitable mindset advocated for a proactive overhaul of existing processes. His unwavering belief in the potential for transformative change through innovation led to the development of a proprietary routing algorithm. This innovative solution not only optimized delivery schedules but also significantly reduced transit times and costs.

Akio's hands-on approach to leadership has been a linchpin of his success. He is known for immersing himself in the minutiae of operations, forging genuine connections with team members at all levels. This accessibility, coupled with an attitude of humility, creates a culture of open communication and fosters a sense of ownership among the team. This instance serves as a poignant reminder that effective leadership is not confined to the boardroom, but rather, it emanates from an empathetic and engaged approach to team dynamics.

Another illustrative example lies in Akio's approach to adversity. When faced with unforeseen disruptions in the supply chain, his response was characterized by a mindset that viewed challenges as opportunities for innovation. By cultivating a culture of adaptability and embracing change, Akio was able to steer the company through turbulent waters, ultimately emerging stronger and more agile.

The integration of emotional intelligence into Akio's leadership style is equally noteworthy. His ability to empathize with team members, understand their perspectives, and navigate complex interpersonal dynamics has been instrumental in building a cohesive and high-performing team. This exemplifies the profound impact that a positive attitude and emotional intelligence can have on organizational culture and performance.

Akio's commitment to continuous learning is yet another facet of his leadership ethos. He approaches each day as an opportunity for growth, viewing setbacks as valuable learning experiences. This growth mindset not only fuels his personal development but also sets a powerful example for his team, encouraging them to embrace challenges with a spirit of curiosity and a thirst for knowledge.

Akio's attitude towards risk-taking is emblematic of a leader who understands the delicate balance between calculated risks and prudent decision-making. He approaches risks with a strategic lens, weighing potential rewards against potential pitfalls. This discerning approach, rooted in a mindset that values calculated experimentation, has been instrumental in propelling the company towards innovative solutions.

The essence of Akio Yamamoto's leadership journey lies in the profound influence of mindset and attitude on organizational success. By scrutinizing key instances in his career, we glean valuable strategies for leaders seeking to effect transformative change within their own spheres of influence. Akio's story serves as a beacon, illuminating the path towards resilient, innovative, and empathetic leadership.

Extracting Insights and Strategies from the Case Study

In dissecting Akio Yamamoto's leadership journey, we unearth a wealth of insights and actionable strategies that can be applied by leaders navigating their own professional landscapes. His story is a reservoir of wisdom, showcasing the transformative power of mindset and attitude in leadership.

One of the most salient takeaways from Akio's experience is the imperative of proactive problem-solving. Rather than passively reacting to challenges, he exemplifies a mindset that seeks out opportunities within obstacles. This proactive orientation towards problem-solving has enabled him to not only navigate crises effectively but also to innovate and drive the company forward.

Akio's hands-on approach to leadership stands out as a key driver of his success. By immersing himself in the day-to-day operations of the company, he fosters a deep understanding of the challenges and opportunities that exist at every level. This hands-on approach not only engenders trust and respect among team members but also allows him to make informed, strategic decisions based on a comprehensive understanding of the organization.

Akio's emphasis on fostering a culture of continuous learning is another pivotal aspect of his leadership philosophy. He views each day as an opportunity for growth and encourages his team to adopt a similar mindset. This commitment to learning not only keeps the organization agile and adaptable but also fosters a culture of innovation and curiosity.

Akio's approach to risk-taking provides valuable insights for leaders seeking to navigate uncertainty. He understands that calculated risks are integral to driving meaningful progress, but also recognizes the importance of conducting thorough assessments before making decisions. This discerning approach to risk management is emblematic of a leader who understands the delicate balance between boldness and prudence.

The integration of emotional intelligence into Akio's leadership style is yet another source of inspiration. His ability to connect with team members on a human level, empathize with their challenges, and celebrate their successes creates a work environment characterized by trust, collaboration, and mutual respect. This emotional intelligence not only enhances team cohesion but also contributes to heightened morale and motivation.

Moreover, Akio's capacity to view setbacks as opportunities for growth and innovation is a testament to his resilient mindset. He understands that failure is not a finality but rather a stepping stone towards greater achievements. This resilience in the face of adversity serves as a powerful example for his team, inspiring them to face challenges with fortitude and a positive outlook.

Akio's unwavering commitment to diversity and inclusion is yet another facet of his leadership approach. He recognizes the value of diverse perspectives and actively cultivates an inclusive work environment where every voice is heard and valued. This commitment to diversity not only enhances creativity and problem-solving but also reinforces the company's reputation as a forward-thinking and socially responsible organization.

In essence, Akio Yamamoto's leadership journey is a masterclass in the profound impact of mindset and attitude on organizational success. By extracting these insights and strategies, leaders across industries can glean valuable lessons for their own leadership journeys. Akio's story serves as a beacon, illuminating the path towards resilient, innovative, and empathetic leadership in an ever-evolving global landscape.

Lessons in Cultivating a Transformational Mindset and Attitude from Akio Yamamoto's Leadership

Akio Yamamoto's leadership journey is a rich source of valuable lessons in cultivating a transformational mindset and attitude. His approach to leadership is underpinned by a deep-seated belief in the potential for positive change, both within individuals and organizations. Through his experiences, several key lessons emerge, providing a roadmap for leaders seeking to foster a transformational mindset.

First and foremost, Akio exemplifies the power of vision and purpose. He understands that a clear, compelling vision provides a north star for an organization, guiding decision-making and uniting teams towards a common goal. This vision acts as a catalyst for transformation, instilling a sense of purpose and direction that permeates every facet of the organization.

In tandem with vision, Akio emphasizes the importance of aligning values with actions. He recognizes that authentic leadership requires a consistent demonstration of core values in day-to-day interactions and decision-making. By modeling these values, leaders can inspire trust and confidence among team members, reinforcing the organization's commitment to its guiding principles.

Akio's leadership also underscores the significance of adaptability and agility in the face of change. He views change not as a disruption, but as an opportunity for growth and improvement. This mindset enables him to lead his team through periods of transition with confidence and poise, ensuring the organization remains resilient in the face of evolving circumstances.

Akio places a strong emphasis on empowerment and delegation. He understands that true transformation requires the collective effort and expertise of the entire team. By empowering team members to take ownership of their roles and contribute their unique skills, he fosters a culture of accountability and innovation that propels the organization forward.

Akio's leadership style also highlights the importance of active listening and open communication. He recognizes that effective communication is a two-way street, requiring leaders to not only convey their vision and expectations but also to actively seek input and feedback from their team members. This approach cultivates a culture of transparency and inclusivity, where every voice is valued.

Akio's leadership exemplifies the power of resilience in the face of challenges. He acknowledges that setbacks are an inevitable part of any transformative journey. However, he views them not as insurmountable obstacles, but as opportunities for learning and growth. This resilient attitude instills confidence in his team, enabling them to face adversity with determination and a positive outlook.

Akio's commitment to continuous learning and development is another cornerstone of his transformational leadership. He recognizes that personal and professional growth is an ongoing process, and he actively seeks out opportunities for learning and self-improvement. This dedication to learning not only enriches his own leadership capabilities but also sets a powerful example for his team.

Akio places a strong emphasis on fostering a culture of trust and psychological safety within the organization. He understands that for transformational change to occur, team members must feel comfortable taking risks, expressing their ideas, and challenging the status quo. This culture of trust empowers individuals to contribute their fullest potential to the organization's transformational journey.

Akio's leadership also highlights the importance of celebrating successes, both big and small. He understands that acknowledging achievements, no matter how incremental, reinforces a culture of achievement and motivates team members to continue their pursuit of excellence. This celebratory approach creates a positive and uplifting work environment.

In summary, Akio Yamamoto's leadership journey provides a treasure trove of lessons in cultivating a transformational mindset and attitude. His visionary approach, alignment of values with actions, adaptability, empowerment, active listening, resilience, commitment to continuous learning, and emphasis on trust and celebration all serve as beacons for leaders seeking to drive transformation within their own organizations. Akio's story is a testament to the profound impact that a transformational mindset and attitude can have on organizational success and the growth of individuals within the team.

Practical Takeaways for Leaders Seeking to Shift Their Mindset and Attitude

Practical takeaways for leaders seeking to shift their mindset and attitude towards a more transformational approach:

- **Clarify Your Vision:** Begin by defining a clear and compelling vision for your organization. This vision will serve as a guiding light, aligning the efforts of your team towards a common goal.
- **Live Your Values:** Actively demonstrate your core values through your actions and decisions. Your consistent adherence to these values will build trust and set a standard for behavior within the organization.
- **Embrace Change:** View change as an opportunity for growth, rather than a disruption. Cultivate an agile mindset that welcomes new challenges and sees them as a chance for improvement.
- **Empower Your Team:** Delegate responsibility and provide your team members with the autonomy to take ownership of their roles. This empowers them to contribute their unique skills and expertise towards the organization's goals.
- **Listen Actively:** Practice active listening by seeking out input and feedback from your team. Create a culture of open communication where every voice is valued and heard.
- **Resilience in Adversity:** Develop a resilient attitude towards setbacks and challenges. See them as opportunities

for learning and growth, rather than insurmountable obstacles.

- **Commit to Continuous Learning:** Prioritize your own personal and professional development. Actively seek out opportunities for learning and self-improvement.
- **Foster a Culture of Trust:** Create an environment where trust and psychological safety thrive. Encourage team members to take risks, express their ideas, and challenge the status quo.
- **Celebrate Achievements:** Acknowledge and celebrate successes, no matter how small. This reinforces a culture of achievement and motivates team members to continue striving for excellence.
- **Promote Growth Mindset:** Encourage a growth mindset among your team members. Emphasize the importance of embracing challenges, persisting through obstacles, and seeing effort as a path to mastery.
- **Set Realistic Goals:** Establish clear, achievable goals that align with your vision. Break them down into actionable steps, providing a roadmap for progress.
- **Lead by Example:** Model the behaviors and attitudes you wish to see in your team. Your actions speak louder than words, and your consistency will inspire confidence and trust.
- **Provide Constructive Feedback:** Offer feedback in a constructive and supportive manner. Focus on areas for improvement while also highlighting strengths and accomplishments.
- **Encourage Innovation:** Create space for creativity and innovation within your team. Foster an environment where new ideas are welcomed and explored.

- **Practice Self-Care:** Take care of your physical, mental, and emotional well-being. A healthy and balanced leader is better equipped to inspire and guide their team.
- **Seek Diverse Perspectives:** Actively seek out input from individuals with different backgrounds, experiences, and viewpoints. This diversity of thought can lead to more comprehensive and innovative solutions.
- **Stay Resilient in the Face of Failure:** Understand that failure is a natural part of any transformative journey. Use setbacks as opportunities to learn and grow.
- **Communicate Transparently:** Foster a culture of transparency by openly sharing information and decisions with your team. This builds trust and ensures everyone is on the same page.
- **Delegate Effectively:** Delegate tasks based on team members' strengths and interests. Empower them to take ownership of their responsibilities and contribute their unique skills.
- **Reflect and Adapt:** Take time to reflect on your leadership style and approach. Be willing to adapt and evolve as needed to best serve your team and organization.

By incorporating these practical takeaways into your leadership approach, you can begin to shift your mindset and attitude towards a more transformational and impactful style of leadership. These actions, when consistently applied, have the potential to inspire positive change and growth within both yourself and your organization.

Leadership Case Reviews: Mastering Situations in Shifting Mindsets

Because the real world is where some of our most valuable lessons are learned, let's now look at instances that illustrate how effective leaders can drive meaningful shifts in mindset within their organizations. By recognizing the need for change, providing the necessary resources and support, and consistently reinforcing the desired behaviors, these leaders successfully influenced their teams to adopt new, more effective ways of thinking and approaching challenges.

Cultural Transformation Initiative

- **Analysis**   A CEO recognized the need for a cultural shift within the organization to foster innovation and adaptability. The leader implemented a comprehensive program that included workshops, mentorship programs, and incentives for employees to embrace a growth mindset. Over time, this initiative led to a noticeable shift in employee attitudes towards challenges, with a greater willingness to take risks and explore new ideas.
- **Lesson**   This instance emphasizes the power of leadership in driving cultural change within an organization. The CEO's recognition of the need for a cultural shift and the implementation of targeted programs showcases how leaders can successfully influence mindset changes. It highlights the importance of providing the necessary resources and reinforcement mechanisms to support the desired cultural shift.

Change Management in a Merger

- **Analysis**   A Senior Executive oversaw the integration of two companies following a merger. Recognizing the need to shift mindsets from competition to collaboration, the executive initiated a series of cross-functional workshops and team-building exercises. By fostering an environment of open communication and emphasizing shared goals, the executive successfully facilitated a change in mindset, enabling a smoother merger process.
- **Lesson**   The Senior Executive's approach to integrating two companies through mindset shift demonstrates the impact of leadership in managing change. By initiating workshops and team-building exercises, the executive fostered an environment of collaboration. This instance underscores the leader's role in guiding teams through transitions and facilitating the necessary mindset shifts for successful mergers.

Agile Transformation in Software Development

- **Analysis**   A Development Manager recognized the need to shift the team's mindset from traditional waterfall methodologies to Agile practices. The manager provided extensive training, coaching, and opportunities for team members to participate in Agile ceremonies. Through consistent reinforcement of Agile principles and a focus on iterative development, the team gradually embraced the new mindset, resulting in increased productivity and higher-quality deliverables.
- **Lesson**   The Development Manager's efforts to shift the team's mindset towards Agile practices illustrate the influence of leadership in driving process change. Through training, coaching, and consistent reinforcement, the manager guided the team towards adopting a more

iterative and flexible approach. This instance highlights how effective leaders can lead teams towards adopting new methodologies and mindsets.

Innovation Program in a Stagnant Industry

- **Analysis**   A Director of Innovation took on the challenge of shifting the mindset of employees in an industry known for its resistance to change. The director introduced an innovation program that encouraged employees to explore new ideas and experiment with novel approaches. By providing resources, recognition, and a safe space for experimentation, the director successfully shifted the mindset towards a more innovative and forward-thinking culture.
- **Lesson**   The Director of Innovation's initiative to instill an innovative mindset within a traditionally resistant industry showcases the transformative influence of leadership. By providing resources and creating a supportive environment, the director empowered employees to explore new ideas. This instance underscores how leaders can drive mindset shifts towards innovation and forward thinking.

Customer-Centric Approach in Sales

- **Analysis**   A Sales Manager aimed to shift the team's mindset from a transactional approach to a customer-centric one. The manager implemented training focused on active listening, empathy, and understanding customer pain points. Through ongoing coaching and feedback, the sales team began to prioritize building long-term relationships over quick wins, leading to increased customer satisfaction and loyalty.
- **Lesson**   The Sales Manager's focus on shifting the team's mindset towards a customer-centric approach highlights

the impact of leadership on sales strategies. Through training, coaching, and feedback, the manager guided the team towards prioritizing customer relationships over transactions. This instance emphasizes how leaders can influence mindset shifts that lead to improved customer satisfaction and loyalty.

Diversity and Inclusion Initiative

- **Analysis**   A Human Resources Director recognized the need to shift the organization's mindset towards inclusivity and diversity. The director implemented diversity training, created affinity groups, and established inclusive hiring practices. Over time, this initiative led to a more inclusive work environment, with employees valuing diverse perspectives and experiences.
- **Lesson**   The Human Resources Director's efforts to shift the organization's mindset towards diversity and inclusion demonstrate the pivotal role of leadership in driving cultural change. Through training, affinity groups, and inclusive hiring practices, the director created a more inclusive work environment. This instance underscores how leaders can champion initiatives that promote diversity and inclusivity, ultimately fostering a more inclusive mindset among employees.

These instances collectively showcase the transformative impact of leadership in driving meaningful shifts in mindset within organizations. Effective leaders recognize the need for change, provide the necessary resources and support, and consistently reinforce desired behaviors. Through their guidance, leaders successfully influence teams to adopt new, more effective ways of thinking and approaching challenges, ultimately contributing to organizational growth and success.

Tools and Techniques for Shifting Mindset and Attitude towards Effective Leadership

A leader's mindset and attitude are critical determinants of their effectiveness. Embracing a growth-oriented mindset not only fosters personal development but also positively influences organizational culture and team performance. This section delves into various tools and techniques that leaders can utilize to shift their mindset and attitude towards more effective leadership, integrating them with the principles of the Holistic Intelligence Model. By embracing these strategies, leaders can cultivate resilience, adaptability, and a proactive approach to challenges.

1. Self-Reflection and Journaling

Deepening Self-Awareness through Introspection

Self-reflection and journaling involve dedicating time to introspect and document thoughts, feelings, and experiences. This practice provides valuable insights into one's mindset, behaviors, and patterns, helping identify areas for growth.

Integration with the Holistic Intelligence Model

- Intrapersonal Intelligence: Enhances self-awareness and self-understanding.
- Emotional Resilience (ER): Allows processing of emotions and building emotional strength.

- Analytical Intelligence (AQ): Facilitates critical thinking about personal experiences.

Practical Strategies

1. Daily Journaling: Set aside time each day to write about experiences, challenges, and feelings.

2. Reflective Questions: Use prompts such as "What did I learn today?" or "How did I handle a difficult situation?" to guide reflection.

3. Pattern Recognition: Review journal entries periodically to identify recurring themes or behaviors.

Case Example

Bill Gates is known for his "Think Weeks," dedicated time for deep reflection and learning, which have been pivotal in his personal development and strategic thinking.

2. Meditation and Mindfulness Practices

Cultivating Presence and Focus

Engaging in mindfulness and meditation enhances self-awareness and promotes a calm, focused mindset. These practices reduce stress, improve decision-making, and increase emotional regulation.

Integration with the Holistic Intelligence Model

- Intrapersonal Intelligence: Strengthens self-regulation and emotional awareness.

- Emotional Resilience (ER): Builds capacity to manage stress and recover from setbacks.
- Practical Intelligence (PQ): Enhances focus and productivity.

Practical Strategies

1. Mindful Breathing Exercises: Practice deep breathing techniques to center yourself.

2. Guided Meditation Apps: Utilize apps like Headspace or Calm for structured meditation sessions.

3. Mindfulness in Daily Activities: Incorporate mindfulness into routine tasks by paying full attention to the present moment.

Case Example

Arianna Huffington advocates for mindfulness and meditation as essential practices for effective leadership and well-being.

3. Positive Affirmations

Reinforcing a Growth Mindset

Positive affirmations are statements that help reinforce beliefs in one's abilities and potential. Regularly affirming these beliefs can reshape attitudes towards challenges and enhance confidence.

Integration with the Holistic Intelligence Model

- Intrapersonal Intelligence: Modifies internal dialogue to be more supportive.

- Emotional Resilience (ER): Increases optimism and motivation.
- Ethical Intelligence: Aligns self-perception with values and integrity.

Practical Strategies

1. Create Personalized Affirmations: Develop statements that resonate with your goals and values.

2. Daily Repetition: Repeat affirmations each morning to set a positive tone for the day.

3. Visual Reminders: Place affirmations where they are frequently seen, such as on a desk or mirror.

Case Example

Muhammad Ali famously used affirmations like "I am the greatest" to build confidence and mental strength.

4. Visualization Techniques

Mentally Rehearsing Success

Visualization involves creating mental images of achieving goals or successfully performing tasks. This technique reinforces a positive mindset and prepares the brain for actual performance.

Integration with the Holistic Intelligence Model

- Intrapersonal Intelligence: Enhances self-belief and motivation.

- Creativity Intelligence (CrQ): Engages imagination and innovative thinking.
- Emotional Resilience (ER): Reduces anxiety by familiarizing oneself with desired outcomes.

Practical Strategies

1. Goal Visualization: Spend time imagining the successful attainment of specific goals.

2. Sensory Involvement: Engage all senses to make the visualization vivid and realistic.

3. Regular Practice: Incorporate visualization into daily routines, especially before challenging tasks.

Case Example

Michael Phelps, the Olympic swimmer, used visualization to prepare for races, mentally rehearsing every detail.

5. Goal-Setting and Action Planning

Providing Direction and Purpose

Setting clear, specific goals and outlining steps to achieve them provides direction, shapes mindset towards achievement, and enhances focus.

Integration with the Holistic Intelligence Model

- Analytical Intelligence (AQ): Involves strategic planning and critical thinking.

- Practical Intelligence (PQ): Translates plans into actionable steps.
- Emotional Resilience (ER): Builds confidence through progress and accomplishment.

Practical Strategies

1. WISE Goals: Set goals that are Well-Defined, Inspiring, Sustainable, and Empowering.

2. Action Plans: Break down goals into smaller, manageable tasks.

3. Regular Review: Monitor progress and adjust plans as necessary.

Case Example

Warren Buffett is known for his focused goal-setting, prioritizing tasks that align with long-term objectives.

6. Emotional Resilience Assessments

Understanding and Enhancing ER

Emotional resilience assessments help leaders recognize their strengths and areas for improvement in emotional competencies.

Integration with the Holistic Intelligence Model

- Intrapersonal Intelligence: Increases self-awareness of emotional states.

- Interpersonal Intelligence: Enhances understanding of others' emotions.
- Ethical Intelligence: Guides personal development in alignment with values.

Practical Strategies

1. Take Recognized Assessments: Use tools like William Stanek's Resilient Growth Self-Assessment and the 8 Pillars of Leadership: Self-Assessment to evaluate emotional resilience.

2. Professional Feedback: Work with a certified coach to interpret results.

3. Develop Improvement Plans: Create strategies to enhance areas needing growth.

Case Example

Organizations like Google incorporate EI assessments in leadership development programs to foster effective leadership.

7. Leadership Coaching and Mentoring

Gaining Insights from Experienced Guides

Seeking guidance from mentors or coaches provides personalized feedback, strategies for development, and support in navigating leadership challenges.

Integration with the Holistic Intelligence Model

- Interpersonal Intelligence: Builds strong professional relationships.
- Practical Intelligence (PQ): Applies learned strategies effectively.
- Ethical Intelligence: Encourages alignment with ethical standards.

Practical Strategies

1. Identify Potential Mentors: Look for individuals whose leadership style you admire.

2. Engage in Coaching Programs: Invest in professional coaching services.

3. Regular Meetings: Establish consistent sessions for guidance and feedback.

Case Example

Sheryl Sandberg credits mentorship as a key factor in her professional growth and leadership effectiveness.

8. Strengths-Based Assessments

Leveraging Personal Strengths

Assessments like StrengthsFinder or VIA Character Strengths help identify inherent talents and strengths, allowing leaders to focus on leveraging what they excel at.

Integration with the Holistic Intelligence Model

- Intrapersonal Intelligence: Enhances self-understanding.

- Practical Intelligence (PQ): Utilizes strengths for effective leadership.
- Emotional Resilience (ER): Boosts confidence and motivation.

Practical Strategies

1. Complete Strengths Assessments: Use tools to identify top strengths.

2. Strengths Application Plan: Develop ways to apply strengths in leadership roles.

3. Strengths-Based Development: Focus professional development on enhancing strengths.

Case Example

Marcus Buckingham popularized the strengths-based approach, influencing leaders to build on their innate talents.

9. Feedback Loops

Embracing Constructive Criticism

Establishing regular feedback mechanisms with team members and peers allows leaders to gain insights into their performance and areas for improvement.

Integration with the Holistic Intelligence Model

- Interpersonal Intelligence: Improves communication and relationships.
- Intrapersonal Intelligence: Increases self-awareness.

- Ethical Intelligence: Promotes transparency and accountability.

Practical Strategies

1. Feedback: Implement comprehensive feedback systems.

2. Open-Door Policy: Encourage team members to share thoughts freely.

3. Act on Feedback: Demonstrate responsiveness to input received.

Case Example

Ray Dalio of Bridgewater Associates emphasizes radical transparency and open feedback in his organization's culture.

10. Conflict Resolution Training

Navigating Challenges Positively

Learning techniques for resolving conflicts constructively helps maintain a positive attitude and effective relationships even in challenging situations.

Integration with the Holistic Intelligence Model

- Interpersonal Intelligence: Enhances communication skills.
- Ethical Intelligence: Ensures fairness and respect in resolutions.
- Cultural Intelligence (CQ): Navigates conflicts arising from diversity.

Practical Strategies

1. Attend Workshops: Participate in conflict resolution training programs.

2. Practice Active Listening: Understand others' perspectives before responding.

3. Develop Negotiation Skills: Learn to find mutually beneficial solutions.

Case Example

Nelson Mandela exemplified conflict resolution, leading South Africa towards reconciliation.

11. Time Management Tools

Enhancing Productivity and Focus

Using time management apps or techniques improves productivity, reduces stress, and fosters a more positive and focused mindset.

Integration with the Holistic Intelligence Model

- Practical Intelligence (PQ): Increases efficiency in task management.
- Emotional Resilience (ER): Reduces stress through organization.
- Intrapersonal Intelligence: Enhances self-discipline.

Practical Strategies

1. Use Productivity Apps: Tools like Trello, Asana, or Time Doctor can help organize tasks.

2. Prioritization Techniques: Apply methods like the Eisenhower Matrix.

3. Set Boundaries: Allocate specific times for focused work and breaks.

Case Example

Tim Ferriss advocates for effective time management strategies in his book "The 4-Hour Workweek."

12. Cognitive Behavioral Techniques

Challenging and Reframing Negative Thoughts

Applying Cognitive Behavioral Therapy (CBT) principles helps leaders challenge and reframe negative thought patterns, leading to a more positive and adaptive mindset.

Integration with the Holistic Intelligence Model

- Intrapersonal Intelligence: Enhances self-awareness and emotional regulation.
- Emotional Resilience (ER): Builds mental strength to handle adversity.
- Analytical Intelligence (AQ): Uses logical reasoning to reframe thoughts.

Practical Strategies

1. Identify Cognitive Distortions: Recognize patterns like all-or-nothing thinking or catastrophizing.

2. Thought Records: Document negative thoughts and counter them with evidence-based responses.

3. Seek Professional Guidance: Work with a therapist trained in CBT techniques.

Case Example

Leaders undergoing executive coaching often utilize CBT to improve performance and mindset.

13. Stress Management Practices

Maintaining a Calm and Receptive Mind

Incorporating stress-reducing activities like exercise, meditation, or deep breathing exercises promotes well-being and makes the mind more receptive to positive shifts in attitude.

Integration with the Holistic Intelligence Model

- Emotional Resilience (ER): Enhances ability to cope with stress.
- Intrapersonal Intelligence: Recognizes personal stress triggers.
- Practical Intelligence (PQ): Maintains productivity under pressure.

Practical Strategies

1. Regular Physical Activity: Engage in exercises like yoga, running, or swimming.

2. Mindfulness Techniques: Practice mindfulness meditation or progressive muscle relaxation.

3. Healthy Lifestyle Choices: Ensure adequate sleep and balanced nutrition.

Case Example

Jack Dorsey, former CEO of Twitter, incorporates meditation and wellness practices into his daily routine.

14. Decision-Making Frameworks

Approaching Challenges Rationally

Implementing structured decision-making frameworks helps leaders approach challenges with clarity and rationality, reducing emotional biases.

Integration with the Holistic Intelligence Model

- Analytical Intelligence (AQ): Enhances critical thinking.
- Practical Intelligence (PQ): Facilitates effective implementation of decisions.
- Ethical Intelligence: Ensures decisions align with values and ethical standards.

Practical Strategies

1. GROW Analysis: Gains, Realities, Opportunities, and Weaknesses.

2. Cost-Benefit Analysis: Evaluate the pros and cons of options.

3. Decision Trees: Map out possible outcomes and paths.

Case Example

Amazon uses data-driven decision-making processes, balancing intuition with structured analysis.

15. Networking and Learning Communities

Expanding Perspectives through Engagement

Engaging in professional networks and communities allows leaders to exchange ideas, gain new insights, and broaden their mindset.

Integration with the Holistic Intelligence Model

- Cultural Intelligence (CQ): Enhances understanding of diverse perspectives.
- Interpersonal Intelligence: Builds relationships and communication skills.
- Creativity Intelligence (CrQ): Stimulates innovative thinking.

Practical Strategies

1. Join Professional Associations: Participate in industry groups or forums.

2. Attend Conferences and Seminars: Stay updated on trends and best practices.

3. Online Learning Platforms: Engage in webinars and virtual communities.

Case Example

Richard Branson values networking and learning from others, attributing it to his entrepreneurial success.

16. Continual Learning and Development Plans

Committing to Lifelong Growth

Creating a personalized learning and development plan demonstrates a commitment to growth and fosters a forward-thinking mindset.

Integration with the Holistic Intelligence Model

- Analytical Intelligence (AQ): Identifies learning needs and strategies.
- Practical Intelligence (PQ): Applies new knowledge effectively.
- Intrapersonal Intelligence: Drives self-motivated growth.

Practical Strategies

1. Set Learning Goals: Define specific areas for development.

2. Educational Courses: Enroll in relevant courses or certifications.

3. Regular Self-Evaluation: Assess progress and adjust plans accordingly.

Case Example

Elon Musk is known for his voracious learning habits, continuously expanding his knowledge base.

17. Books and Thought Leaders

Inspiring New Ways of Thinking

Reading books and following thought leaders in leadership and personal development provides insights that can inspire mindset shifts.

Integration with the Holistic Intelligence Model

- Analytical Intelligence (AQ): Enhances knowledge and critical thinking.
- Creativity Intelligence (CrQ): Stimulates innovative ideas.
- Intrapersonal Intelligence: Promotes self-reflection.

Practical Strategies

1. Curate a Reading List: Include books that challenge and inspire. Start with William Stanek's *Building Resilience*

Foundations and *Thriving Amidst Flux: Navigating Change and Uncertainty*.

2. Follow Thought Leaders: Engage with their content on social media or blogs.

3. Reflect on Learnings: Apply insights to personal leadership practices.

18. Accountability Partnerships

Holding Each Other to High Standards

Establishing partnerships with peers or colleagues to hold each other accountable promotes adherence to personal and professional development goals.

Integration with the Holistic Intelligence Model

- Interpersonal Intelligence: Strengthens relationships through mutual support.
- Intrapersonal Intelligence: Encourages self-discipline.
- Ethical Intelligence: Fosters responsibility and integrity.

Practical Strategies

1. Regular Check-ins: Schedule meetings to discuss progress and challenges.

2. Set Shared Goals: Collaborate on objectives to motivate each other.

3. Provide Constructive Feedback: Offer honest insights to facilitate growth.

Case Example

Mastermind groups, like those formed by Napoleon Hill, utilize accountability partnerships for mutual success.

19. Gratitude Practices

Cultivating a Positive Outlook

Regularly acknowledging and appreciating positive aspects of the leadership journey fosters a gratitude mindset, enhancing overall positivity.

Integration with the Holistic Intelligence Model

- Emotional Resilience (ER): Increases happiness and reduces stress.
- Intrapersonal Intelligence: Promotes self-awareness of positive experiences.
- Interpersonal Intelligence: Enhances relationships through appreciation.

Practical Strategies

3. Gratitude Journals: Write down things you are thankful for each day.

4. Express Appreciation: Communicate gratitude to team members and colleagues.

5. Mindful Moments: Pause to reflect on successes and positive events.

Case Example

Oprah Winfrey credits her gratitude practice as a key to her success and well-being.

20. Cognitive Restructuring Techniques

Transforming Limiting Beliefs

Cognitive restructuring involves identifying and challenging irrational or unhelpful thoughts, replacing them with more constructive ones.

Integration with the Holistic Intelligence Model

- Intrapersonal Intelligence: Enhances self-awareness and thought management.
- Emotional Resilience (ER): Reduces negative emotional responses.
- Analytical Intelligence (AQ): Applies logic to modify thought patterns.

Practical Strategies

Identify Negative Thoughts: Be attentive to self-limiting beliefs.

Challenge Assumptions: Question the validity of these thoughts.

Develop Alternative Perspectives: Replace them with positive, realistic beliefs.

Case Example

Cognitive restructuring is a core component in executive coaching to enhance leadership effectiveness.

—

By incorporating these tools and techniques into your leadership approach—integrated with the Holistic Intelligence Model—you can actively work towards shifting your mindset and attitude for more effective leadership. Consistency and a genuine commitment to growth are key to making lasting positive changes. Embracing these strategies fosters not only personal development but also positively impacts your team and organizational culture.

Reflection Questions

1. Personal Assessment: Which tools and techniques resonate most with you, and why?

2. Implementation Plan: How can you incorporate these strategies into your daily leadership practices?

3. Impact Evaluation: What changes do you anticipate in your mindset and leadership effectiveness as a result?

Action Plan

1. Select Key Strategies: Choose a few techniques to focus on initially.

2. Set Specific Goals: Define what success looks like for each strategy.

3. Create a Timeline: Establish a schedule for implementing these practices.

4. Engage Support Systems: Involve mentors, coaches, or accountability partners.

5. Monitor Progress: Regularly review your development and adjust as needed.

Empowering Leaders through Mindset and Attitude Shifts

In the ever-evolving landscape of leadership, one truth remains constant: the transformative power of mindset and attitude. These twin forces shape not only how leaders perceive challenges but also how they navigate through them, influence others, and drive organizational success. Throughout this book, we have delved deep into the critical role of a positive attitude and a growth-oriented mindset in effective leadership. We have explored how these attributes impact resilience, organizational culture, emotional intelligence, and overall leadership effectiveness.

This concluding section brings everything we've discussed together, emphasizing how embracing a growth-oriented mindset and cultivating a positive attitude are not merely commendable endeavors—they are essential attributes for effective leadership. By integrating these concepts with the Holistic Intelligence Model, leaders can unlock new levels of performance, influence, and innovation.

The Transformative Power of Mindset and Attitude

Shaping Perception and Reality

A leader's mindset forms the foundation upon which decisions are made, strategies are devised, and teams are rallied. It is the lens through which opportunities are recognized, challenges are tackled, and setbacks are viewed as stepping stones. Similarly, a positive attitude serves as the fuel that propels leaders forward, even in the face of adversity.

Integration with the Holistic Intelligence Model:

- Intrapersonal Intelligence: Enhances self-awareness and self-regulation, allowing leaders to understand and manage their thoughts and emotions effectively.
- Emotional Resilience (ER): Builds the capacity to recover from setbacks and maintain a positive outlook.
- Ethical Intelligence: Ensures that a leader's mindset and actions align with core values and principles.

Key Points:

- Mindset Determines Approach: A growth mindset fosters adaptability, learning, and innovation.
- Attitude Influences Culture: A positive attitude from leadership permeates the organization, influencing morale and productivity.
- Perception Shapes Reality: Leaders who perceive challenges as opportunities create an environment conducive to growth and success.

Inspiring Change and Driving Organizational Success

Embracing Growth and Positive Attitudes

Inspiring leaders to embrace change and drive organizational success through shifted mindsets and positive attitudes is the charge of this book. It is a call to action, urging leaders to recognize the incredible potential that lies within their own mental framework.

Integration with the Holistic Intelligence Model:

- Interpersonal Intelligence: Enhances the ability to communicate vision and inspire others.
- Cultural Intelligence (CQ): Enables leaders to navigate and leverage diversity within their teams.
- Creativity Intelligence (CrQ): Fosters innovation and problem-solving.

Strategies for Embracing Change:

1. Lead by Example: Demonstrate a commitment to personal growth and a positive attitude.

2. Communicate Vision: Clearly articulate the benefits of change and how it aligns with organizational goals.

3. Empower Teams: Encourage team members to adopt a growth mindset and provide opportunities for development.

4. Recognize and Reward: Acknowledge efforts and achievements that reflect a positive shift in mindset and attitude.

Case Example:

Satya Nadella, CEO of Microsoft, transformed the company's culture by fostering a growth mindset, leading to renewed innovation and success.

Unlocking New Levels of Performance and Influence

Harnessing the Power of Belief and Positive Outlook

By understanding the intricate interplay between mindset, attitude, and behavior, leaders can unlock new levels of performance and influence. They can harness the power of belief in growth and the art of maintaining a positive outlook, fostering an environment of continuous learning and boundless potential.

Integration with the Holistic Intelligence Model:

- Analytical Intelligence (AQ): Supports strategic thinking and informed decision-making.
- Practical Intelligence (PQ): Enhances the ability to implement strategies effectively.
- Emotional Resilience (ER): Sustains motivation and perseverance.

Practical Strategies:

1. Set Stretch Goals: Challenge yourself and your team to exceed expectations.

2. Cultivate Learning Opportunities: Encourage ongoing education and skill development.

3. Promote a Feedback Culture: Foster open communication and constructive criticism.

4. Celebrate Successes: Recognize both individual and team achievements to reinforce positive behaviors.

Overcoming Challenges on the Journey to Transformation

Commitment, Self-Awareness, and Embracing Discomfort

As we conclude this exploration, remember that the journey towards a transformed mindset and attitude is not without its challenges. It requires dedication, self-awareness, and a willingness to embrace discomfort.

Integration with the Holistic Intelligence Model:

- Intrapersonal Intelligence: Facilitates self-reflection and personal growth.
- Emotional Resilience (ER): Helps manage the discomfort associated with change.
- Ethical Intelligence: Guides leaders to stay true to their values during transformation.

Strategies for Overcoming Challenges:

1. Self-Reflection: Regularly assess your thoughts, beliefs, and reactions.

2. Seek Support: Engage with mentors, coaches, or peers for guidance and accountability.

3. Embrace Failure as Learning: View setbacks as opportunities for growth rather than obstacles.

4. Maintain Focus on Goals: Keep the bigger picture in mind to stay motivated.

Case Example:

Oprah Winfrey overcame significant personal and professional challenges by transforming her mindset, ultimately becoming a global influencer and philanthropist.

Empowering Leaders to Inspire, Innovate, and Lead

Propelling Organizations Toward Limitless Potential

Empowered leaders, armed with a renewed perspective, have the capacity to inspire, innovate, and lead their teams towards unprecedented heights of success.

Integration with the Holistic Intelligence Model:

- Interpersonal Intelligence: Enhances the ability to motivate and connect with others.
- Creativity Intelligence (CrQ): Encourages innovative solutions and approaches.
- Cultural Intelligence (CQ): Allows leaders to effectively manage and leverage diversity.

Key Actions for Leaders:

1. Inspire Through Vision: Share a compelling vision that aligns with organizational values and goals.

2. Foster Innovation: Create an environment where new ideas are welcomed and explored.

3. Develop Others: Invest in the growth and development of team members.

4. Lead with Integrity: Model ethical behavior and decision-making.

Case Example:

Elon Musk inspires innovation and pushes boundaries in technology and space exploration through his visionary leadership and relentless pursuit of goals.

Conclusion: A Call to Action

May this discussion serve as a catalyst for you to embark on your own transformative journey. It is an invitation to transcend limitations, both self-imposed and external, and step into the realm of visionary leadership.

Key Takeaways:
- Mindset and Attitude are Critical: They influence every aspect of leadership effectiveness.
- Transformation is a Journey: Embrace the ongoing process of growth and development.
- Empowerment Leads to Success: Leaders who invest in their mindset and attitude empower themselves and their organizations.

Final Thoughts:

Empowered leaders, armed with a renewed perspective, have the capacity to inspire, innovate, and lead their teams towards unprecedented heights of success. By shifting your mindset, cultivating a positive attitude, and integrating the principles of the Holistic Intelligence Model, you can propel your organization toward a future defined by limitless potential and enduring achievement.

Reflection Questions

1. Self-Assessment: How has your current mindset and attitude influenced your leadership effectiveness?

2. Areas for Growth: In what ways can you shift your mindset and attitude to become a more effective leader?

3. Action Steps: What specific actions will you take to begin this transformative journey?

Action Plan

1. Set Personal Development Goals: Define clear, measurable objectives for shifting your mindset and attitude.

2. Create a Learning Plan: Identify resources, courses, or mentors that can support your growth.

3. Implement Strategies: Apply the tools and techniques discussed in this book.

4. Engage Your Team: Share your journey with your team to foster a culture of growth and positivity.

5. Monitor Progress: Regularly assess your development and adjust your approach as needed.

Thoughtful Exploration: Shifting Mindsets for Effective Leadership

These thought-provoking questions aim to stimulate reflective contemplation and meaningful discussions regarding the concepts presented in this book. They prompt readers to explore the practical implications of emotional resilience in leadership and its interconnectedness with various aspects of intelligence.

- Why is mindset considered a critical factor in effective leadership? Can you share an example from your own experience where a shift in mindset positively impacted a leadership situation?

- The book emphasizes the importance of adopting empowering mindsets. What are some specific empowering mindsets that leaders can cultivate, and how can they contribute to improved leadership effectiveness?

- Reflect on a time when you or a leader you know had to navigate a challenging situation. How did their mindset influence their approach and decision-making in that situation?

- The book discusses the concept of a growth mindset. How can leaders develop and nurture a growth-oriented mindset within themselves and their teams? What are the potential benefits of doing so?

- Consider the role of self-awareness in mindset shifts. How can self-awareness help leaders identify and challenge limiting beliefs or attitudes that may hinder their effectiveness?

- Share an example of a leader who successfully implemented a mindset shift in their leadership approach. What were the outcomes of this shift, and how did it impact the team or organization?

- How can leaders proactively foster a culture of continuous learning and adaptability within their teams? What strategies or practices can be employed to encourage a growth-oriented mindset among team members?

These questions can serve as discussion prompts to foster thoughtful reflection and meaningful conversations about the concepts covered in the book. They can be customized to suit various learning environments and objectives, making them a versatile resource for diverse audiences.

For Book Discussion Groups, Reading Discussion Groups, and classrooms dedicated to leadership development, these prompts provide invaluable resources. They provide a structured framework for engaging and enriching discussions about the content, enabling participants to share their insights and perspectives.

Additional Suggestions:

- Encourage participants to draw from personal experiences or real-world examples when responding to the prompts.

- Cultivate a safe and inclusive environment for sharing thoughts and opinions.

- Consider assigning specific questions to different individuals or groups to ensure a well-rounded discussion.

- Customize the questions to align with the specific context and learning goals of your group.

Remember, the aim of these discussion prompts is to deepen understanding, foster critical thinking, and facilitate meaningful exchanges among participants. Feel free to adapt them to best serve your unique learning or teaching environment.

Enjoy your discussions!

About the Author: William R. Stanek

Meet the Visionary, the Storyteller, and Your Guide on the Journey to Intentional Living

Biography

William R. Stanek is no ordinary author in the world of personal growth. With a background that's woven with more experiences than can be counted, Stanek is known for his straightforward wisdom, practical insights, and a talent for helping others build lives that align with their core values. His work speaks to those who seek authenticity and a real connection to their purpose, bringing an inspiring yet realistic approach to the journey of self-discovery.

Throughout his journey, Stanek has played many roles—teacher, innovator, mentor, and artist—each experience adding to the perspective he shares in his books. He is known for being the voice people turn to when conventional advice falls short and when what's needed isn't a quick fix but a path to meaningful change. Over his career, he has helped countless individuals rethink their relationship with success, personal growth, and what it truly means to live a purposeful life.

As a leader and technologist at the intersection of business, technology, and leadership, William's work extends far beyond the written word. He has spent years inspiring action, driving meaningful change, and guiding others on how to create impact that resonates, endures, and honors each individual's unique journey. His influence spans professions and walks of life, providing a grounding perspective in a world that often encourages us to chase everything at once. In this book, William shares his experiences, insights, and deep conviction in the power of intentional living with a broader audience.

Connect with William R. Stanek

Join William in exploring new ideas, challenging conventional wisdom, and pushing the boundaries of what's possible in personal growth. Connect with him here:

LinkedIn: Follow William for updates, articles, and perspectives on intentional living and personal growth.

https://www.linkedin.com/in/williamstanek/

Facebook: Like his author page for daily insights, reflections, and updates.

http://www.facebook.com/William.Stanek.Author

Twitter: Follow for thought-provoking tweets and personal growth tips in 280 characters.

http://www.twitter.com/WilliamStanek

Website: Visit http://www.williamrstanek.com to learn more about his books, workshops, and other projects.

Comprehensive Professional and Collegiate Reference Edition

William R. Stanek

Esteemed author, renowned worldwide bestseller, and trusted consultant to Fortune 100, 500, and 1000 companies for over three decades.

THE RESILIENT LEADER
EMBRACING RESILIENCE FOR SUCCESS

REIMAGINING LEADERSHIP BEYOND THE EQ VS IQ PARADIGM

Actionable Leadership Principles - Straightforward and Effective

The "Comprehensive Professional and Collegiate Reference Edition" offers enhanced value through additional comprehension aids, including comprehensive insights, holistic analysis, discussion prompts, independent study notes, and teacher/facilitator guidance.

THE NEW LEADERSHIP LANDSCAPE

WILLIAM'S EXPERTISE IS THE BEST-KEPT SECRET AMONG TOP MANAGEMENT, DELIVERING UNPARALLELED IMPACT.

"The Resilient Leader, Embracing Resilience for Success" stands out in the crowded landscape of leadership and emotional intelligence books by offering a fresh, holistic approach to leadership that transcends traditional models. This groundbreaking work by William R. Stanek redefines the essence of effective leadership in the modern era, distinguishing itself through several key differentiators:

- **Holistic Integration of Multiple Intelligences**   While most leadership books focus on emotional intelligence (EQ) or traditional cognitive intelligence (IQ), "The Resilient Leader, Embracing Resilience for Success" introduces readers to the 8 Pillars of Leadership. This innovative framework encompasses Emotional Resilience, Creative Intelligence, Practical Intelligence, Cultural Intelligence, Intrapersonal Intelligence, Interpersonal Intelligence, Ethical Intelligence, and Analytical Intelligence. By embracing a broader spectrum of intelligences, the book equips leaders with a multifaceted toolkit, enabling them to navigate the complexities of the contemporary landscape more effectively than ever before.

- **Emphasis on Emotional Resilience**   "The Resilient Leader, Embracing Resilience for Success" delves deep into emotional resilience, offering readers actionable strategies to cultivate this essential trait. The book presents emotional resilience as the bedrock of leadership excellence, enabling leaders to withstand challenges, adapt to change, thrive in adversity, and so much more. Whereas most literature on emotional intelligence or emotional resilience treats resilience as a narrow set of traits or a subset of emotional intelligence, "The Resilient Leader, Embracing Resilience for Success" reconceptualizes it as a multifaceted intelligence in its own right. This book goes far beyond the typical definitions and presents emotional resilience as a complex, dynamic intelligence that is critical for effective leadership.

- **Rigorous Self-Assessment Tool**   Distinct from other leadership books that offer generalized advice, "The

Resilient Leader, Embracing Resilience for Success" integrates a cutting-edge self-assessment tool. This personalized assessment allows readers to evaluate their strengths and areas for growth, providing a tailored roadmap for personal and professional development. This actionable, data-driven approach ensures that readers can make concrete progress on their leadership journey.

- **Case Studies and Real-World Application**   While many books on leadership and emotional intelligence rely on theoretical principles, "The Resilient Leader, Embracing Resilience for Success" grounds its insights in practical reality. Through a series of detailed case studies featuring real-world scenarios and leadership challenges, the book illustrates how the principles of resilient leadership can be applied in various contexts. From crisis management in the financial sector to navigating complex mergers and leading through global pandemics, these case studies offer readers a window into the transformative power of resilient leadership in action.

- **Future-Oriented Leadership Vision**   Stanek's book critically examines the evolution of leadership theories and practices, from ancient times through the industrial revolution to the present day, offering a visionary outlook on the future of leadership. Unlike books that dwell on past or current leadership models, "The Resilient Leader, Embracing Resilience for Success" charts a course for the future, advocating for a comprehensive, adaptable leadership approach that meets the demands of an ever-changing world. This forward-thinking perspective encourages leaders to not only adapt to the new normal but to thrive within it, paving the way for a new era of leadership excellence.

In summary, "The Resilient Leader, Embracing Resilience for Success" offers a unique, comprehensive guide that goes beyond traditional leadership tenets, providing readers with the insights and tools needed to excel in today's dynamic environment. By combining a holistic view of intelligence, a focus on emotional resilience, practical tools for self-assessment, real-world applicability, and a visionary leadership approach, this book is an essential resource for anyone looking to lead effectively in the 21st century.

www.ingramcontent.com/pod-product-compliance
Lightning Source LLC
Chambersburg PA
CBHW051707160426
43209CB00004B/1050